東京の都心部は、世界最大の都市だ。成長が手に取るように見える場所である。ここは人工的環境だ。
アスファルトとガラスとコンクリートで書かれたフィクション。自然な景観が遠い夢になる場所。

The Tokyo Metropolitan Area is the biggest city in the world. It is a place where growth is palpable. It is a man-made environment. A fiction written in asphalt, glass and concrete. A place where the natural landscape has become a distant dream.

この都市では、宇宙の光は、進歩がもたらす人工的な明るさにかき消されてしまう。星々は、ゆっくりと瞬く飛行機やヘリコプター用の赤い航空障害灯にとってかわられた。

In this city the light of the cosmos is pushed aside by the artificial brightness of progress. The stars have been replaced with slowly pulsating red lights, warnings for airplanes and helicopters.

この都市は、無限に広がる内部空間のように思える。肌に突然雨つぶを感じて、驚いてしまうこともあるだろう。そこでは、すべてのものがあるべき場所と目的をもっているかのようだ。

The city can feel like an infinite interior. You might be surprised to suddenly feel drops of rain on your skin. Everything seems to have its place and purpose.

東京は世界で最も安全な都市の１つでもある。東京では、ゴミのポイ捨てや軽犯罪、暴力的なデモやフーリガン、公共物破壊行為はほとんど見られない。東京の子供たちは、幼少のころから、巨大な都市のインフラを使って一人で移動することを学ぶ。

Tokyo is also one of the safest cities in the world. In Tokyo there is almost no littering, no petty crime, no violent demonstrations, no hooliganism and no vandalism. From a young age, children learn to navigate the vast urban infrastructure on their own.

東京は、高齢化が進み、経済成長が止まった国の首都である。この都市で、人々はどうやってくつろいでいるのだろうか？みなさんはどうだろうか？

Tokyo is the capital of an ageing nation, where economic growth falters. How do people make themselves at home in this city? And how do you?

TOKYO TOTEM

A Guide to Tokyo

トーキョー・トーテム

主観的東京ガイド

A project by Monnik

Edited by Christiaan Fruneaux and Edwin Gardner

Designed by Jasper van den Berg

TOKYO
IS
YOURS

DEAR READER,

Tokyo offers a lot of spectacle and confusion. This is just a façade. Behind the neon glare lies a steady, rhythmic and miraculous everyday world that can be yours if you want it to be. *Tokyo Totem* can guide you through this realm, made as much of souls as of stones. A city that exists as much "out there" as it does "in here". To help you navigate this slippery slope, stretched between imagination and reality, you will occasionally find your path marked by a totem. It may be the recognizable chime of your train-stop, waking you from your morning slumber. Or the taste of your favorite food, lingering in your mouth, evoking pleasant childhood memories. Or perhaps it will be the faces that you can't help seeing in the façades of this city. These totems signify the effort of your imagination to reach out into the world and connect to it.

It is perhaps good to state what this book is not. This book will be of little use if you want to know where to eat or what to see. There are other very good guidebooks available for that purpose. Instead this is a subjective guidebook that is intended to help you navigate and read this city in a way that evokes both a sense of adventure and a feeling of belonging.

Throughout this guidebook, flaneurs, artists, designers, anthropologists, architects, bathhouse connoisseurs and many, many other seasoned urban explorers will invite you to look, read and experience Tokyo differently. They offer insights, angles and imaginations that will hopefully assist you to make this seemingly never-ending metropolis your own. *Tokyo Totem* is both an investigation of how home is understood and experienced in this city and an imaginarium for personal exploration and home making—processes that we think are deeply connected.

Cities are notoriously difficult to navigate. And we are living in an increasingly urbanized world. More and more cities resemble interiors, artificial places where the natural outside world is withdrawing. It is not too far-fetched to suppose that the art of urban reconnaissance (and thus of home making), once a purely artistic and intellectual endeavor, will one day become an accepted part of everyone's education. It will be a craft that teaches us to make

読者の皆さまへ

東京は、スペクタクルと混乱にあふれる都市だ。しかし、それは表層にすぎない。輝くネオンの裏側には、着実に、リズミカルに展開する奇跡のような日常世界があり、その一部になりたいと思うならそれも可能だ。『トーキョー・トーテム』は、石と同じくらいたくさんの魂でできたこの世界に皆さまを案内する。「ここ」にも「あそこ」にも存在する世界。イマジネーションと現実の間に広がるとらえがたい世界を進んでいくと、ときおり、進むべき道を記した「トーテム」を見つけることになるだろう。

トーテムとは、ある集団にとっての自動誘導装置、方位測定地点、あるいは結集点となる個人的なガイドまたはエンブレムである、と私たちは理解している。東京には、たくさんのトーテムがある。東京にある無数の通りを歩いていると、例えば、ある種の精神、神々、ファッション集団、地域、消費傾向、職業、企業への帰属性といった意味を示すエンブレムに遭遇する。あなたにデザインの素養があるなら、東京の典型的な色彩スペクトラムが目についてしかたないだろうし、音楽的な感性があるなら、学校の終業を知らせる5時のチャイムに耳をふさぎたくなるだろう。本書のタイトルは、東京人たちが果てしなく広がる街並みを歩きまわるときの助けとなっている、こうした数多くの社会的、そして非常に個人的な記号への頌歌（オード）である。また、読者の皆さまにも自分自身のトーテムを見つけてもらえたら、という私たちの希望も込められている。

『トーキョー・トーテム』は、この都市を見歩き、読み解いていくうちに、冒険のような感覚と帰属意識の両方を感じさせる、主観的なガイドブックだ。どこで何を食べるかとか、何を見るべきかといったことを知りたいなら、この本はほとんど役に立たない。東京も含め、都市というものはどれも、客観的な立場で近づいていくことのできないものだと私たちは考える。あまりにも多くの物事がおきているし、計算に入れておかなければならないことがあまりにもたくさんある。都市というものを説明する公式は、無数にあるだろう。建物、人々、仕事、思想、会話、ファッション、テクノロジーが、前触れもなく現れては通り過ぎ、都市を変えていく。主観的なコンパスがあるからといって、この大都会が理解しやすくなるわけではない。しかし、大都会にもっと近づくことはできるようになる。そして、もっと大事なことは、このコンパスがあれば、この大都会を自分のものにできるということだ。たとえ立ち位置というものがあったとしても、それを自ら進んで明かすことはないのが都市である。見えてくるのは、都市の立ち位置ではなく、自分自身の立ち位置だ。自分の立ち位置をコンパスにすれば、都市はその驚きと神秘に満ちた豊かな姿を明かしてくれるだろう。

『トーキョー・トーテム』は、4.5章で構成されている。0.5章は「自分自身を見出そう」というタイトルの短い章で、家づくりや都市再生を主観的な視点から考察している。客観性をコントロールし、主観的なコンパスを見出す必要がある。その後、「大地を歩き回ろう」「リズムに乗ろう」「都市を見出そう」「くつろごう」という章が続く。つまり、章を追ったプロセスの背後にあるロジックとは、まず自分自身を見出し、次に時間のリズムを発見し、人々がそれに寄り添って生活している様子を知り、それから自分自身の都市をつくりだし、最後にようやくくつろぐことができる、ということだ。もちろん、実際に探究をしてみると、これらの段階は、突然一度に起こったり、あるいはランダムに起こったりすることになる。

本書を通して、都市散歩者（フラヌール）、アーティスト、デザイナー、文化人類学者、建築家、銭湯通など、本当にたくさんの都市探検の達人たちが、読者のみなさんを、今までとは異なる東京の見方、読み解き方、体験の仕方に誘っていく。しかし、自分自身のトーテムや、道の途上で出会うかもしれない新しいトーテムを、恐れず信頼してほしい。それは、あなた自身のためだけでなく、世界の他の人たちのためでもある。なぜなら、この世界を自分の居場所にしてくつろぎ始めることができたときに、はじめて私たちはこの世界に対する責任を果たし始めることができるのだから。

Edwin Gardner &
Christiaan Fruneaux

sense of our man-made world and to find our bearings in a physical and social labyrinth that is constantly changing. You will have to learn to make your own kingdom in a cityscape where everything is already claimed on many different levels, and to derive meaning from a place where everything already has a purpose and where nothing is just there—like a mountain is just there.

Unfortunately this craft doesn't exist yet. It still has to be invented. And the knowledge on which it will be based is still scattered across the minds of the many millions of urbanites who feel inspired, amazed and at home in their cities. Knowledge that would be of great use to the many more millions of urbanites who feel lost in the maelstrom. To help construct and formulate this new craft, we asked many seasoned urban explorers, both outsiders as insiders, to join us in investigating the largest urban agglomeration the world has ever witnessed. A place where urban expansion is tangible: the Tokyo Metro Area, consists of 37 million people try to make themselves at home.

Tokyo represents a unique urbanism because of two simple and straightforward facts: it is both the biggest metropolis the world has ever seen and the safest. Millions of people are crammed together in one of the most unremitting urban landscapes man has ever created, but there is almost no petty crime, no vandalism, no littering, no hooliganism and no violent demonstrations. Although we belong to that naive tribe of people who, despite the overwhelming body of evidence to the contrary, are optimistic about humanity's future, we are continually amazed by this truly astounding phenomenon.

Although all cities are difficult to relate to, Tokyo in particular seems to baffle people. When we started our investigation we quickly realized that Japan, and thus by default Tokyo, provokes a lot of academic, artistic and ideological interpretations of its culture that in some way or another emphasize its separateness. These interpretations come from both foreigners and the Japanese themselves. The idea of Japan as a unique and monolithic culture is widespread, but there are also many who reject it. There is an acute and growing sensitivity towards any kind of generalization, Orientalism, Occidentalism, exoticism or cliché about what makes Japan tick. Starting a sentence with "The Japanese are" often elicits a sharp reprimand, and rightly so. Therefore when we came to Tokyo to ponder Tokyo's uniqueness, we had a lot of explaining to do.

Having gotten to know Japan a little better over the years, we can only say, in our modest estimation, that it has its fair share of unique qualities and wondrous features. But, like any other culture, Japan, and thus Tokyo, is no homogeneous, monolithic whole. It is divided by class, gender, generation and caste, by regional differences, subcultures and political flavors. Japanese culture is just one of many unique, diverse and dynamic incarnations of human togetherness on the planet—the product of people working together and making a home together.

That many foreigners and Japanese think of Japan as somehow separate also cannot be ignored, however. Ideas on about identity, whether they be expressed by outsiders or insiders, are powerful forces inside any culture. If you think you are different, or if others think you are different, you may start to behave different. These kinds of ideas have a self-fulfilling quality about them.

At any rate, we didn't come to Tokyo to acknowledge its monolithic nature. In some ways this guide proposes to do exactly the opposite. Its proposition is to break the city up into everyone's city. It is intended to help you engage with this city in a way that makes sense to

you, allowing you to create your own Tokyo. To overcome the confusion that cities evoke, perhaps this city most of all, we want you to imagine and experience a Tokyo that you can call your home.

Cities are impossible to approach from an objective standpoint. There is just too much going on, too much to take into account. The formula that could explain a city would be endless. Buildings, people, jobs, ideas, conventions, fashions and technologies come and go unpredictably, leaving a changed city in their wake. We think that in these bewildering circumstances you can do only one thing: trust the subjective. A subjective compass does not make the metropolis more understandable. It does, however, make the metropolis more approachable. And, more importantly, it makes it yours. Cities will never reveal their position, if they have any. The only position you can learn is your own. With your own position as your compass, the city will reveal itself to be a deeply wondrous, mysterious, and enriching place.

A totem can be understood as a personal guide or an emblem that serves some group as a homing device, an orientation or a rallying point. In Tokyo there are many totems. Walking its many streets one encounters emblems that signify, for example, certain spirits or gods, fashion tribes, neighborhoods, consumer preferences, professions, or corporate affiliations. But these totems also exist within you. Perhaps your designer eye can't help seeing the typical color spectrum of the city, or perhaps your musical ear is eager to block out the 5 o'clock tune that signals the end of school. The title of this book is an ode to these many social and deeply personal signifiers, which somehow help Tokyoites navigate their infinite cityscape, and it also represents our wish that you may find your own totems.

The *Tokyo Totem* guide has 4.5 chapters or steps. Chapter 0.5 is a very small chapter called *Find Yourself*: it explores the subjective quality of home making and urban reconnaissance. You need to reign in your objectivity and find your subjective compass. The next chapters are called, in consecutive order, *Walk The Land, Follow the Rhythm, Choose Your City* and *Make Yourself at Home*. The logic behind these steps is this: Before you can make yourself at home you have to know who you are. Then, to get a sense of where you are, you have to walk the land to know the land. Next, you need to discover the rhythms of time and how people inhabit them before you can actually create your own city, and finally make yourself at home in it. Of course, when actually out there exploring, these steps occur all at once or in random order.

We hope that you enjoy this guide and find it helpful in your urban explorations. Most of all we hope that you enjoy Tokyo. Don't be afraid to trust your own totems and the new ones that may cross your path. Be curious, explore, and make the world your own. You will not only do yourself a favor, but the rest of the world as well. Because only when you start making yourself at home in this world, can you start taking responsibility for it.

Edwin Gardner &
Christiaan Fruneaux

TABLE OF CONTENTS / 目次

TABLE OF CONTENTS / 目次

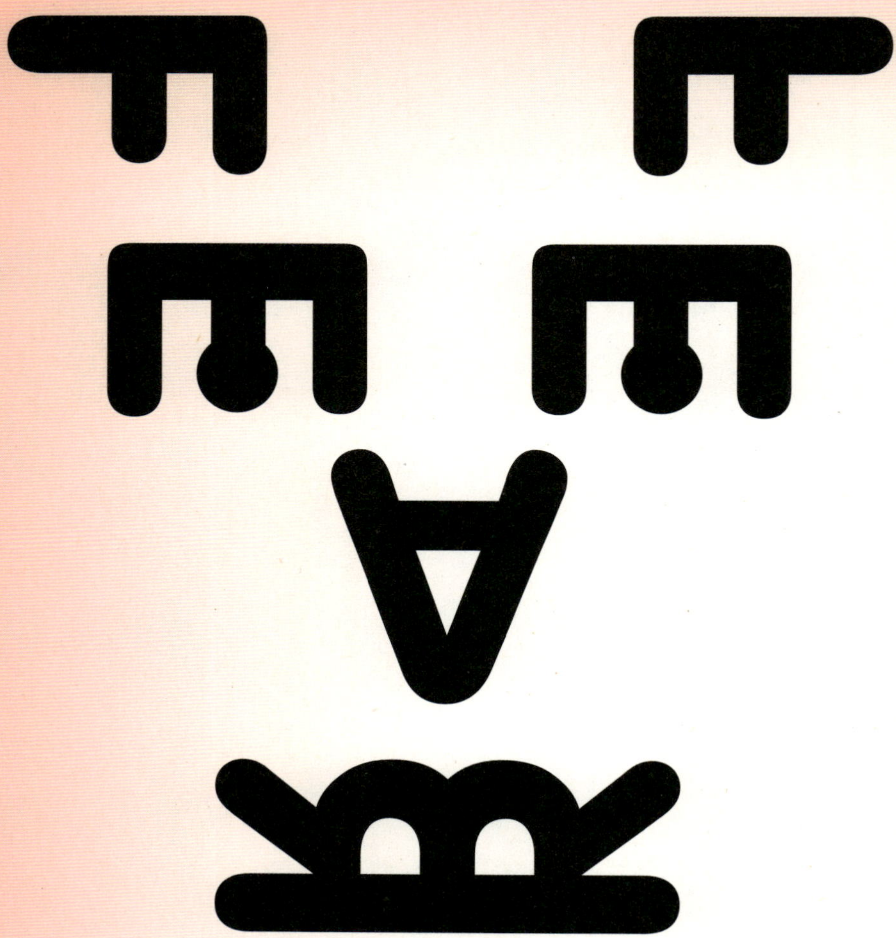

自分自身を見出そう

都市は自分のポジションを決して明らかにはしないだろう。自分で学べるポジションは、自分自身のポジションでしかない。自分自身のポジションをコンパスにすれば、都市は非常に驚きに満ちた、神秘的で豊かな場としての姿を見せてくれるだろう。プロフェッショナルな見方や態度は捨てよう。懐疑主義も手放そう。自然に任せること。自分のものにすること。自分自身を見つけよう。そうすれば、街の姿も見つかるだろう。

FIND YOURSELF

Cities will never reveal their position. The only position you can learn is your own. With your own position as your compass the city will reveal itself as a deeply wondrous, mysterious, and enriching place. Loose your professional gaze and attitude. Lay down your skepticism. Be spontaneous. Take ownership. Find yourself and you will find your city.

赤レンガ通り
祝30周年

餃子房
601

家餃子房
春日 ㊌16 02

区一廃第77号
㈱要興業
0120-66-5341

126
UBE
26

I took to the streets to sell my T-shirts. A white T-shirt with the text "I am not from here".

私は自分でつくったTシャツを売るために街に出た。白いTシャツには「わたしはここの人ではありません。」という言葉がプリントされている。

FOREIGNERS OF THE WORLD, UNITE!

Everybody knows the feeling. When you are in another country — relaxing or partying — the pressure to "be someone" seems to dissipate. When you're abroad, you're on the outside. You speak another language, you don't share the same experiences, and you have habits that differ from those of the people around you.

This sense of being on the outside may also occur on a regular Monday morning when you commute to work with the other briefcases, when you sit with your family at the kitchen table, or when you are unable to express yourself in your native tongue. Sometimes you're so far removed from where you are that you feel like you don't exist in a world that is clearly there. The rhythm of your day, the things you have to do, even your own reflection in the mirror. For a moment it may seem unrecognizable. You feel like a stranger in an absurd reality that enfolds you.

I invite you to join this group of strangers. The bigger the group, the freer the movement. Break through your discomfort, relief yourself from appropriate behavior and the oppression of standard patterns. Come home to the strangeness of yourself.

世界中の外国人よ、連帯せよ!

誰もが知っているあの感覚。外国人、アウトサイダーとして感じるあの感覚。見知らぬ国にいるときだけでなく、日常生活のなかでも感じる感覚だ。一時的に感じる、世界から切り離されたような感覚。自分の内なる外国人を見出すこの瞬間に、私たちは解放される。自分の中の外国人としての感覚を受け入れよう。勇気をもって、世界に広がる「外国人コミュニティ」に参加しよう。

Arthur van Beek はヴィジュアルアーティストであり、アムステルダムにあるエディ・ジ・イーグル・ミュージアムの共同設立者である。2012年に東京に滞在し、路上でTシャツを販売した。

The 'I am not from here' T-shirt licences the wearer to embrace the stranger within and broadcasts the alienation of the traveler as a liberating message.

「わたしはここの人ではありません。」と書かれたこのTシャツを身につければ、その間は、1日だけ、あるいはお好きなだけいつまででも、自分の中の外国人を受け止めて、旅行者の抱える疎外感を、解放へのメッセージとして広めることができる。

THE NOBLE ART OF SUBJECTIVE EXPLORATION

An interesting episode unfolded the first time I visited Tokyo, in July 2012. We were preparing the Still City workshop, whose outcome would form the basis of this guide. We had two and sometimes three meetings a day with people we hoped would join the workshop, or who could tell us something about their city. We were zigzagging through Tokyo, going in and out of subways, trying to navigate a unique address system that doesn't use street names. We spent our days meeting people, sitting in coffee shops trying to connect to the Internet, and traveling in subterranean metro cars. After two weeks, Tokyo weighed heavy on me. I didn't know why, but I felt claustrophobic. Trapped. Lost inside a seemingly endless, perfectly organized city.

主観的探検という高貴な芸術

自分が属していない場所に関わることは、臆病者には向いていない。旅をしているときには、自分自身、アイデア、期待、オブセッション、偏見を携えたままでいざるをえない。しかし、ひとつの場所に本当の意味で関わろうとするときには、自分というものを一度失い、再発見しなければならないかもしれない。自分がしっていると思っていたもの、正しいと思っていたものを、もう一度とらえ直さなければならなくなるだろう。これは、東京に来たときに、自分の内なるコンパスがゆらぎ、再調整することになった私の実体験の物語だ。東京という無限の内部空間のような都市で感じた閉所恐怖症をいかにして克服し、東京に広がる建築環境によって生じた疎外感のなかで、いかにしてこの都市のリズムを再認識していったかを描写している。そしてついに私は、ある都市において自分をくつろがせてくれるものについて、より深い洞察を得たのだった。

Christiaan Fruneaux は、作家、歴史家であり、人工的世界の探検家である。Monnikの共同設立者であり、ジャカルタ、ダマスカス、ベイルート、アムステルダム、東京、ラゴスの「主観的探検」を行っている。

I felt the need to confirm that Tokyo was not all that there was. I persuaded my fellow Monnik companions to join me in my search for a physical end to the city. We took the Chuo line westwards to Takao station, an hour by JR-train from Nakano, where we were staying with a friend. From the train-car window, the vast cityscape flowed unremittingly past. When we arrived in Takao we walked north for 20 minutes, towards a green rise on the horizon, and found a fence, demarcating the end of the city. This fence stood at the foot of a hill. On one side of the fence was Tokyo; on the other side, a forest. It was the end of the city. I felt relieved. Behind a small opening in the fence we found an old stone stairway that led to an abandoned Shinto shrine. It was raining, and through the leaves you could see the Metropolis, not so endless after all.

The second time I visited Tokyo, in October and November 2012, the oppressive heaviness returned, and with a vengeance. I felt unwanted, like I had hit an invisible wall. As though Tokyo didn't appreciate my presence. And this feeling was increasingly mutual. Again it was a busy time; we were working hard to get the Still City workshop organized. Though, I was conscious of the fact that I couldn't host a workshop about Tokyo if I felt so out of place in the city, I wasn't able to shake off my sense of alienation. After some soul searching, some making an ass out of myself, and a lot of discussion with my colleagues, I came to suspect that there were a couple of things—let's call them first impressions (although they differed very little from prejudices)—about this city that were throwing me off balance. First there was Tokyo's extraordinarily generic cityscape; second there was an apparent lack of urban turmoil and individual temperament; third came my impression that Japan was a country of role-playing and decorum; fourth was my estimation that Tokyo was not a cosmopolitan city; and finally it seemed to me that a large part of Tokyo's populace was chronically exhausted. Together these impressions were somehow offensive to me. But why?

First impressions are, of course, mostly projections. You don't actually have the knowledge to make a sensible interpretation of what you are seeing. First impressions, in short, will tell you more about yourself than the other. So why did these first impressions leave me deeply confused? What did that say about me? Was I so easily unhinged? Was there a deeper narrative that I believed about myself, one that was colliding with what I observed about Tokyo?

Once upon a time I was trained as a historian, and if someone were to ask me about my background I'm always sure to mention my master's degree in history. My love affair with history is as old as my capacity to read. In my free time, I still read historical biographies or browse historical atlases. You can say it's ingrained in my consciousness. I also happen to live in Amsterdam, a city where you can easily read the built environment within its historical framework.

Perhaps like many who are interested in history, my knowledge of the past generates a sense of belonging in the present. I take comfort in the idea of continuity and historical narrative. It makes me feel part of something. In Tokyo, my habitual sense of belonging did not recognize anything it could hold on to, or make sense of. I realized that my uneasiness was a direct result of me being a hopeless Romantic—indeed, with a capital R.

In the 18th and 19th centuries Romanticism, an artistic and intellectual movement, was searching for more meaningful ways to connect to the natural and social environments. The Romantics were trying to make sense of a world disturbed by individualism, secularization, the rationalization of work and chaotic urban growth. Their emotional and intellectual search for belonging focused on genuine feelings and the raw experience of the external environment and the subjective self. In a world that was becoming more and more artificial, the Romantics were looking for the uncontaminated, in themselves and in the world.

FIGHTING MASTER

adidas

I can relate to this. And I'm not the only one. In many ways Western cities have never been as Romantic as they are today, with our interest in authenticity, craftsmanship, honest food, fun jobs, creative hubs and pure experiences. In this sense, I'm no more than a product of my time. For me old stones symbolize historical roots, while my own spontaneity provides me with a kind of rootedness in myself. Both entities provide me with a sense of belonging, anchoring me in a world based on relentless technological innovation and economic growth. For me cities are places of reinvention—technologically, socially, but most of all personally.

With my newly discovered inner lens of Romanticism, my unease suddenly made more sense. My inner Romantic was obviously not pleased with Tokyo's nonspecific and non-historic cityscape. I couldn't distill any kind of narrative from the buildings. My Romantic inclination towards spontaneity, which presumed a certain unexpectedness and chaos to be part of any city, made it difficult for me to accept that Tokyo was both the biggest city in the world and the safest and cleanest. This seeming lack of mayhem, and ostensible lack of individual temperament, was not how the Romantic in me typically understood cities to work. In my mind cities were engines of creative destruction, tumultuous but virtuoso, elegant but rowdy, deeply unfair but also hopeful—places were anything could happen. Tokyo appeared to represent another kind of urbanism. Or so it seemed at least.

In short, because I couldn't recognize anything, these first impressions left me confused about how exactly Tokyoites made sense of their city and how they felt at home within it. My confusion wasn't helped by all the tired people I saw. I seemed to encounter them everywhere, sleeping in restaurants or in subway cars. I got a strange impression that half the town was jetlagged.

In the back of my rational head I knew that there must be an explanation. That Tokyoites must have the same love/hate relationship with their metropolis as any other urbanite. But in the moment I couldn't see it. I could only see an outwardly perfectly organized city, inhabited by very tired people, in very generic homes. It made my presence sad and negative. I needed to snap out of it, which I eventually did.

Out of my initial confusion and unease, and out of the subsequent discussions I had with my colleagues, interest gradually emerged in the notion of "home", and how this is structured in different cities and cultures. My unease transformed into fascination and curiosity. Discomfort faded and only questions remained: How do Tokyoites engage with their city? How do they take personal ownership and responsibility over their surroundings? How do they try to make the city work for them?

I've transcribed the above anecdote because it reminds me of two things. It reminds me that exploration and investigation, perhaps of any kind, are always very subjective affairs. They have as much to do with personal intuitions, inclinations, and fascinations as they have to do with rationality. They are as much an art as a craft. And the anecdote also reminds me of the blind spot that most urban explorers have towards the behavioral aspects of society. Most look at the hardware of cities, but the software is just as important. Cities are governed not only by infrastructure, laws and buildings but by conventions, etiquettes, ideas and expectations as well. Cities are foremost a gathering of people and only secondarily a heap of man-made objects. Cities are more about how people come together than about where they come together.

What I experienced in Tokyo resembles an experience I had years ago, an experience commonly known as a culture shock. As a student I lived for a while in Indonesia. I was doing research for my master's thesis and learning the Indonesian language. My father was born in the former Dutch East Indies, present-day Indonesia, and for the first six months I lived with relatives in Malang, East Java. For the last six months I lived on my own in Jakarta. Culture shock is an interesting phenomenon because it occurs when you are confronted with different behavioral patterns and social expectations to those you're used to. Looking back at my attempt to internalize Indonesian language and customs, it felt like moving through a thick, unseen barrier.

Culture shock makes something that is in normal circumstances implicit and imperceptible suddenly very solid, almost tangible. Culture shock has four distinct phases, whose reality I can attest to: the honeymoon phase, where you experience the differences between the old and new culture as "exotic" and alluring; the comparison phase, where the excitement eventually gives way to unpleasant feelings of frustration, loneliness and anger, as you interpret events as strange and offensive to your own attitudes and worldviews; the adjustment phase, where you grow accustomed to the new culture and develop new routines and understandings in line with it; and the bicultural phase, where you accept the cultural logic of the new place and become part of it (without shedding the old one). The whole process, if one perseveres, takes about two years.

The experience of culture shock is probably one of the most insightful experiences a person can have. It makes you aware that you are embedded in a cultural force field of shared habits, expectations, ideologies and conventions, from body language to political worldview, none of which you have ever been explicitly taught. These cultural elements are an implicit part of you. Like a fish that does not notice the water he swims in, most people are unaware of the cultural space they inhabit. They only become aware of it when they are confronted with another cultural system.

Subjective exploring is thus as much about observing the other as it is about observing yourself, because whenever you feel strongly about something—positively or negatively—there is something in that feeling that's worth looking into. Making yourself at home inside a city is an internal process. It has to do with making sense of your new surroundings but also with adapting to them, to the cultural logic of the place you're in. It is not an easy task. It can be full of confusion, misunderstanding, frustration and angst. But it's definitely worthwhile.

The last time I visited Tokyo, in June 2015, this guide was almost finished. I had read all the contributions. The city, although still as mysterious as it was the first time I visited, made much more sense to me now. I felt very much at ease and comfortable in it.

On one particularly warm night I was riding the bicycle I had borrowed from a friend. During the day Tokyo can be hot and humid but the nights are pleasant. A nice breeze brushed against my body. I was on my way to have dinner with friends. Above my head an artificial firmament of slow flashing red lights stretched out. Warnings for airplanes and helicopters, so they wouldn't fly into the skyscrapers, -or those dark concrete mountains that occasionally rise up above you. Tokyo felt like a dream. Interspersed within the metropolitan expanse were intimate residential areas. I was constantly cycling through barriers, from shadowy almost suburban neighborhoods to light metropolitan high-rises. I felt myself falling in love with the city for the first time. It wasn't love at first sight, but that doesn't matter. Perhaps it makes the relationship even more precious.

Aukje Dekker はアーティストであり、アムステルダムにあるエディ・ジ・イーグル・ミュージアムの共同設立者である。2012年に東京に滞在し、自分がこの都市を把握し理解することができないという事実を、言葉と画像で表現しようと試みた。

THERE I WAS
私はそこにいた

There I was
a wandering mind
trying to understand
mapping and connecting the way I always do
in a world that doesn't think like that
where "I" has a different meaning
and logic an opposed axis.
But I tried
I had my findings
I fought to capture
and Tokyo fought back
can't catch it in one breath.

私はそこにいた
さまよえる心となり
理解しようと試みていた
いつものわたしのやりかたを、
それが通じない世界でマッピングし、接続しようとしていた
わたし」という言葉が異なる意味や
対立する論理をもつ場所で
でも、私はこころみていた
発見もあった
東京をとらえようと戦いを挑むと
東京もこちらに戦いを挑んでくる
一息にとらえられるものではない

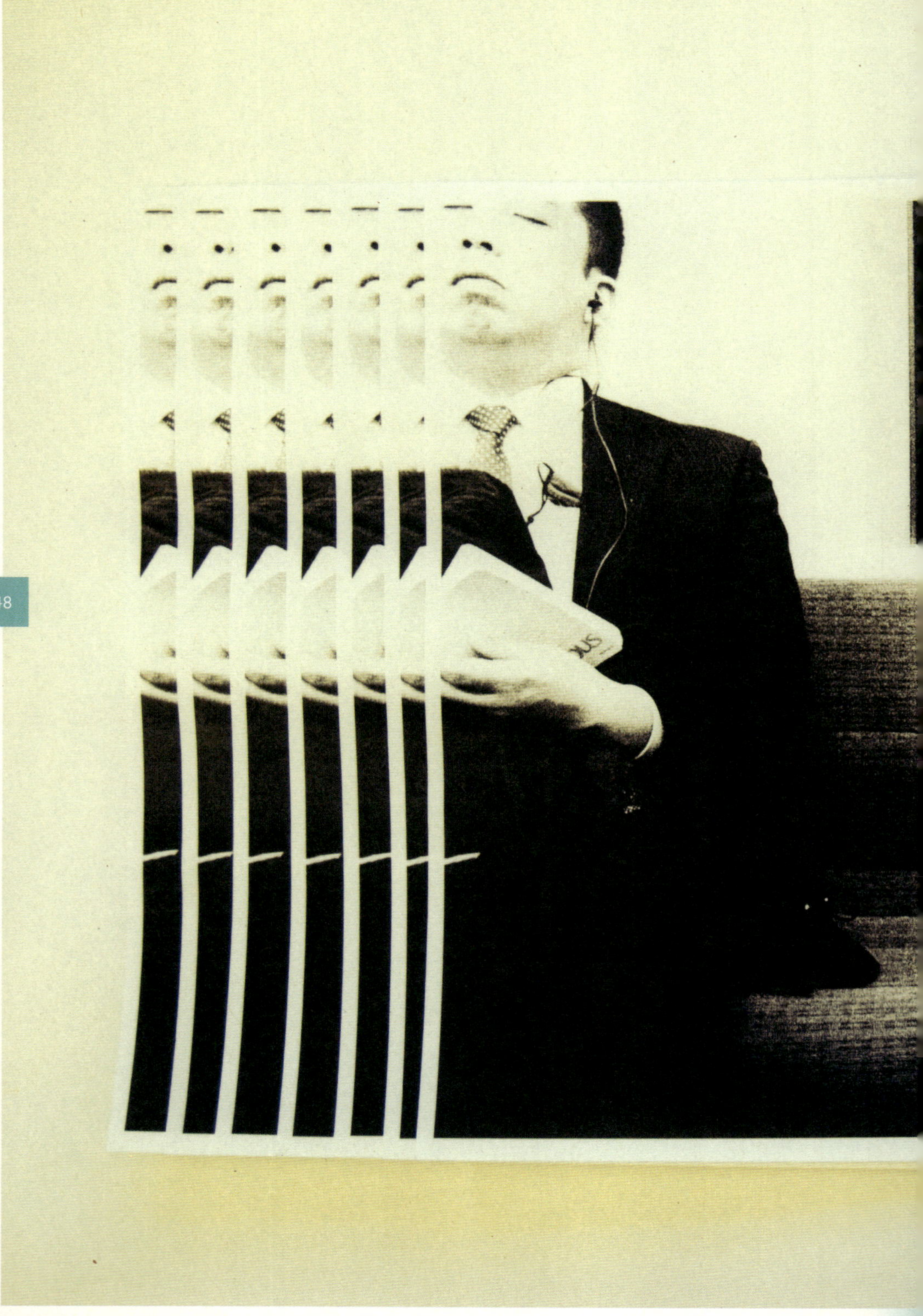

旬彩料理
炭火焼
TOBACCO

TSIM TSUM

Initially I couldn't find my place in Tokyo. So I went into a department store called Tokyu Hands. I bought a very large piece of white vinyl and cut it into a circle. Rolled up, it looked like a big cigarette. I walked around carrying it on my shoulder, until I saw a place that I liked and placed the circle there. It functioned as a lens. The city came into focus.

ツィムツーム

当初、私は東京で居場所を見つけることができなかった。そこで、東急ハンズというデパートに行った。大きな白いビニールシートを買い、それを円形にカットした。くるくると巻いてみると、大きなタバコのようだった。これを肩かけて歩きまわり、ついに気に入った場所が見つかったので、ビニールの円を置いてみた。それはまるでレンズのような機能を果たした。東京という都市を見るための焦点が定まったのだ。

Arne Hendriks はヴィジュアルアーティスト。東京には数回滞在している。

横倉屋
NO LITTER

クリニック

大地を歩き回ろう

東京のランドスケープは、人類がこれまで生み出したなかでもっとも苛酷な都市のランドスケープのひとつだ。大地の自然な曲線はビルとタッチスクリーン、道路とサイドウォークの背後に隠されている。ここでは、摩天楼の上にゆっくりと点滅する赤いライトが星々にとってかわり、熱気がドームとなり風をとめてしまうこともある。東京は、ほとんど屋内にいるかのように感じる場所だ。しかし、この都市の背後に、向こうに、そして下に、大地が横たわっている。そして、この大地が今も、東京という都市の成り立ちと機能を決定している。大地を歩くことは、この都市を知ることだ。

WALK THE LAND

Tokyo has one of the most relentless urban landscapes ever created by man. It is a place where the natural contours of the land are hidden behind buildings and touch screens, underneath roads and sidewalks. It is a place where the stars are replaced by the slow pulsating red lights adorning skyscrapers, and where the wind is sometimes deflected by the heat dome. Tokyo almost feels like an interior. But behind, beyond and below the city lies the land. And this land is still defining how Tokyo is buildt and how it functions. To walk the land is to know the city.

201

301

通り
25

熊野
久間淑太郎
廣瀬信二

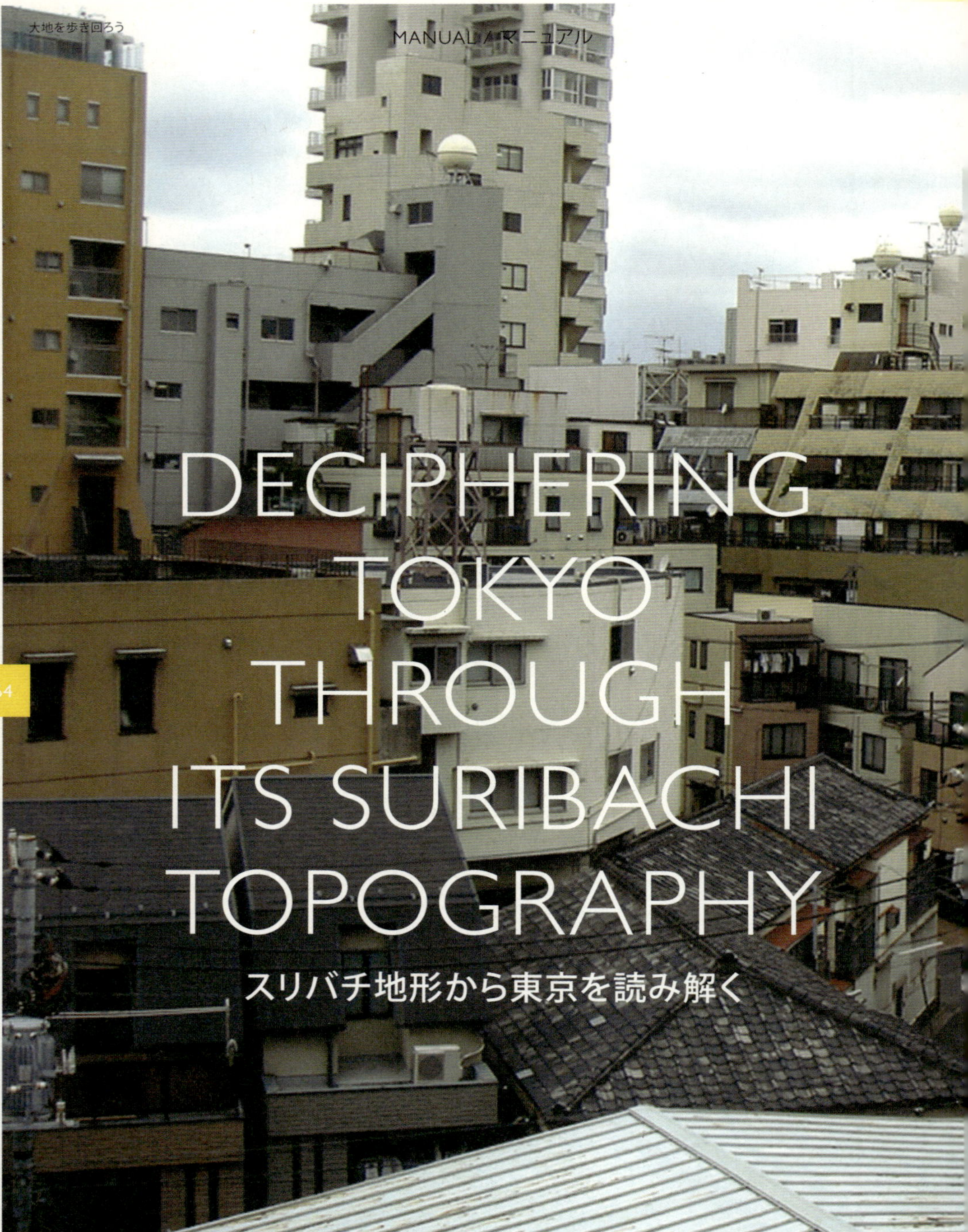

DECIPHERING TOKYO THROUGH ITS SURIBACHI TOPOGRAPHY

スリバチ地形から東京を読み解く

皆川典久は東京スリバチ学会会長。東京都内の凹凸地形に着目してフィールドワークと記録を続けている。2012年『凹凸を楽しむ東京「スリバチ」地形散歩』（洋泉社）を上梓。2014年には町の魅力を再発見する手法や取組が評価され、東京スリバチ学会として日本グッドデザイン賞を受賞。テレビ番組「タモリ倶楽部」や「ブラタモリ」などに出演。

Looking down on the Araki-cho Basin
スリバチの第1法則の典型例、荒木町の窪地。丘の上の建物が取り囲んでいる

東京の市街地は、武蔵野台地と呼ばれる台地面と海岸平野にまたがって広がる。台地の東端エリアは「山の手」と呼ばれ、海岸沿いの低地に比べ10m〜20m程度の比高を持つ。ほぼ平らな台地面は、西から東へと蛇行した川によって幾筋もの谷が刻まれ、複雑な起伏を持つ。都心の山の手地区に坂道が多いのは、この特殊な凸凹地形に起因している。台地を刻んだのは都市河川と呼ばれる石神井川・神田川・渋谷川・目黒川などで、台地面に水源を持つのが特徴だ。川の上流は樹枝状に分かれし、その先端部分（谷頭）では、3方向を丘で囲まれた谷あるいは窪地を成し、元々は水の湧き出るスポットでもあった。その特殊な形状から「スリバチ」と名づけ、探索と記録を続けるうちに、自分たちはすっかりその虜になってしまった。なぜならスリバチ地形が東京ならではの都市文化を育み、東京の魅力を再発見する手がかりとなり得るからだ。

まずはフィールドワークで気がついた、スリバチ地形が育んだ東京の都市景観に潜む秩序あるいは法則性について紹介したい。

スリバチの第1法則

台地には高い建物が立ち、低地では低い建物が密集する。
または、建物のスカイラインは土地の起伏を強調する。

台地では敷地の区画が大きく、ゆとりある広い敷地を利用して大学や病院、官舎など高層の建物が立地する。一方スリバチの底では、敷地が小さいために低層の町家型の建物が密集している。これは江戸時代の町割り（台地は武家地・低地は町人地や職人地）が継承されている証しだ。

スリバチの第2法則

断崖が台地と低地を隔てるように、町も不連続である。

スリバチ状の窪地は崖で囲まれているために、台地との行き来が制限されている。そして土地の高低差によって、町の様相や空気感には明瞭な隔たりが存在する。これも江戸時代に行われた土地の高低差による棲み分け、身分制度の名残である 。

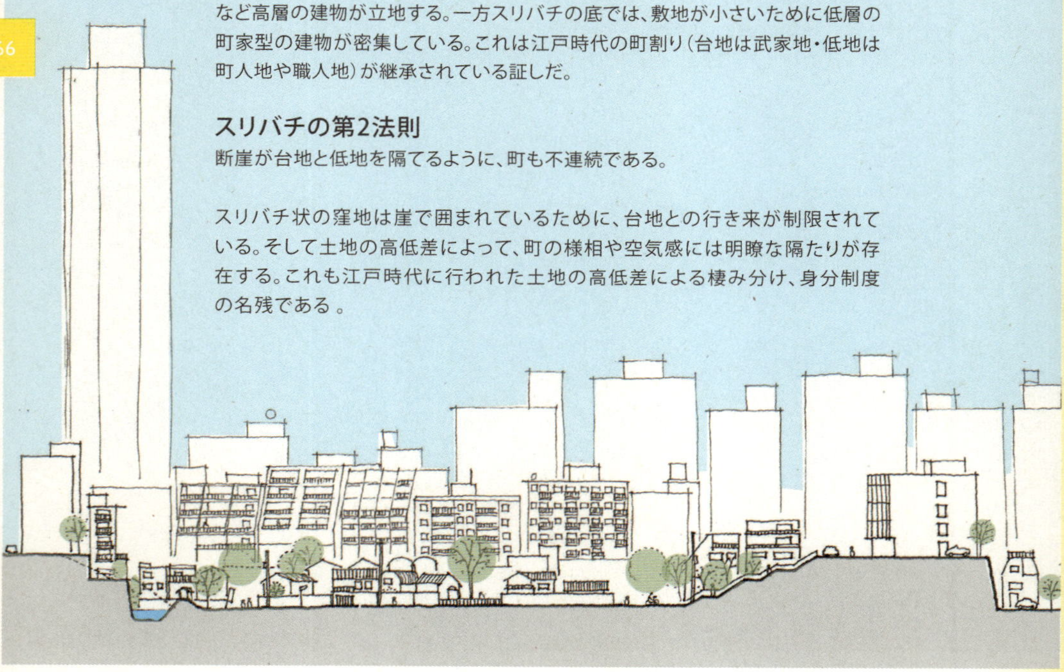

The cross sectional view of the Araki-cho Basin, Shinjuku-ku

新宿区・荒木町の断面展開図

Tokyo's urban area extends across a surface known as the Musashino Plateau and the lower coastal plain. The easternmost area of this plateau is referred to as Yamanote (the highlands), and lies approximately 10 to 20 meters higher than the lowlands along the coast. Numerous meandering rivers, running from west to east, make their incisions in this near-flat plateau, resulting in a complex undulating surface. The hills you find in the city center's Yamanote district are the result of this unique, uneven topography. The rivers that cut into the plateau are Shakujii River, Kanda River, Shibuya River, and Meguro River. They are known as municipal rivers, their shared characteristic is that their sources are located on the plateau. Upstream these rivers branch out and have their own valleys, terminating in depressions surrounded by hills on three sides. It is here where water accumulated in spring water pools and these rivers find their origin. We refer to these as suribachi (basins) due to their unique form. Researching and recording them, we have found ourselves to be completely captivated by this topography. The suribachi-shaped terrain has essentially nurtured Tokyo's distinctive urban culture and has the potential to serve as a key to rediscovering Tokyo's appeal.

I would like to introduce what I, throughout the course of my fieldwork, have come to recognize as a sense of order or set of rules that exist within Tokyo's urban landscape and that has been nurtured by the suribachi topography.

THE FIRST RULE OF SURIBACHI

Tall buildings stand on the plateau, and low-rise buildings are concentrated in the lowlands. The buildings' skyline serves to emphasize the undulations of the land.

In the plateau the land is subdivided into large sections, and these vast spacious sites are used for the allocation of high-rise buildings such as universities, hospitals, and official residences. Conversely, low-rise townhouse-type buildings, machiya, are concentrated at the bottom of the suribachi, where the plots are much smaller. This system is a consequence of inheriting the town layout of the Edo Period (the plateau designated as land for the samurai, the lowland area as land for the townspeople and artisans).

THE SECOND RULE OF SURIBACHI

Since the transition between the plateau and the lowlands is articulated by cliffs, the city itself is discontinuous.

As suribachi-shaped depressions are surrounded by cliffs, access between the valley and the plateau is limited. Because of differences in height between the lands, there is also a distinct sense of contrast in the atmosphere of the city. This is reminiscent of the segregation and class system implemented during the Edo Period, which was also based on the height differences of the land. Next, I would like to trace the transitions of land usage for suribachi by introducing two representative patterns.

The valley topography of Arisugawa Memorial Park
有栖川宮記念公園の谷地形

The transformation of the depression currently used as the park

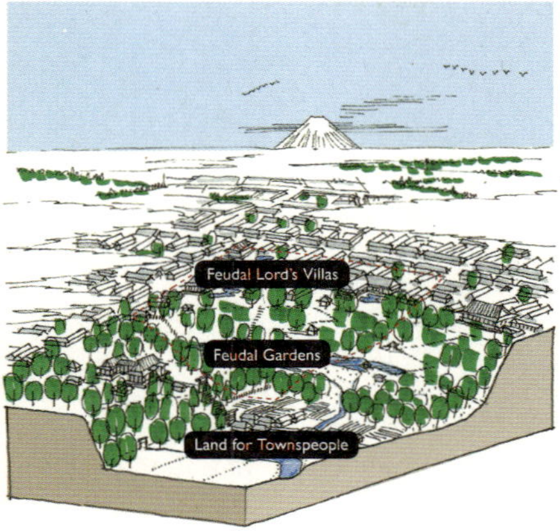

The land use in the Edo Period
江戸期の土地利用の模式図

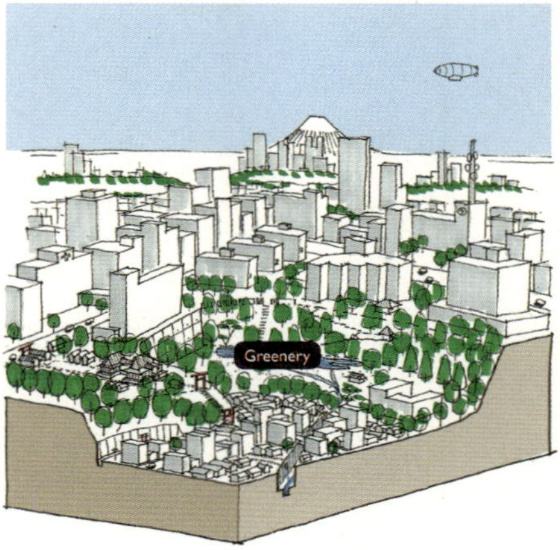

The modern land use
近現代の土地利用の模式図

PATTERN 1.
PARK-TYPE SURIBACHI: PARK PONDS ARE OASES IN THE TOKYO DESERT

Suribachi-shaped depressions that remain in certain parks

Many of the inner-city parks have ponds that were originally created with the spring water from the valley heads. Their origins date back to land usage during the Edo Period. The numerous feudal villas of Edo were built on the plateau, and the valley topography with its sources of spring water was used to create circuit-style feudal gardens. Upon the collapse of the shogunate system and the establishment of the new Meiji government in the second half of the 19th century, the vast grounds of the feudal villas were confiscated. These estates became the receptacles for government facilities, mansions for royal families and nobility, and they were appropriated for embassies and other urban facilities. Furthermore, a number of feudal villas were granted to the private sector and transformed into residences for capitalists, state-guest facilities, and hotel gardens, some of which are open to the general public. While serving as urban heritages sites where our current generation can learn about Edo's garden culture, these sites are simultaneously geoparks that reveal a great deal about Tokyo's topographical features.

1. 公園系スリバチ ～公園の池は東京砂漠のオアシス。その多くがスリバチにある

都心部に点在する公園の池とは、もともとスリバチの湧水を利用して造られたものが多い。

それらの起源は江戸時代の土地利用に遡る。江戸の昔、武士の住む大名屋敷では、水の湧くスリバチを利用し回遊式の庭園を築いていた。それらが明治の時代になって新政府に収用され、軍や政府、大学などの用地に転用された。または民間に払い下げられて、ホテル用地や邸宅などに利用されていった。それらの幾つかが公園として開放され、身近に接することができるわけだ。それらは江戸の庭園文化を今に伝える都市遺産であると同時に、東京の地形的特色を示すジオパークでもある。

The small path to Ichiyo Higuchi House, Bunkyo-ku
樋口一葉が住んでいたとされる本郷・菊坂の路地

The transformation of the Depression on which the Shitamachi area extends

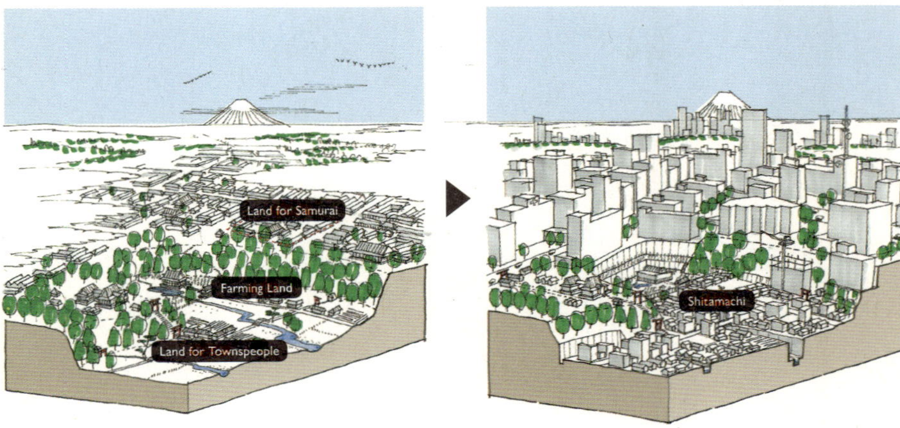

The land use in the Edo Period
江戸期の土地利用の模式図

The modern land use
近現代の土地利用の模式図

PATTERN 2.
SHITAMACHI-TYPE SURIBACHI: TOWNS WITH A HISTORIC ATMOSPHERE

Suribachi-shaped depressions that retain the Shitamachi townscape

In certain cases, suribachi-shaped depressions have been designated as traditional shopping districts and dense residential areas (shitamachi). The reason for their formation traces back to the Edo period, and is closely related to the division of life based on height differences in the topography. The lower lands were originally used as paddy fields, yet many of these places eventually became sites for residential land development. Edo-era Japan repeatedly suffered disastrous fires. In the ensuing reconstruction, farmlands were developed into residential districts. During the reconstruction period, after the Great Kanto Earthquake and World War II, there where several cases where rivers were transformed into ditches, and valleys leveled to make way for new residential areas. The residential and commercial areas were subdivided into small plots that could not be easily consolidated. Thus, the contrast between the traditional shitamichi landscape, with its meticulous layout in the valley, and the spacious plotting of the city on top of the higher land, is still preserved today.

2. 下町系スリバチ ～歴史的な風情が漂う町。その多くがスリバチにある

下町と呼ばれる商店街や住宅密集地は、坂の下のスリバチに立地することが多い。

スリバチは元々、湧水を使って水田に利用されていたが、時代の転換期にそうした農村が短期間に都市化されていった。江戸の大火や関東大震災、あるいは第2次大戦の復興期に、郊外の水田地が宅地化され、商業地や住宅地へと変わっていった。土地の確保が急務であったため、区画割りは小さいものが多かった。時代を経ても土地の集約は進まなかったために、台地の華々しい大規模再開発とは対照的な小さな区画のままに建物が更新され、下町風情が温存されたのだった。

Aoyama-itchome Station
青山上水
Shin-zaka
Inari-zaka
赤坂サカス
TBS
Akasaka Station
種徳寺
Sampun-zaka
乃木神社
Hikawa-zaka
Nogi-zaka
5 Nogizaka Depression
赤坂氷川神社
乃木坂陸橋
4 The Valley of Hinokicho Park
アメリカ大使館宿舎
青山葬儀所
Nogizaka Station
檜町公園
東京ミッドタウン
Chiyoda Line
妙像寺
国立新美術館
Oedo Line
六本木通り
天祖神社
Nadare-zaka
円林寺
Roppongi Station
Tanbadani-zaka
3 Tanbatani
笄川支流
六本木
共同墓地
Roppongi Station
星条旗通り
法典寺
Imoarai-zaka
外苑東通り
6 Higakubo
飯倉片町
首都高速三号渋谷線
六本木ヒルズ森タワー
毛利庭園
西麻布
テレビ朝日通り
テレビ朝日
Nezumi-zaka
桜田神社
Keyaki-zaka
Otafuku-zaka
Torii-zaka
正光院
Hibiya Line
Azabu-juban Station
新一の橋
麻布十番商店街
Kurayami-zaka
長玄寺
Tanuki-zaka
一ノ橋JCT
本光寺
Daikoku-zaka
大法寺
Azabu-juban Station
善福寺
Suribachi Topography
Slope
Culvert / Ruin of River
Waterway in the past
Shrine / Temple

A RECOMMENDED TOUR OF ROPPONGI'S UNEVEN TOPOGRAPHY

六本木・凹凸めぐりのすすめ

I would like to introduce Roppongi and its vicinity as an area where one can enjoy Tokyo's unique uneven topography. It allows us to glimpse the history of this town as constituted through the topography. It is a place where we can observe the dynamism of the city that, despite being at the mercy of the topography, finds itself in a continuous flux of transformation.

東京ならではの凹凸地形を楽しめるエリアとして六本木界隈を紹介したい。地形が紡ぎ出した町の歴史が垣間見られ、地形に翻弄されながらも変貌を続ける都市のダイナミズムを観察できるからだ。

The uneven topographic map of Roppongi
六本木の凹凸地形図
Map by Kimiko Sugiura
地図制作：杉浦貴美子

N

0 100 200 500m

❶ The stairs-shaped valley of Izumi Garden
泉ガーデンの階段状の谷

❷ Looking down on Gazenbotani from Sannen-zaka
三年坂から我善坊谷を俯瞰する

❷ The contrastive townscape from Gazenbotani
我善坊谷から見た対比的な町なみ

❸ The cemetery in Tanbatani / 丹波谷の共同墓地

❶ A REDEVELOPMENT PROJECT THAT REVEALS THE SURIBACHI TOPOGRAPHY (The Valley of Izumi Garden)

"Izumi Garden" that directly connects to Roppongi-Itchome subway station was established on land where there had formerly been a concentration of wooden houses. The subway station's concourse had been provided on the very bottom of the Suribachi-shaped valley in light of redevelopment, and the commercial facilities arranged in a stair-like formation appear to convey the memories of the site. The skyscrapers that stand adjacent to the commercial facilities are separated from the ground by columns and float in the air (a piloti format), delivering natural light to the commercial facilities and the glazed concourse.

❷ GAZENBOTANI THAT RETAINS THE TOWN LAYOUT FROM THE EDO PERIOD

The Suribachi-shaped land formerly referred to as "Gazenbotani," has a history of being developed into residences (Kumiyashiki) for low class samurai in correspondence to Edo's urban expansion in the wake of the Great Fire of Meireki. The strip-shaped plots that align both sides of Ochiaizaka (slope), directly inherits the land use of the Edo Period. The high-rise apartments and the large facilities on top of the hill appear as if overlooking the densely populated residential areas situated in the bottom of the valley. Moreover, steep cliffs surround the Nishikubo Hachiman Shrine that had been enshrined on a hill to the south of this valley, giving the impression of the premises being a cape within a peninsula. It is also a typical example of shrines that are generally built on unique points within the topography.

❸ THE FUNERAL GROUNDS OF YATO (TANBATANI) THAT LURK IN THE DEPTHS OF ROPPONGI

"Tanbatani" is a depression that is seemingly symbolic of Ura-Roppongi. The land had been gifted in the Edo Period by Okabe Tanbamori[1], a direct retainer of the shogun, and temples had used to line the boundaries between the valley and the plateau. Currently a common cemetery referred to as the Roppongi Cemetery remains at the bottom of the valley. Various stairs named after terms pertaining to the temples connect the hills and bottom of the valley such as Enmazaka and Fudozaka, known for its legend of an evil serpent that lived in the swamp, yet these stairs appear as if connecting the divine and worldly realms.

❶ スリバチ状の地形を露わにした再開発（泉ガーデンの谷）

地下鉄の六本木一丁目駅と一体的に整備された「泉ガーデン」のある土地は、木造家屋が密集する窪地だった。再開発によってスリバチ状の谷底には地下鉄駅のコンコースが設けられ、階段状の商業施設が土地の記憶を伝えている。商業施設の横に立つ超高層ビルは柱によって地上から切り離され宙に浮かび（ピロティ形式）、商業施設とガラス貼りのコンコースに自然の光を送り届ける仕掛けとなっている。

❷ 江戸由来の町割りが残る我善坊谷

「我善坊谷」と呼ばれたスリバチ状の土地は、明暦の大火後の江戸の都市拡大に伴い、禄高の低い武士たちの宅地（組屋敷）として開発された歴史を持つ。落合坂の両側に並ぶ短冊状の区画割は江戸の土地利用を継承したものだ。丘の上の高層マンションや巨大な施設が、谷底の住宅密集地を見下ろしているかのようだ。また谷の南の高台に祀られた西久保八幡神社は、切り立った断崖で囲まれ半島の岬のような土地となっている。地形の特異点に建立される神社の典型例でもある。

❸ 六本木の裏に潜む、弔いの谷戸（丹波谷）

「丹波谷」は裏六本木を象徴するかのような窪地だ。江戸時代、旗本岡部丹波守が拝領した地で、かつては谷と台地の境界周囲に寺院がならんでいた。現在は谷底に六本木墓苑という共同墓地が残されている。沼地に悪蛇がいたという伝説が残る不動坂や閻魔坂など、寺院にまつわる名のつく階段が丘と谷底を結ぶが、あたかも聖と俗の世界を繋いでいるかのようでもある。

❹ The Suribachi-shaped Hinokicho Park / スリバチ状の檜町公園

❺ The lost landscape of the depression in Nogi-zaka / 失われた乃木坂の窪地の景観

❻ Mori Teien that inherits the legacy of the feudal gardens / 大名庭園の記憶を伝える毛利庭園

❹ A FEUDAL GARDEN RECREATED IN A SURIBACHI-SHAPE (the Valley of Hinokicho Park)

The land where Tokyo Midtown and Hinokicho Park are currently situated had used to be the grounds of the villa residence for the Mori Clan in the Edo Period, and is the former location of the Ministry of Defense. The spring water pond that traces its origin to the feudal garden had been left to remain, however the site was redeveloped in correspondence to the relocation of the Ministry of Defense, and the Suribachi-shaped Hinokicho Park was established in honor of the former garden.

❹ スリバチ状に再現された大名庭園（檜町公園の谷）

東京ミッドタウンと檜町公園のある土地は、江戸時代には毛利家下屋敷が置かれた場所で、かつては防衛省の敷地であった。大名庭園に由来する湧水池が残されていたが、防衛省の移転にともない、その跡地が再開発され、大名庭園に因んでスリバチ状の檜町公園が整備された。

❺ DISAPPEARANCE OF THE SHITAMACHI AT THE BOTTOM OF THE SURIBACHI (Nogizaka Depression)

I would like to keep a record of the depression that could be observed from a corner of Tokyo Midtown. It was a typical example for Shitamachi-type Suribachi. Unfortunately, this unique Tokyo landscape has now disappeared. In the past a grand landscape comprising of a vast spread of Iraka roof-tiles that adorned the traditional wooden houses could be observed from the top of the hill. All these houses have now been removed, and a tower apartment is currently in construction where they had once stood.

❺ 失われたスリバチの底の下町（乃木坂の窪地）

東京ミッドタウンの一角から眺められた窪地を下町系スリバチの典型的な風景として、ここでは記録にとどめておきたい。今は残念ながら、その東京独特な景観は失われてしまった。
かつては木造家屋の甍の波が広がる絶景が丘の上から眺められたが、すべての家屋は撤去され、現在はタワーマンションが建設中である。

❻ THE DEPRESSION RECONCEIVED AS ROPPONGI HILLS (Higakubo)

The whole area that had been redeveloped as Roppongi Hills in 2003 had once been known as "Higakubo," and like Gazenbotani, a densely populated low-rise residential area had extended across the bottom of the valley. The inclining area had used to be the site of the Kamiyashiki (the main Tokyo villa) belonging to the Mori Clan of the Chofu Domain, Nagato Province, and the deep forests of the former feudal gardens had remained on site until recently. Although the landscape has been completely renewed in light of redevelopments, the legacy of the land is passed onto the Mori Teien.

❻ 六本木ヒルズに生まれ変わった窪地（日ヶ窪）

2003年に六本木ヒルズとして再開発された一帯は、かつて「日ヶ窪」と呼ばれ、我善坊谷と同様に低層の住宅密集地が谷底に広がっていた。斜面地は長門長府藩毛利家の上屋敷だった場所で、大名庭園に由来する深淵なる森が近年まで残されていた。再開発によって湿気を含んだ窪地特有の風景は一新されたが、土地の記憶は毛利庭園へと引き継がれている。

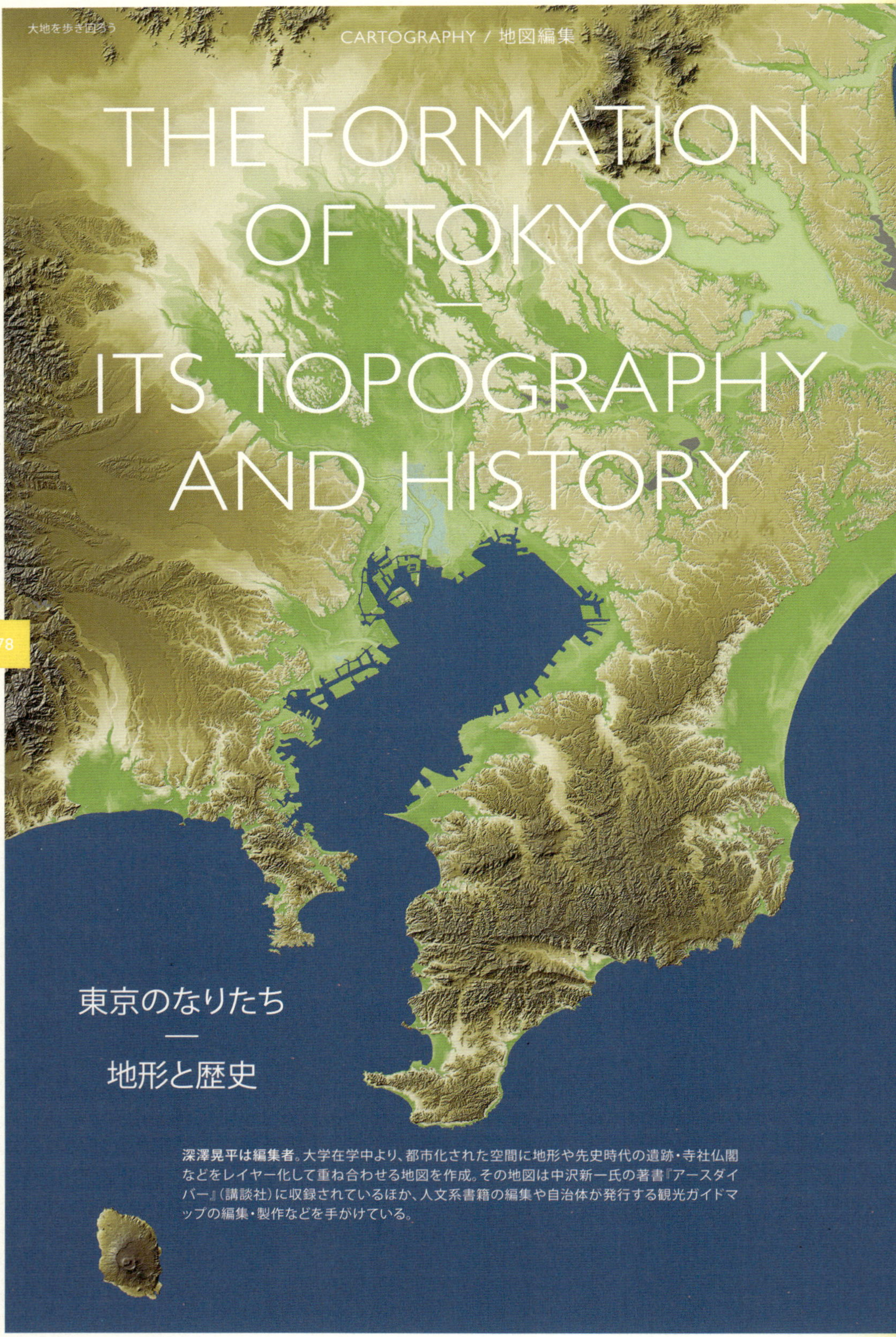

THE FORMATION OF TOKYO — ITS TOPOGRAPHY AND HISTORY

東京のなりたち — 地形と歴史

深澤晃平は編集者。大学在学中より、都市化された空間に地形や先史時代の遺跡・寺社仏閣などをレイヤー化して重ね合わせる地図を作成。その地図は中沢新一氏の著書『アースダイバー』(講談社)に収録されているほか、人文系書籍の編集や自治体が発行する観光ガイドマップの編集・製作などを手がけている。

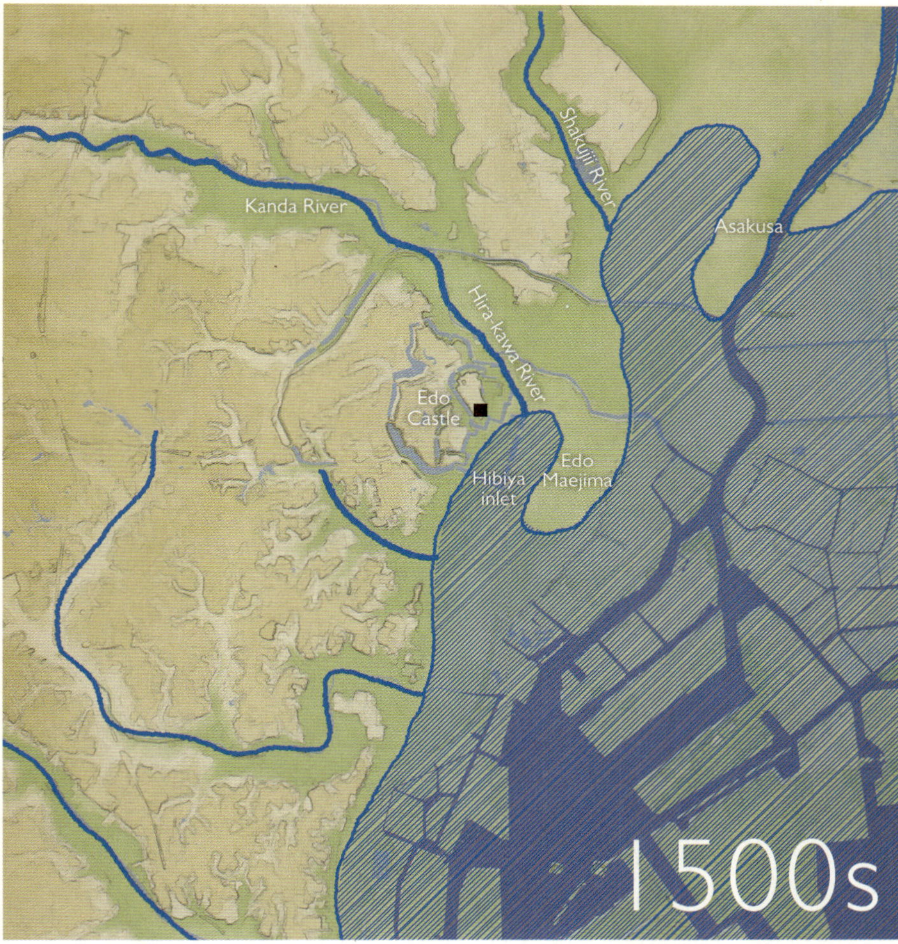

Approximately 6,000 years ago in the Jomon Period, the ocean covered about half of what is currently Tokyo's city center. Numerous prehistoric monuments were discovered on the tongue of the plateau that forms a promontory pointing south towards the ocean. Edo, modern-day Tokyo's predecessor, emerged in the 12th century. The area stretching between what is now Nihonbashi and Shinbashi used to be a small peninsula known as Edomaejima, and the area in the vicinity of Hibiya and Marunouchi used to be a bay. The prototype for Edo/Tokyo was a medieval port city that was established on this peninsula. By the mid-15th century, citadels were being built on the tongue section of the plateau overlooking Edomaejima.

現在の東京の都心の半分は、6,000年ほど前の縄文時代には海が広がっていた。当時、海に突き出た岬をなしていた台地の突端部では、先史時代の遺跡が数多く発見されている。東京の前身である「江戸」が歴史に登場するのは12世紀。現在の日本橋から新橋にかけては「江戸前島」と呼ばれる小さな半島で、日比谷や丸ノ内のあたりは海が入り込んだ入江だった。江戸・東京の原型は、この半島にできた中世の港湾都市。15世紀頃になると、江戸前島をのぞむ台地の突端部に城館が設けられるようになった。

Early in the 17th century Edo became the stronghold for the samurai government that unified early modern Japan. The easternmost section of the Musashino Plateau was developed into a large castle that became the center of Edo. The lowland area on the east side of the castle was developed into land for the townspeople, and the plateau area on the west side was developed as land for the samurai. As land was reclaimed from the sea, a waterway distribution system was established throughout the lowland area. The city is said to have reached a population of one million by the early 18th century. The city developed. Its urban districts expanded into the intensely undulating plateau section, and overland transportation networks, including the Gokaido (five highways), were established, creating the precursors for present-day towns such as Shinjuku and Shibuya.

17世紀初頭、江戸は近世日本を統一した武家政権の本拠地になった。武蔵野台地の東端部は大規模な城郭へとつくり変えられ、これを中心に東側の低地部が町人地、西側の台地部が武家地として開発されていった。低地部は埋め立てが進むとともに縦横に水路が張り巡らされ、18世紀初頭には人口100万に達したと言われる都市の流通を担った。都市の発展にともなって起伏の激しい台地部にも市街地は展開、五街道をはじめとする陸上交通も整備され、現在の新宿や渋谷といった町の原型がつくられていった。

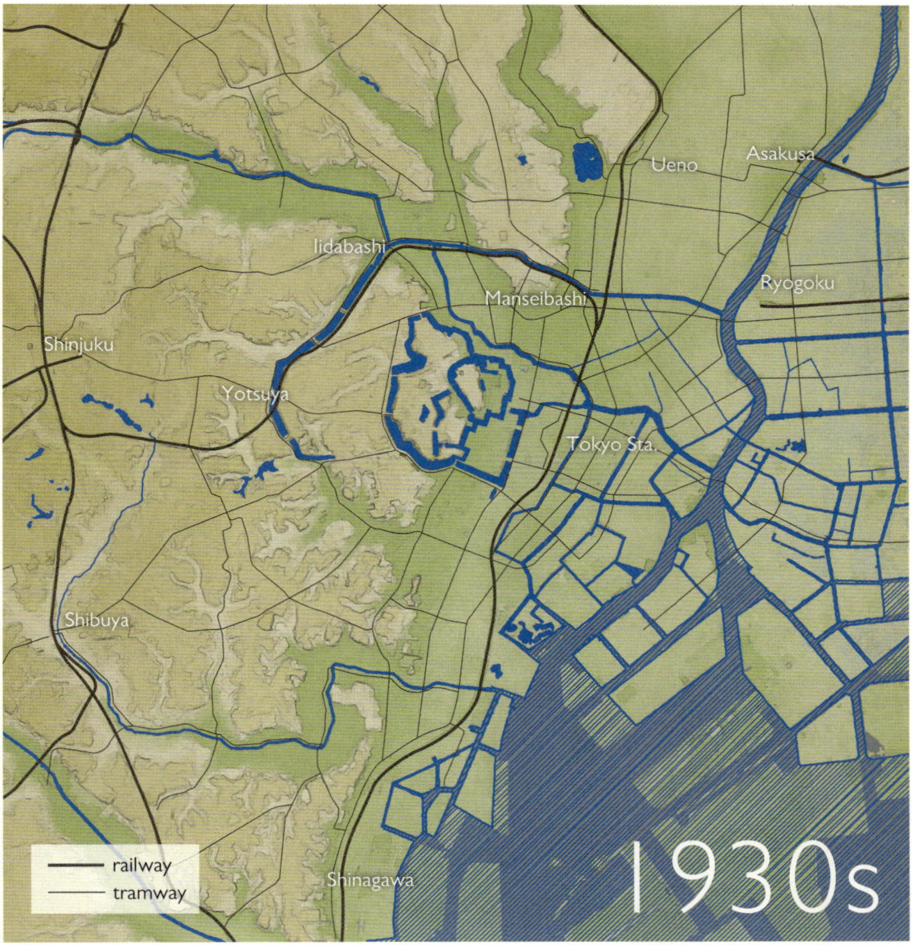

In 1868, the city that had changed its name from Edo to Tokyo began to explore the conditions of a modern city. Overland transport was developed further, and a transportation network that centered on the railway was implemented. In 1925 the current Yamanote Line began to operate in a circular formation, spanning the plateau from the west to the lowlands. Two years earlier the Great Kanto Earthquake had devastatingly struck the central urban district in the lowlands, and the population had progressively sprawled towards the plateau to the west, which had suffered little damage. As a result, the areas surrounding terminal stations such as Shinjuku, Shibuya, and Ikebukuro had gradually taken on the appearance of new central urban districts.

1868年、「江戸」から「東京」へとその呼び名を変えた都市は、近代都市の姿を模索していった。陸上交通の整備が進み、鉄道を中心とする交通網が形成されていく。現在の山手線が西側の台地と低地にまたがって円を描いて走るようになったのは1925年。その前々年に起きた関東大震災で低地部に広がっていた中心市街地が壊滅的な打撃を受けたことによって、被害の少なかった西側の台地部へ人口のスプロールが進み、新宿、渋谷、池袋といったターミナル駅周辺が新たな中心市街地としての様相を見せるようになっていく。

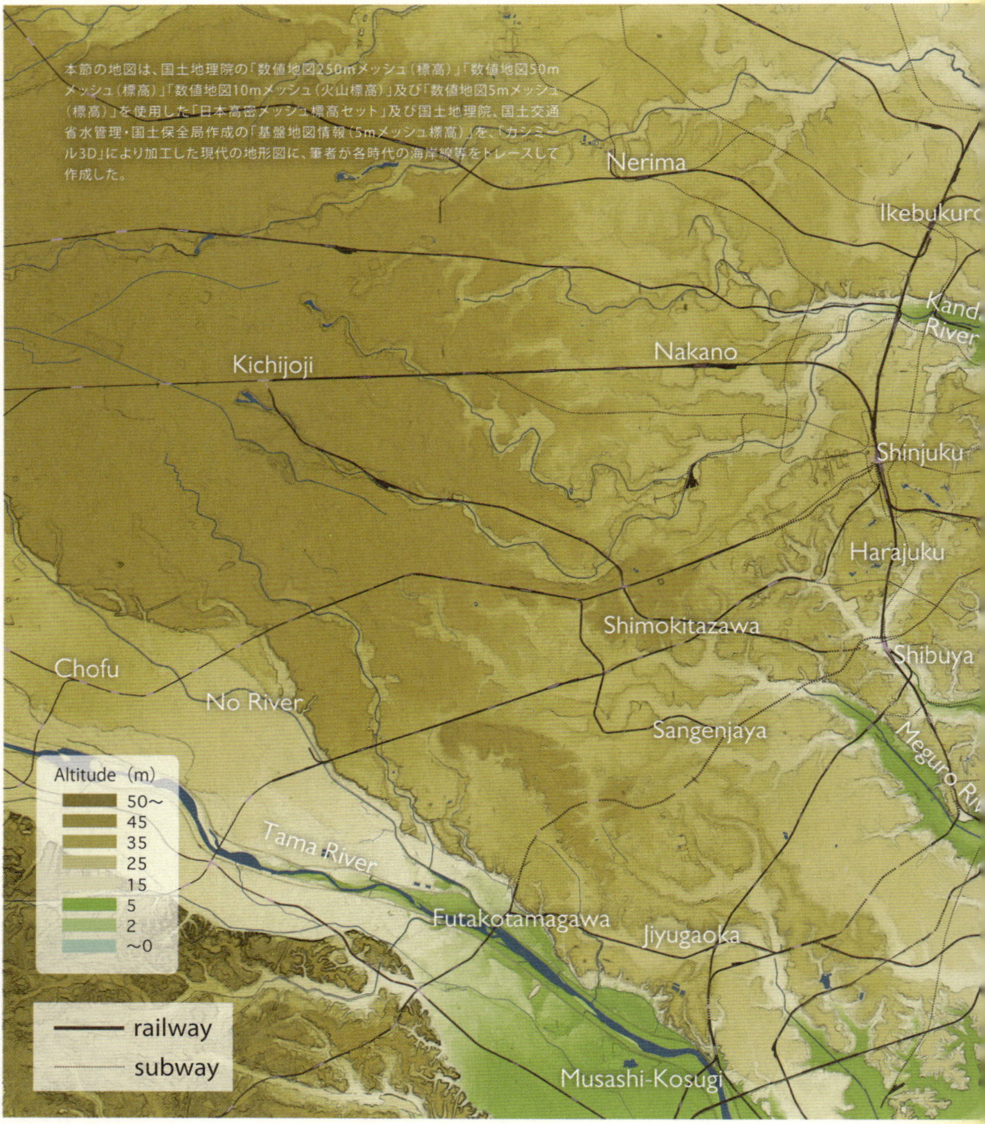

After World War II, the waterways that formerly served as infrastructure for the central urban districts of Edo were landfilled and converted for use in overland transportation. The landfills in the bay area consequently increased in elevation with each passing year. The current population of Tokyo's metropolitan area exceeds 30 million people, and the city is recognized as the world's largest megacity. One important factor that facilitates the vast metropolitan area we see today is Tokyo's location within the largest plain in Japan, known as the Kanto Plain. However, this plain is by no means flat when observed on a human scale. The sprawl that has continued for over 400 years, until today, essentially unfolds upon a richly undulating topography.

第二次世界大戦後、かつての江戸の中心市街地のインフラであった水路は埋め立てられて陸上交通への転換が進み、湾岸の埋立地は年を追うごとにその比高を増していった。現在、東京の都市圏人口は3000万人を越し、世界最大のメガシティと言われている。今日のような巨大都市圏が成立する重要な要因の1つは、東京が、日本で最も大きな平野である関東平野に位置していたことにある。しかしその「平野」は、ヒューマンスケールで見れば決して平らではない。今日まで400年以上に渡って続くスプロールは、その起伏に富んだ地形の上で繰り広げられている。

参考文献：久保純子「東京低地水域環境地形分類図」(1993)、鈴木理生『江戸の川・東京の川』(井上書院、1989)、鈴木理生『江戸はこうして造られた』(筑摩書房、2000)

RECOMMENDATION / お薦め

TOKYO JISOU MAPS

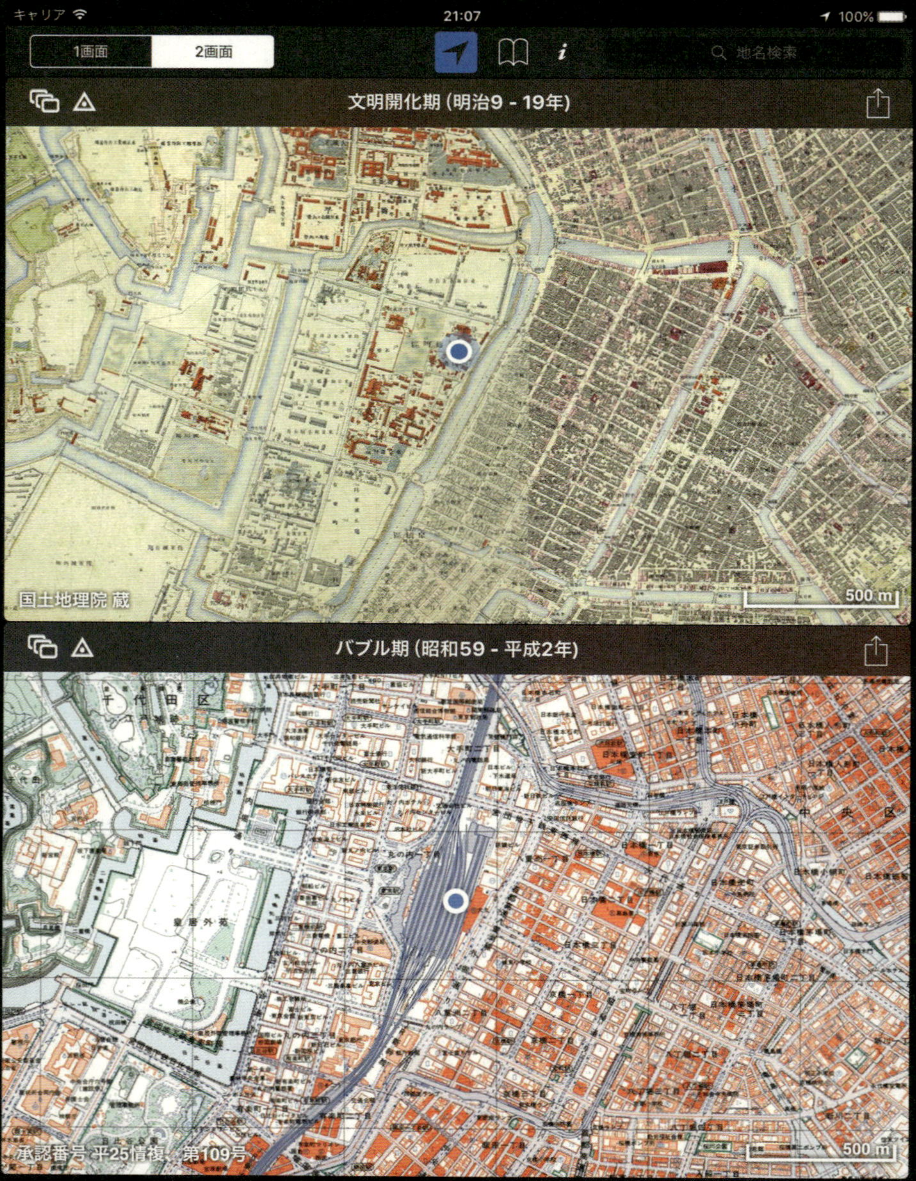

Tokyo Jisou Maps is an iPhone/iPad app that allows users to switch between and compare old and current maps of the same location. Seven varieties of maps are provided, spanning from the Meiji Period to the present. The user can simply tap on a period of their choosing to be instantly transported back in time to that era. Through the use of GPS information, it is possible to indicate where one currently is within the context of the old map. If the user moves with the device, the map also moves in synchrony. The app allows you to walk through different cities from different times.

Jisou is an invented term that refers to the "overlapping of time". By viewing a location through the overlapping of old maps, it becomes possible to capture the changes in the site similar to studying various jisou (strata) of the land.

There are historical maps from the time of civilization and enlightenment (1876-1886), the end of the Meiji Period (1906-1909), just before the Kanto Earthquake (1916-1921), the pre-war Showa Period (1928-1936), the period of Japan's high growth (1955-1960), and the time of the economic bubble (1984-1990). But a contemporary topographical map, aerial photography, and a hybrid aerial photographic map combined with a normal map are also provided. Together they allow access to a total of ten different maps. In the latest version, recently released on the iPhone, aerial photographs from each period are further included to provide a total of eighteen maps.

The app supports both a single-screen display and a dual-screen display, allowing users to freely pair the ten different maps and view them side by side. It is also possible to freely expand and reduce the scale of the maps by zooming in and out.

Tokyo Jisou Maps and Yokohama Jisou Maps are currently available for the iPhone, and Tokyo Jisou Maps is also compatible with the iPad. English versions releases are anticipated in the near future.

東京時層地図

「東京時層地図」は、同じ場所の古地図と現代地図を、切り替えて見比べることができるiPhone／iPad用アプリ。地図は明治期から現代まで、7種類を用意。見たい時代を選んでタップするだけで、瞬時にその時代へタイムスリップ。GPS情報を利用し、今、自分がいる場所を古地図上に示すことができる。端末を持って移動すると、それに合わせて地図も移動。まち歩きがより一層楽しくなるアプリ。

「時層」は「時間の重なり」を意味する造語で、古地図を重ねて見ることで、地層のように、その土地の変遷を捉えることができる。

文明開化期、明治のおわり、関東地震直前、昭和戦前期、高度成長前夜、バブル期、現代の7種の地図のほか、現代の地形図、航空写真、航空写真＋地図の計10種類を用意。先ごろリリースされたiPhone向けの最新版ではさらに各時代の航空写真などを加え計18種類となっている。

一画面表示と二画面表示があり、10種類を自由に組み合わせ、並べて表示することができる。ピンチイン・ピンチアウトで拡大縮尺も自由自在。

現在、iPhone版の「東京時層地図」「横濱時層地図」、iPad 版の「東京時層地図 for iPad」があり、英語版も近日中にリリース予定。

HIDDEN TERRAIN

Tokyo appears to be hyper-modern in many ways, but beneath this spectacle lies the landscape of the old city, which is the metropolis' basic layer. Its built form was replaced almost four times in the last century. Traces of history seem to be absent from Tokyo's architecture. Nevertheless, historical meaning and character are very much alive throughout the city's 23 wards. The form changes constantly, but the rituals of everyday life are strongly connected to specific places, and these places are in turn shaped by the underlying terrain - the landscape on which Tokyo was built. Once you start to read the landscape that lies beneath the tarmac and beyond the concrete, a new urban logic reveals itself to you. These ten views of the city of Tokyo form a toolbox, a starting point that can be used for reading this hidden topography, which lies beneath the cityscape.

❶ PLOTS
❷ NAMES
❸ PARKS
❹ SLOPES
❺ HIGH TREES
❻ TRAINS
❼ RIVERS
❽ STAIRS

隠された地形

東京の都市の論理を理解するための重要な鍵の1つは、東京の街がその上に立つランドスケープにある。東京という都市に対するこれら9つの視点は、東京の街並みの下に横たわる隠された地形（トポグラフィー）を読み取るための道具箱、出発点となる。

Niklas Fanelsa は建築家であり、かつて東京に暮らし研究をしていた都市の散策家。東京スリバチ学会のメンバーでもあった。現在はベルリンに仕事と生活の場を写し、ベルリナー・ベルク（ベルリンの山）という名の都市景観研究グループを設立した。

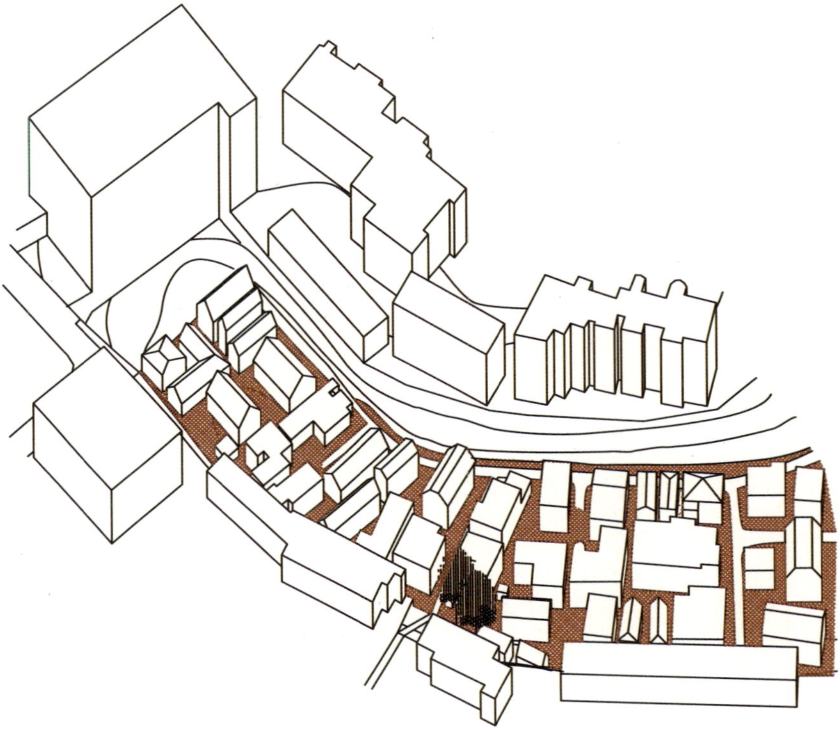

❶ PLOTS

The chaotic appearance of Tokyo results from the fact that the layout of Edo was based on height differences in the natural landscape. This is still visible in the city's fabric today. Although the buildings are very different, the original spatial arrangement has not changed much since Edo times. High-lands and valleys defined where Samurai houses and merchant quarters were built. With the abolishment of the Samurai system during the Meiji Restoration (1868-1912), the Samurais' large estates became the grounds for public buildings and government facilities. The number of small plots belonging to houses in the low-land made it difficult to develop large buildings on them. This smaller scale of housing still exists in the valleys of central Tokyo.

❶ 敷地

山の手にある大きな公共建築物は、武士や大名の大きな屋敷があった敷地に建てられている。谷あいの地にある、商人たちが暮らしていた敷地は狭い。

名前の由来
渋谷
Origin Name Map
Shibuya

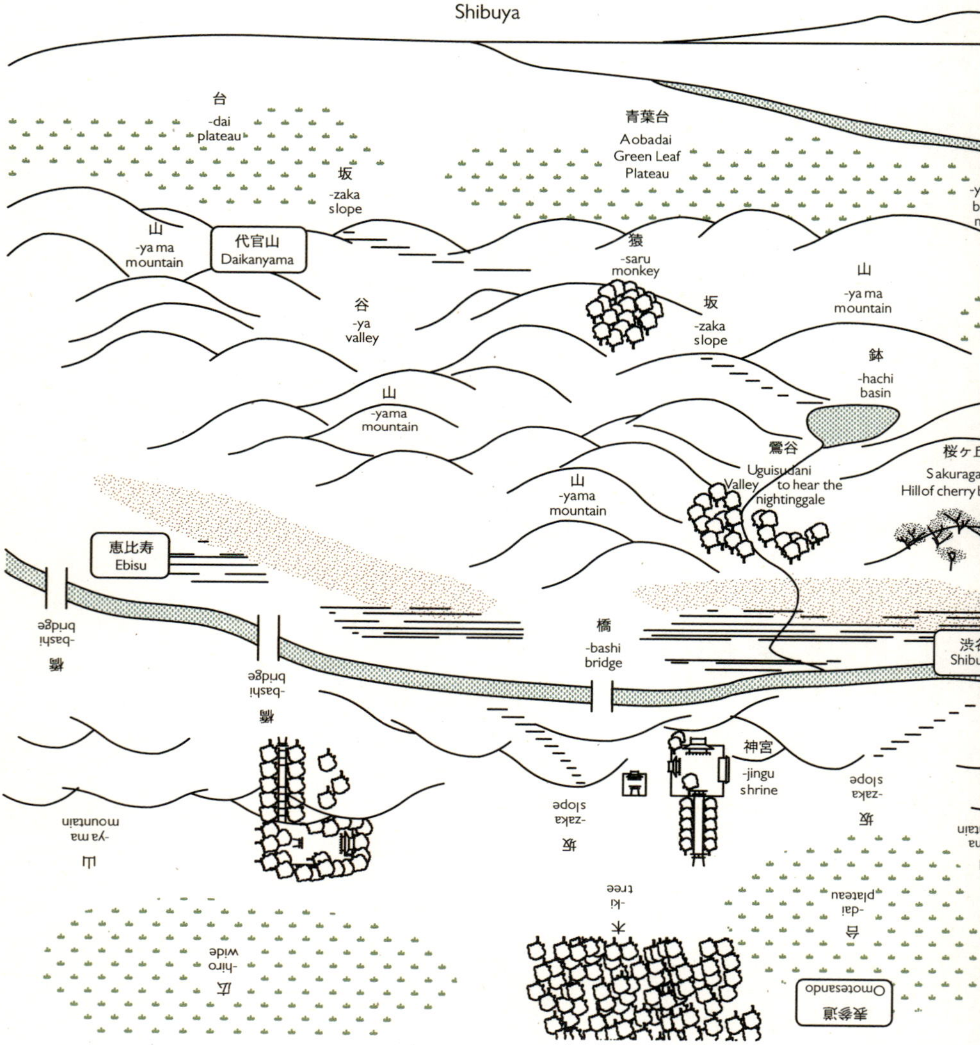

❷ NAMES

The Japanese admiration for nature, its seasons and the rich landscape of Edo has left its trace in the names of streets, neighborhoods and city quarters. Most places in Tokyo contain references to the hills, valleys, rivers and trees. With knowledge of a few basic words it is possible to read this hidden landscape simply from how places are named. This map of the

area around Shibuya was drawn using only the names of the places or a part of the name containing a topographical reference. The result is a very accurate image of the actual topography.

❷ 名前

東京の地名の多くは、山、谷、川や木を含んでいる。場所の名前を観察するだけで、隠されていたランドスケープが目の前に立ち現れてくる。この地図は、渋谷を取り巻く地域を、地形に言及する地名や、地形に言及する言葉を含む地名だけを使って描いたものだ。

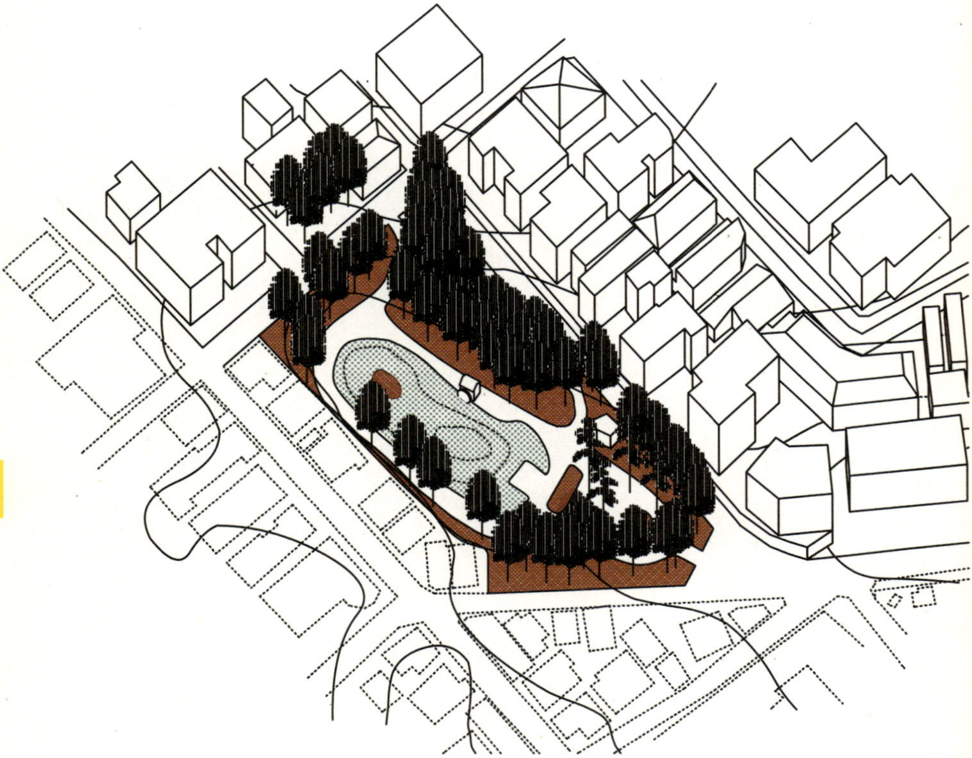

❸ PARKS

In the Edo era, Samurai estates were often situated on the edges of hills, with large gardens along the slopes. A lot of these gardens were transformed into public parks during the Meiji era; this is the reason parks are often situated in unique spatial settings today. Incorporated water bodies indicate a low point surrounded by higher ground.

❸ 公園

山の手の端にある武家屋敷の多くは、スロープに沿って大きな庭園を有していた。こうした庭園の多くは明治時代に公立公園になった。

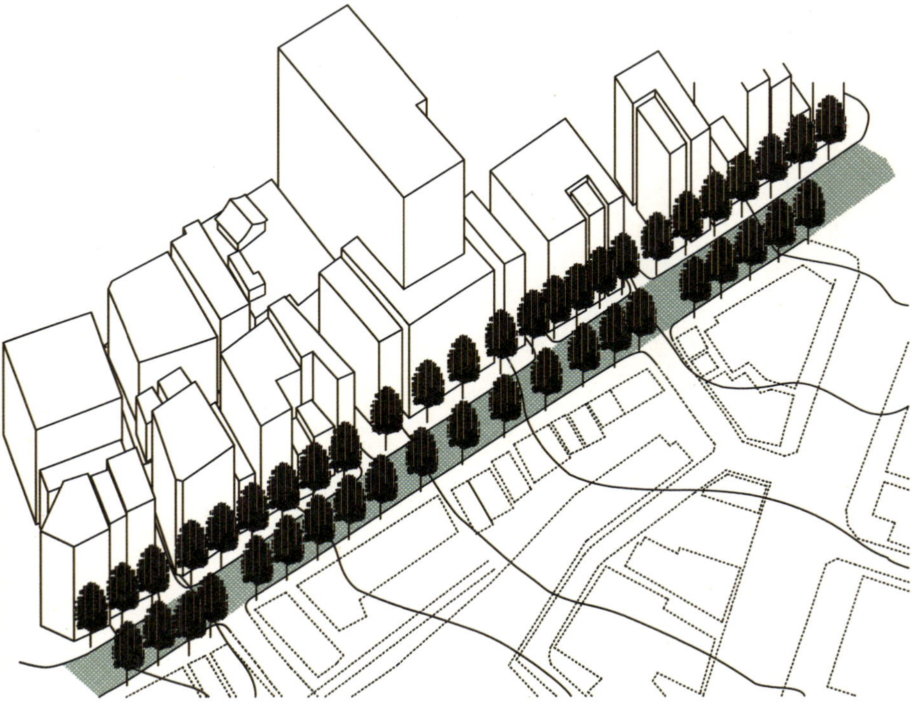

❹ SLOPES

Tokyo consists of many hills and thus also of streets that run up and down its slopes. These streets were often laid out to frame the view of a scenic landscape setting or monument. The name of a slope would tell you what you'd see when you descended the hill. Thus many slopes in Tokyo that descend westwards, for instance, are called "Mount Fuji Viewing Slopes". Today high buildings on the horizon obscure the scenery, but the name of the street might tell you about the view that was once visible.

❹ 坂

今日では、地平線上に立つ高層ビル群のせいで見えなくなっていても、通りの名前からは、かつてはそこからあの眺めが見えたことがわかる。

❺ HIGH TREES

On a small scale, Tokyo is a very green city. Narrow, intimate streets are filled with potted plants that form personal gardens. The larger-scale green parks and the boulevards that are lined with trees were made during the Meiji era, but the oldest and highest trees you will find on shrine grounds. So look out for tall trees at the skyline and you'll most likely find a shrine

❺ 高い木立

東京で最も古い木立は神社の境内にある。スカイラインに背の高い木立が見えたら、そこにはきっと神社がある。

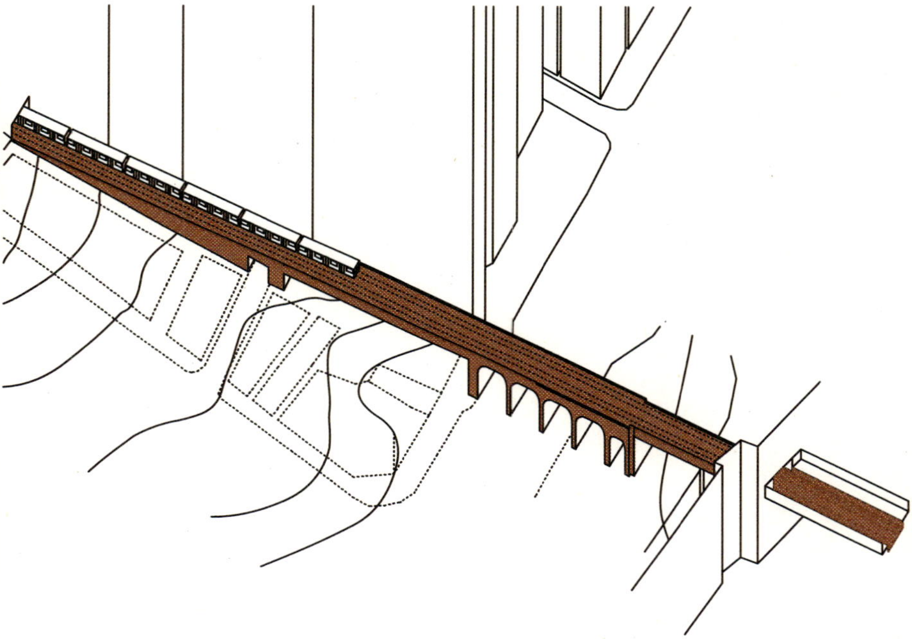

❻ TRAINS

For most residents and visitors of Tokyo the train map is the main reference for understanding the complexity of this city. Unfortunately the train and metro networks basically negate the topography. But there are a few places where topography is revealed and may be experienced from the train. The approach to Shibuya Station on the Ginza Line is one of them. Being the first subway line constructed in Tokyo, the Ginza Line generally stays close to the surface, but in the sudden depression of Shibuya Valley the line surfaces and goes over a viaduct before entering the station, which is far above the ground.

❻ 電車

東京で最初に建設された地下鉄線である銀座線は、大部分が地中の浅いところを走り、急激に深くなる渋谷の谷底に近づくにつれて地上に姿をあらわし、最後は地面よりはるかに高い位置にある駅に入っていく。

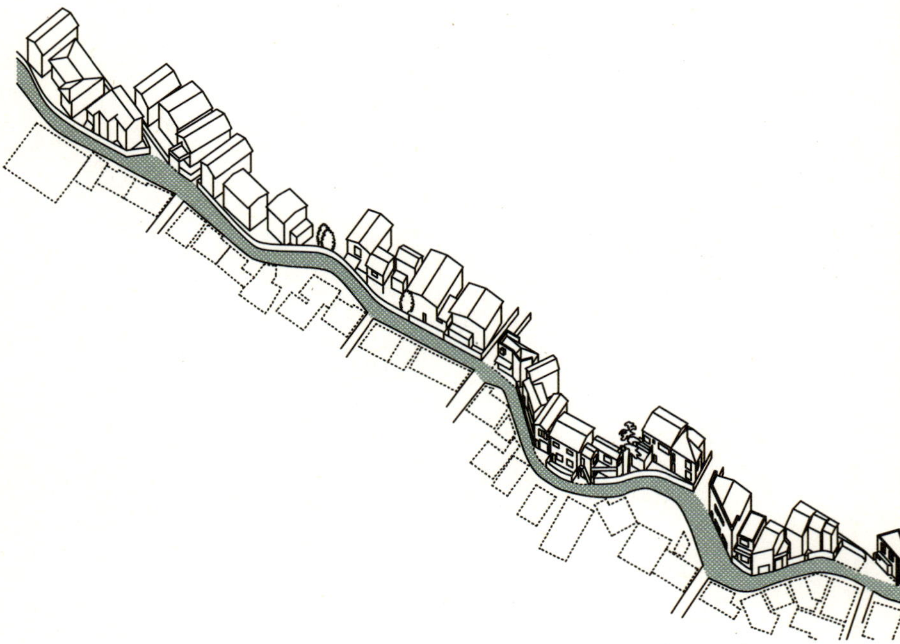

❼ RIVERS

Old Edo was a city of water. Canals and rivers formed a dense network for the transportation of goods and people. Small rivers running along the valleys were used for agriculture. Most houses built on the river had their backsides turned to the water; this is still true today, giving these little rivers a back-alley feel. In the post-war period most tributaries have been canalized, but their character remains: they wind and curve through the city. Sometimes you can only sense the winding in the streets, and you hear only the sound of water. Or you see the snaking movement of highways, above you or on a map. Both indicate that one of Edo's old waterways is close by.

❼ 川

江戸は水の都だった。谷間を縫うように流れる小さな川は、農業と輸送に使われていた。川沿いに立つ家の多くは、今日でも水辺に背を向けて立っているため、こうした小さな川には裏通りのような風情がある。

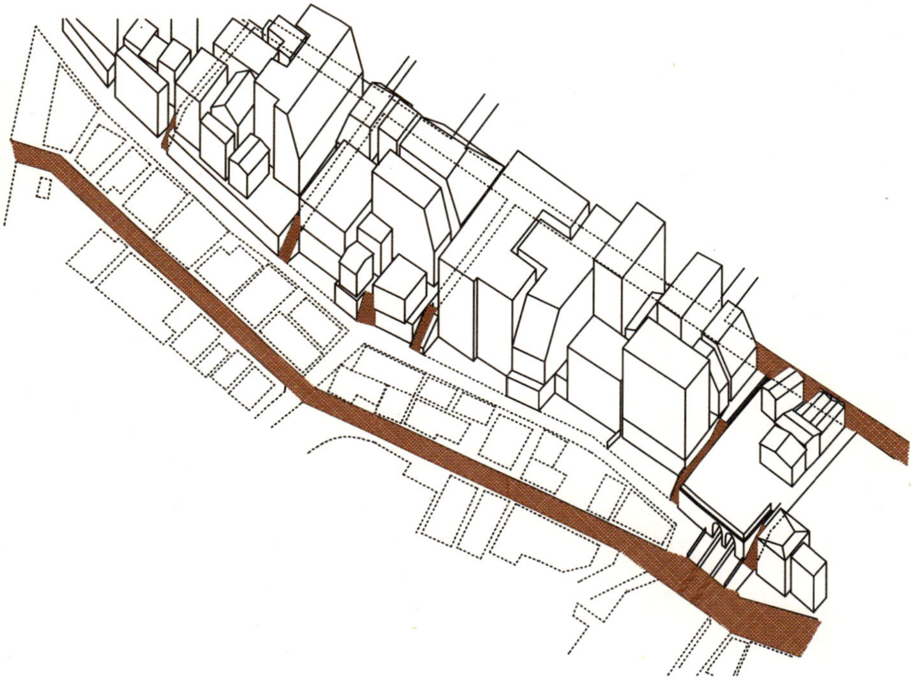

❽ STAIRS

The distinction between high-land and low-land was very clear during the Edo era (1603-1868). On the higher plateau, which is called Yamanote, were the living areas of the Samurai and Daimyos. In the Shitamachi valleys lived lower-class people and merchants. The areas were separated and were not connected directly by streets. This layout of the city is still present today. Most large streets run along the ridge or valley but do not go directly down or up, linking the high- to the low-city. Often only staircases allow you to go from one area to the other.

❽ 階段

東京の山の手と山の下の地域を行き来する場合、階段しかない場所も少なくない。

OKINA KUTSU, BIG SHOE

ピンク・ポニー・エクスプレスはアムステルダムを拠点に活動するデザイン集団。2012年11月に東京に滞在し、自分の足よりも大きな靴を履く人たちに着目し、観察。この現象の背後にある理由を調査・推測した。

大きな靴

東京では、ビジネスマンも芸者もファッション戦士たちもみんな大きな靴を履いている。たいていは3サイズぐらい大きすぎる。男性は革靴を強制されているが、女性にはもっと選択肢がある。

In Tokyo, the businessmen, the geisha girls and the fashion commandos all wear big shoes. A big shoe is usually worn three sizes too big. A leather shoe is mandatory for men, while women have more choices.

Watch the video at / 動画を参照。www.tokyototem.jp/bigshoe

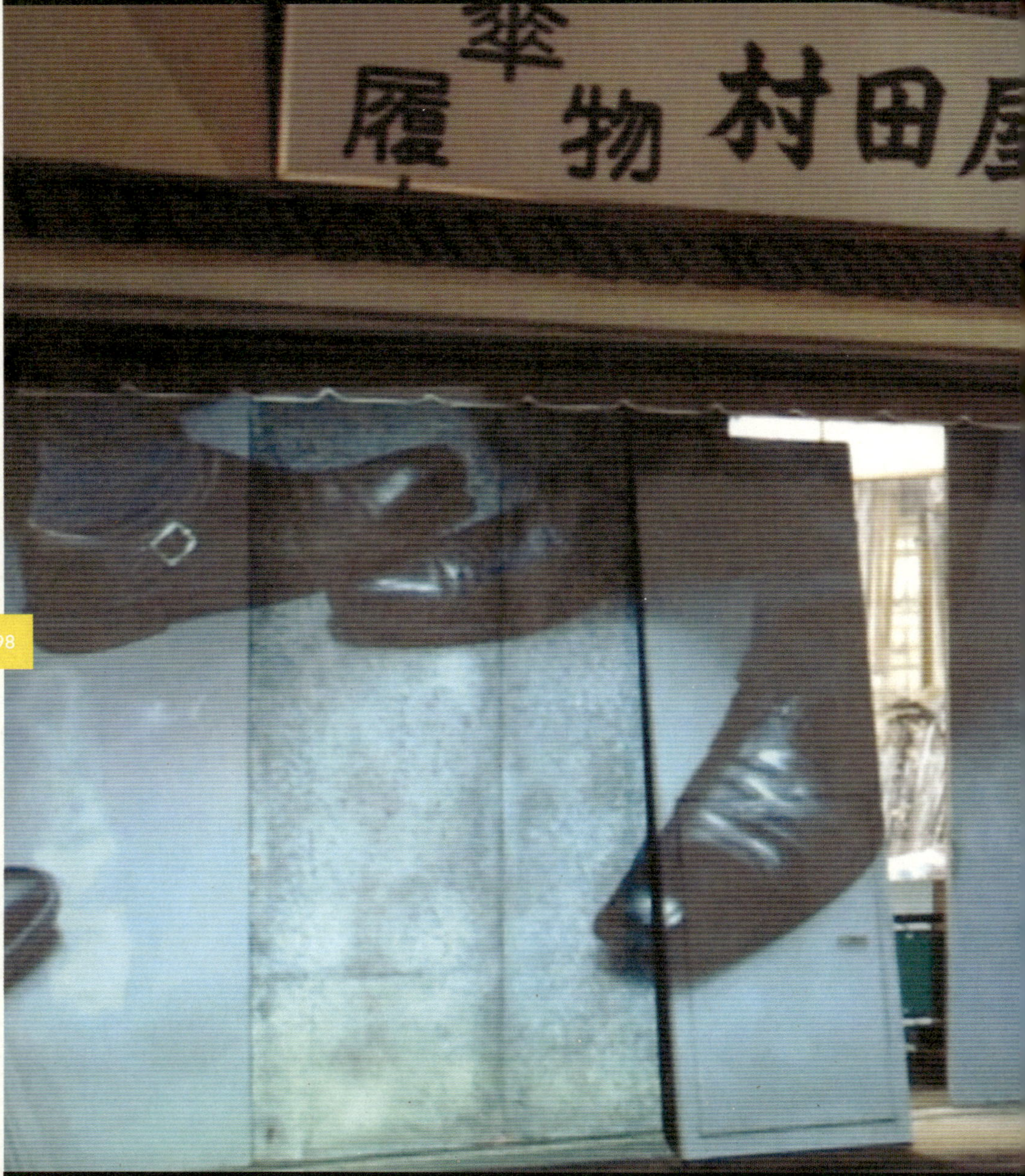

東京という都市の有機体は、その最大サイズに達してしまっている。個別の各地域はそれぞれ異なるペース、異なる規模の発展パターンに従っている。継続的かつ流動的に内部の再構成が進行している。次第に、自動車はガレージのサイズを超え、人間はドアを通れなくなっている。かつては基準とされていた人間のサイズまでもが―何もかもをひっくるめて―変化しつつある。

The urban organism of Tokyo has reached its maximum size. Its individual parts are taking on their own patterns of development, at different paces, and different scales. There is a constant and fluid internal reorganization taking place: gradually, the car doesn't fit into the garage; the man doesn't fit through the door. Even the size of man, which used to be the point of reference—holding it all together—is changing.

モデュロールマンは、一個人となった。そして、彼のサイズが大きくなる一方、都市の諸基準が分解されていく。常に変化し続けるこの都市のダイナミクスを、さりげなくくつろぎながら旅する彼は、もっと個人的な空間を求めている。かかとと靴の端の間に3センチの隙間があるということは、彼は個人的な成長を期待しているのだ。

The modular man has become an individual; and while his size increases, the standards of the city dissolve. Traveling with subtle ease through the ever-changing dynamics of the city, he claims more personal space. With the three centimeters between his heel and the backside of his shoe, he anticipates personal growth.

CONVERSATIONS IN A TEASHOP

This is the story of a personal quest for a place that felt homely—a place that resonated with my ideal of a city neighborhood. What does it mean to feel at home in Tokyo? What does community involvement mean in this massive, never-ending, 24/7 metropolis? Since it was also a personal quest, I thought a good idea would be to start by searching for neighborhoods in which I myself could dwell pleasantly and feel at ease: somewhere sheltered from the endless festival of consumerism. In short: If one is interested in the soft side of the city, where can one go, as a short-time visitor?

Thinking of my ideal inner city neighborhood, I imagined it would resemble a small village, without the downsides of severe social control and intolerance. It would have plenty of green, benches, open squares and playgrounds. There would be a peaceful and open atmosphere; interaction with neighbors would include sharing responsibility for the environment and for community members. On top of this it would be close to the city center, where all the action takes place.

Yanaka soon caught my attention. It is an area in which I thought there was a real chance I might find my neighborhood utopia. It was considered a place where community organizing had a relatively long history (since the 1980s), strong and capable enough to keep skyscrapers and other massive, horrifying constructions at bay. It is a relatively green and spacious area, where storytelling and local festivals celebrate the meaning of public spaces, where commoners and locals inform one another and outsiders through neighborhood tours, magazines, websites, and blogs.[1, 2]

Time Out magazine calls Yanaka "Tokyo's slow lane": "When the frantic pace of Tokyo starts to wear you down, head to Yanaka, a picturesque spot where life seems to potter along just as it did a century ago." When I searched Lonely Planet I found that it did not really pay attention to Yanaka; they mentioned it simply as part of a walk through Ueno. This was a very positive finding in my view: perhaps there would be no tourist crowds.

I went to a tourist information office to find out how Yanaka was presented by the Tokyo Tourist Board. The lady behind the counter gave me a map of the area. She pointed me to the shopping area, the many temples and the famous graveyard. She also mentioned cats.

喫茶店でのおしゃべり

谷中の喫茶店に入り、オーナーや地元の店の主人たちと長時間話し込むうちに、東京に対する恐怖心が消えていった。数日間、果てしなく続くショッピング街を歩きまわり、東京の摩天楼を見物した後だったので、このときのおしゃべりは、人と触れ合う本物の体験だと感じられた。この日以降、東京は機械のような街だという感じが減っていき、もっと人間らしさを感じるようになった。世界一の大都市は、こじんまりとした親しみを感じさせる街でもあったのだ。心の通う近所づきあい、人のつながりのある場所なのだ。

Willemien Dorresteijn はアムステルダム応用科学大学の教師、研究者。2012年11月に東京を訪れた。

Apparently it is an attractive hangout not just for people, but for cats as well. The map also showed a community center.

I took the metro to Yanaka. After taking the west exit of Nippori station, I arrived at a small shopping street with a mix of souvenir shops, teashops, grocery stores, little restaurants and cafes. On the streets I saw mainly Japanese people: some were obviously tourists, walking with street maps in their hands; there were also plenty of residents—elderly people and mothers with child-seats fixed to their bikes. It was a grey day and the streets and houses seemed pretty gloomy, though there were many more flowers and plants in pots than elsewhere in Tokyo, and it was also much quieter.

In an article on meaningful spaces in Tokyo, Sorensen—a professor of Urban Planning at the University of Toronto—mentions a festival known as Geikoten.[3] Geikoten celebrates the neighborhood with its little streets and public areas. Local artists show their work on the streets and visitors from in and beyond the neighborhood can enjoy the exhibits, as well as become acquainted with less familiar spots in the area. Geikoten was originally a festival initiated by former students of the University of Fine Arts, which is located in the southeast part of the neighborhood, close to Ueno, the museum quarter.

In order to find out more about how people felt about Yanaka, I thought it would be interesting to go to the University Mensa to eat and talk with some students. None of the four students I talked to separately knew about the festival. They Googled it for me so they could draw on my map where it was supposed to have taken place, but they also told me that it had finished a week ago. (That year was the 25th anniversary. The festival was held from 7-21 October 2012.) When talking about Yanaka in general they told me they thought it was "cute": an important historical area with low buildings; nice to walk through from the subway to university. They also said they believed it would remain the same for a long time, for the government would protect such historical sites.

Later that day I tried talking to people in the shops. As the Geikoten festival had just finished a week ago I thought it might make a good conversation starter:

Me: "Excuse me. May I ask you something about Yanaka?"

Shopkeeper: "Yes. Yanaka, yes? Yanaka, yes?"

Me: "Yes, Yanaka. I was wondering if you could tell me something about this neighborhood."

Shopkeeper: "Yanaka?"

And then we looked at each other, realizing the conversation could not continue across the language barrier. He did give me a map of Yanaka, however.

Walking away from the shops through the narrow little streets I found many small temples and shrines. Most temples were closed, but their gates were open and I was able to enter the small graveyards surrounding the temples. The fact that there are many temples gives the whole atmosphere a sense of serenity and loftiness. The enormous graveyard just behind Nippori station, which has many cherry blossom trees, and whose graves are well-kept, generates a beautiful, melancholic atmosphere. In the residential area I saw many bikes and children playing in the streets. I imagined that it would be quite easy to walk out of one house and into another; the doors are very close together and face each other.

Cats are clearly a theme in the commercial area: many shops sell cups, bags, pictures and calendars emblazoned with pictures of cats. I saw only three real cats. Apparently they take preference to the graveyards.

I decided to go to the community center, wondering what kinds of activities were held there and who would join in these. However, as I stood before this grim and grey concrete building it did not seem as lively as I had expected. There was a small square—the first and only square I saw—in front of it with a small playground. A few old men entered the building. I saw some pictures of children hanging close to the windows. When I entered I found a small reception where three clerks sat typing on computers. Paperwork surrounded them. One lady came up to me; however, since we did not speak the same language, it became quite an awkward situation. The other clerks seemed to ignore us; they did not help the lady who had been brave enough to approach me. In the end I was given another map of the Yanaka area, and the conversation ended.

Out in the street near the main shopping area, I found a cultural information center. When I entered I encountered an American sitting at the counter. He wore a traditional Japanese robe. Relieved—for here, finally, was someone to whom I could make myself understandable—I asked him about the center, Yanaka, and Geikoten. The center appeared to be a private initiative launched by a local resident who thought it was important that Japanese traditions in Yanaka be shared with people from Japan and elsewhere. English and Japanese language lessons were taught with a particular focus on Japanese culture and customs; introductory courses in flower arranging, calligraphy, tea ceremonies, etc., were also offered. They arranged for tourists to visit an artist, accompanied by a translator along.

While I was talking to the American, who told me that he was one of the English teachers, the owner came into the center. When I asked about Geikoten, he told me it means "art-making event". When I asked about the organizers he offered to arrange a meeting with one of them. When the American went up after a young boy was brought in by his mother for an English lesson, the owner began phoning people. Unfortunately he could get hold of anyone then, but he asked for my email address and promised to get back to me.

Two days later I went to the center again. I had not heard anything yet but I thought I might find a translator at the center if I went there in person. There were two Japanese women sitting there. The first one remembered her boss mentioning my request and told me he was still working on it. When I asked if she knew anyone who could assist me in talking to some people in the streets the other lady told me she had time. I asked the first lady if that was okay: Was it not rude to try to just talk to people in the streets? She said that people in Yanaka would be more than happy to talk to us. She immediately put her stuff away and, after a quick introduction, we went out. I felt very lucky.

On approaching the first elderly lady we saw, my translator, Ayako (a woman in her fifties or thereabouts), asked if we might ask her something. The elderly lady immediately said she was not the right person to give information. We had better ask the man at the flower-shop; he would be far better than her at giving information. And then she rushed off. There was only one woman at the flower shop and Ayako decided not to ask her as she was eating.

Then she said she knew somebody who would like to talk: the owner of a small cafe that mainly served tea. She did not know the woman personally, but she did know that the owner was very talkative. Ayako herself was a Japanese teacher and lived in another suburb of Tokyo. Except for her colleagues, she did not know anyone in this area.

On our way to the teashop Ayako showed me the old stores, the sake terrace (which was currently unoccupied), and the places famous Japanese people had visited. She showed me their pictures and autographs; these were quite visible from the street. Ayako was clearly quite impressed by the pictures, although she also showed me the high prices these restaurants asked for the cakes and dishes popstars had eaten there. One could tell that it worked, however: these eateries were more crowded than others.

When we entered the teashop Ayako asked the owner, Masako Okawa, a lady in her sixties, if we could talk to her about Yanaka. She replied quite cheerily: "I love Yanaka!" We began laughing.

As it was quite busy in her small shop, we ordered cups of green tea and —with people all around us—began chatting. I think there were about eight people in total, all chattering to one another. There were a few elderly men seated in the corner and, next to us, a couple who were perhaps in their mid-sixties. We began speaking to the couple. They asked why I wanted to know more about Yanaka. I explained that I was interested in the way people felt at home in the biggest city in the world, and that Yanaka seemed so different from the rest of Tokyo.

The lady explained that they came from a village not far from Tokyo. The village was famous for its handmade paper; I was more than welcome to visit them there and take a look around. She also told us that they had been to Yanaka once before, for they had been curious about this historical site; the houses date back to the Showa period. And because she had recently seen a TV program in which a puppeteer from Yanaka was broadcasted (he animated small handmade puppets, representing Japanese presidents, in a hilarious half-hour show), they wanted to see it for themselves. The lady asked me about my thoughts on Tokyo; she asked what I thought of these girls who wore tiny dresses (of which she was very ashamed). Her husband explained to me that every temple and shrine is devoted to a particular deity. In Yanaka there is a deity for fishing, for good luck in work, and for good health; there is also one for good fortune, and another, which the couple could not remember. Next to the couple sat another elderly man. He did not say anything but gave Ayako a map, on which the deities and temples of Yanako were all detailed. We thanked him.

Meanwhile, a big disabled man had come toward the shop. He sat outside first; one of the ladies who helped Masako then helped him to a seat inside, next to us. He ordered an ice-cream, ate it, and then, just before leaving (without paying), he gave me a small, chocolate panda bear. I looked at Ayako out of curiosity and asked her why? She asked him and he said it was a gift for me and then he went his way again.

Between orders Masako told us that she had come from a village from the northern part of Japan 30 years ago to look for a job. After living in different, very busy areas in Tokyo, she passed through Yanaka one day and thought: This is it. I want to stay here. Now she owns her own teashop (not the land, however); her husband runs the souvenir shop next-door. They live in a small apartment across the street.

The reason Masako loves Yanaka so much is it looks much like the countryside in which she was brought up. Yanaka is in a valley, and it is not busy like Shinjuku. The area is calm and the people who live here are calm too. It's different here. Many people come here to shop, and she likes talking. Masako explained that she liked the air in Yanaka. It felt like the countryside, it smelt similar—though she knew it was not the same. She liked the atmosphere; it was calm and peaceful around here. While talking, she treated the people in her shop with fried sweet potatoes and sesame seeds on the house. When I told her I liked them very much she immediately gave me the recipe. At that point one of the elderly men in the corner stood up, saying that a lot of foreigners lived in Yanaka nowadays, and then he left the shop.

Masako told us that many people came to her shop—not just elderly people from the neighborhood. Though when I was there I saw only Japanese people of a certain age, young people and tourists would visit Masako's shop as well.

The shops have changed very little over the years, according to Masako. The mentality of new members in the commercial street society is different. Chain stores are entering Yanaka and their owners do not have the right mindset. For them Yanaka is just a commercial area, but Masako and the other older members feel they have to stay mindful of how Yanaka wants to present itself: as a historical site and as a calm and peaceful place. In addition, shop owners used to live in Yanaka; nowadays many shop owners come from elsewhere and feel less connected. This worries Masako. She lives right across the road with her husband and is also a member of the residence society. When I tried to ask about her interactions with neighbors and social life she only tells me about the residence association, that she received a gift on the Day for the Elderly. It became hard for me to formulate the right questions and she clearly did not understand what I was getting at, or else did not want to talk about it, so I let it go.

A lady in the corner suddenly jumped up. She shouted something to Masako, and everybody began laughing. The lady ran to her bike and took off. Ayako explained that the lady had forgotten to prepare lunch for her husband and that it was already half past two.

When the conversation grew quiet for a moment the man who had given us the deities map earlier began talking. "During the war, many people fled and to the temples of the Samurai here to plead protection." As this remark seemed to have come from nowhere, I asked Ayako to ask him why he had shared this. She looked at me in a funny way and asked: "Really? You want me to ask?" I said: "Yes." She asked him and everybody started to giggle. The man told her that he had seen so many people giving me information; he had wanted to tell me a few things too, and join our conversation.

The man told us he was a businessman who worked in Ueno and that he lived 20 minutes from here. Every day he passed Nippori and then would come around this teashop. He explained that he came here because of Masako's good character and that of her husband next door.

Later, Masako explained that there was a big problem with elderly people in Yanaka: many of them lived by themselves. There was a lady who watched over them and when they were in need she would call the government and arrange for somebody to take care of them. She only checked and visited, however; she did not take care of them herself. Masako does not take care of other elderly people either for she is too busy in her shop (where she works six days a week). She loves it however. She loves receiving people and talking to them.

"The graveyards are open spaces and they make Yanaka a special place," Masako said when I asked her what the rest of Tokyo could learn from Yanaka. She explained that the temples have small "gardens," which give the area plenty of open space. "The rest of Tokyo is so crowded and there is no space left. Each neighborhood has its own character and uptown some people are very proud and hide themselves. This way they have little contact, unlike in Yanaka, where there is a lot of interaction."

I thanked them both and when I went back to my room via the subway I felt happy for the first time in Tokyo. I felt that I had made real personal contact for the first time and I felt very relieved. The next day Tokyo felt less overwhelming, less detached and less mechanical—and more human. Talking to Masako and Ayako, I realized that the biggest city in the world was also a small and intimate place, a place with meaningful neighborhoods.

TOKYO SLIDE

I find myself immediately fascinated by the fire escapes, balconies and staircases of this building, SHIBAURA HOUSE, whose alternating floors are connected by stairs as objects, doubly heightened volumes and diagonal beams. Since it's my first encounter with quintessential architecture in Tokyo, I take note of the details. And I wonder what these signs tell me…

The building, by Kazuyo Sejima, a Japanese architect, is exceptionally light and transparent and convincing in its argument of existing within a long line of typical Japanese architecture. The circulation within it, and the relation between outside and inside spaces is carefully considered.

A little knowledge of local building and fire codes reveals the other solutions: the semi-spiral staircase and the external openings framed by a mesh. The first is required by law to ensure a system of escape routes; the second is supposed to provide air circulation.

トーキョー・スライド

東京を歩いていると、火災避難用の出入口やバルコニー、階段がたくさん目につく。中には、完璧な滑り台（スライド）になるものもある。それは、養老ホームに設置された美しい火災避難危惧だ。ポスト経済成長時代の東京において、これから数十年間はおそらく雨後の筍のように養老ホームが増えるだろう。都市のいたるところで、滑り台を滑るおばあちゃんたちの子供のような笑い声が響き渡る光景は、思い浮かべるだけですばらしい。想定された用途が、都市全体に楽しいファンタジーが生まれるのは、素敵なことだ。

Anneke Abhelakh はフリーランスのキュレーター、ライター。

I decide to follow my newly established preoccupation of staircases and fire escapes. I start noticing a multitude of them. The graphical language of their verticality is trying to tell me a story. I have yet to discover what that story is.

There were two catastrophic fires that devastated the city: the Kanto earthquake in 1923 and the bombing in 1945. In their aftermath, new building codes and fire regulations mandated an obligatory fire-escape route to ensure a safe escape in a possible emergency.

I perpetually encounter straight stairs, with or without intermediate landings, L-shaped, double L-shaped and U-shaped winder stairs, and spiral stairs, in colors or tiled. When added to existing buildings, the platforms and stairs are made of open steel gratings that prevent the build up of snow, ice and leaves.

In the midst of all these fire escapes, I see a perfect slide and wonder. From a practical and architectural perspective, slides transport people, quickly and safely, and they are relatively cheap to construct.

I think of Carsten Höller, a Belgian artist, and his description of slides as devices for experiencing a unique emotional condition somewhere between delight and madness. He refers to Roger Caillois, a French writer, who writes about "a kind of voluptuous panic upon an otherwise lucid mind".

So what about this slide?

It is a beautiful fire escape attached to an elderly home. In post-growth Tokyo, elderly homes will appear like mushrooms in the next decennia. The thought of a city filled with childlike, giggling grandmothers on slides excites and delights me, and makes my mind invent a new playground.

It's nice when preoccupations turn into joyous and grand-scale urban fantasies...

The slide

THE CITY OF CHILDREN

"Don't ever laugh at the child jumping along the road trying not to step on the cracks between the paving stones; he is probably inventing a rite."

Superstudio, 1982 [4]

Tokyo. Off the busiest connective carways and exhaust streams run dense and conjunctive footways and well-worn tracks. Streets without raised footpaths that necessitate the jostled, personal negotiation of people, bicycles, unicycles, walking sticks, wheelchairs, and the occasional powered vehicle. Cars are at a distinct disadvantage on Tokyo's narrow, winding internal corridors where potplants and pedestrians often trump automobiles, as limited space and personal preference bring gardens across driveways and side streets.

These safe and slow pathways are perfect for tiny feet and their larger commute-weary companions. Dense greens and colorful, scented collages reside at the height and scale of little eyes and noses. Irrepressible hands thrive on the mixture of gravel, sand, grass, rocks, sticks and fallen fruit that compose Tokyo carpets. In summer, developing ears drink in crickets, cicadas and neighborhood rustlings.

I envy my children, their everyday environment: its flowers and vegetable plots, insects and pets, informal structures, fruits, berries and edible greens. The human(e) scale and pungent personality of Tokyo's neighborhoods distill the exquisite refinement of sight, taste, smell and touch in a shifting stream of experience that comprises sensation, memory and anticipation.[5]

Children don't just own their environment; they invent it. Their instinct and curiosity turn the urban landscape into a vital resource to be exploited (often to the discomfort of the adult world) in pursuit of a fluid "repertoire of playthings"[6] that values activity and things over spatial relations.[7] It is from these "normal" aspects of everyday life—capabilities, relationships, and resources—that resilience grows.[8, 9]

Children do not need the "extraordinary", the "specialized" or the "kiddy-fied". On the contrary, the directness and intimacy with which children interact with people and objects should be the envy of adults bruised by life. Consider: The child looks up and says "Bow-wow" every time it sees a dog. It jumps up and down in its stroller, waving its arms: "Bow-wow! Bow-wow!" We who are older and wiser may feel somewhat exhausted by the child's enthusiasm. "All right, all right, it's a bow-wow," we say, unimpressed. "Please sit still." We are not enthralled. We have seen a dog before.[10] Children are oblivious to the harsh light of reason illuminating the adult world, a seemingly alien way of reasoning that rejects the relevance of places it does not create. Children carve out pockets of the hidden and familiar, furnishing their daily paths with acts and memories, dense, amplified detail, discontinuous islands of habitable space—all infused like orange sugar syrup with makeshift stories and strange happenings.[11]

子供たちの都市

車が行き交う道路網、大量の人波であふれる歩道、いつもの道を少し離れてみる。安全で人の行き来もスローな道は、小さな足で探検するにはうってつけの場所だ。小石、砂、雑草、石、棒きれ、落ちた果実など、東京のじゅうたんをなすものたちに、子供たちは心赴くままに手をのばす。子供たちにとって、都市のランドスケープとは、遊び、暮らし、冒険するために活用されるべき、いきいきとしたリソースだ(大人の世界にとっては不快さのもとであることも多いものだが)。子供たちは身の回りの環境を自分のものにするだけでなく、新しい工夫を加えていく。そのようすを見て、学んでいこう。

Chris Berthelsen は、都市、組織、人間にとってクリエイティブな気候を研究している。東京に居住し、仕事をしながら、子供たちが東京の街並みを使いこなすようすを観察し、また、タヌキの扮装をして東京の人々と関わりながら、研究を続けている。

FINE-GRAINED CONSTRUCTIONS

Tokyo parks are covered in gravel and dust. Grass is rare—it's too expensive and difficult to maintain. A space that is hot, dirty and uncomfortable for adults provides a flexible, fine-grained and almost limitless construction toy for little hands—in this case, for cooking birthday cakes.

サラサラなものづくり

東京の公園は砂とホコリで覆われている。芝生はあまり見かけない。芝生の設置は膨大な費用がかかり維持するのが難しい。大人にとって暑くて汚くて不快な場所は子供達の小さな手の中で柔軟性のある微粒子でできた自由自在なおもちゃとなる。この遊びではバースデイケーキになっている。

FINE-GRAINED TREASURES

Gravel, rocks, sticks, mud—the "bits of unconsidered clutter"[12] that comprise our streets add a rich and dense tactile layer to the rut of "visual appreciation" that adults are stuck in.

小さな宝物

私達の町の路上にある砂利、石、枝、どろなどの"散らかり放題のかけら"は型にはまった大人の視感に贅沢で濃い触感の層を加える。

FINE-GRAINED TREASURES

Abundant and resilient plants (known to adults as weeds) are an important part of children's lives because they are always close and no one cares if you mess around with them.

貴重な雑草

繁殖力が強く丈夫な植物(大人は雑草と呼ぶ)は子供達の生活の中で重要な一部となる。なぜなら雑草はいつも身近にあり、めちゃくちゃにしてしまっても誰も気にしないからである。

PLAYGROUND HACKS

It's incredibly easy to hack your neighborhood playground for competitive sports. Here, a rock and a set of swings are the required elements for the intensely competitive "Ishi-tori ge-mu" (Grab the Rock Game).

公園のハッキング

近所の公園を競争的なスポーツの場に変えるのは信じられないほど簡単だ。この激しい"いしとりゲーム"の必須要素は石とブランコ2台のみ

FRUGAL THRILLS

A desolate park in the middle of a monolithic and depopulating apartment complex provides ample space for dangerous fun. A grassy car park slope combines with cardboard from a nearby supermarket to form a handmade roll-ercoaster. Junk paired with unobserved children often escalates to thrill seeking.

円スリル

手作りローラーコースターは草に覆われた駐車場の斜面と近くのスーパーから持ってきたダンボールを組み合わせればできる。ガラクタと大人の目を盗んだ子供が一つになると、しばしばスリルを求める行動はエスカレートする。

FRUGAL PEACE

For children, the possibilities for quiet time are easy to create—a cardboard box can provide a dark and cool spot for rest from heavy-duty play.

質素な場所

子供たちにとって静かな時間をつくる事は簡単だ。ダンボールは激しく疲れる遊びから休息を得るための暗くて涼しい場所を提供する。

COZY INFINITY

At child scale, curved paths and routes are wide and flat. They appear to go on forever, making them feel both cozy and less claustrophobic at the same time.

心地よい地平線

子供のスケールではカーブした小道や通路は広くて平らたくみえる。まるで地平線のようだ。心地よくそれと同時に狭苦しくない気持ちにさせる。

WASTE OF LEARNING?

Water fountains foster knowledge of refreshment, ballistics and raw, near out-of-control power. Permissive, indeterminate design of water is important.[13]

無駄遣い？それとも学び？

水飲み場はリフレッシュできる場所でもあれば弾道学の基本知識、コントロール不可能な力とのふれあいができる場所にもなる。許容的であいまいな水のデザインが重要。

STRANGE ENCOUNTERS (GENERATIONS)

Gentle negotiations while feeding ducks create a brief but relaxing and secure moment between an elderly gentleman and a young girl, meeting for the first time. Fleeting encounters across generations foster the sharing of energy, experience and trust.

不思議な出会い（世代間）

カモの餌やり中の穏やかなやりとりは、短くも心地よい老人と少女の初めての出会いの瞬間を創造する。世代を超えたつかの間の出会いは活力・知識・信頼の共用を育てる。

STRANGE ENCOUNTERS (ANIMALS)

Neighborhood animals are mysterious, elusive, and sometimes friendly. Regular yet unschedulable and thus highly anticipated meetings take place.

不思議な出会い(動物達)

ご近所の動物達は不思議で神出鬼没そしてたまに人懐っこい。規則的ではあるものの、会う約束が出来ないので心待ちな出会いになる。

HUMBLE ROUTINES

Child-scale routines are marked by simple elements of the street: patterns, cut-outs, hints. It's good to have something to align yourself with. Tuan taught us that "place is in the pauses"—a sense of routine; moments of stability; transition points.

小さな決まり事

子供達の決まり事は路上の単純な要素によって形成される。ー模様、ある物の形、町が教えてくれるヒントー自分自身を何かに合わせる事は気持いい。Tuanは「プレイスの本質はちょっとした静かな時間で作られる」と教えてくれた。決まり事の感覚;安定の瞬間;過渡期。

These selections from an ongoing investigation of child use of the environment begin to illustrate the rich and vibrant usership of the streets that children enact. We can learn from children if we follow, appreciate, and stifle reflexive NO's. Stop and listen. Forget about time and your pressing tasks. Simply watch and listen: you will develop a reverence for their inexhaustible ingenuity.[14]

THE EMPTY SIGN

The first time I visited Tokyo, I was accompanied by my then-seven-month-old baby. The city, and maybe the entire nation, seemed to reflect innocence in all its surfaces. I wondered whether it was my personal pink cloud that colored my perception, or something larger than that.

Drawing on his visit to Japan, the semiologist Roland Barthes guides us through an analysis of his "imagined" Japan in *The Empire of Signs*. He explains with great care that it is not the real Japan that he describes, but one constructed from his subjective semiotic reading of the country, his personal constructed image of Japan—semiology being, of course, the science of signs within society.[15] One could read the book as a study of a hypothetical society where things possess innocence.

For Barthes, Japan is a test, a challenge to think the unthinkable, a place where meaning is finally banished.[16] A named meaning is a dead meaning since the beauty of imagination is lost. I collected the images that I came across, and that fuelled my thoughts of the city. Hesitant to assign meaning, I present you here with some empty signs to beguile your imagination on the city.

空虚な表象

東京、あるいはもしかしたら日本という国全体が、あらゆる表層においてイノセンスを装っているようにも思える。ロラン・バルトは、『表象の帝国』の中で、彼が「想像した」日本の分析を通して、私たちに示唆を与える。バルトの説明によれば、彼が描くのは本当の日本ではなく、彼の主観的な読みによって構成された日本である。あの本は、イノセンスな物事がつくる仮想の社会の研究として読むことができるかもしれない。イメージは、東京という都市に対する私たちの想像を欺く空虚な表象として提示されている。

Anneke Abhelakh はフリーランスのキュレーター、ライター。

フリクション
カラーズ
NO.1

東京都公認
台東初音幼稚園

平成25年度
区立幼稚園・区立こども園
園児募集
(3歳児～5歳児)
入園案内
申込書配付
各幼稚園・こども園
にて配付
申込み受付
各幼稚園・こども園
にて受付
あら坊

2012年のテーマ
ありがとう
POST

ひろげよう！
青色！！
青色申告

ゴミのポイ捨て
禁止です!!
タバコを吸いながら歩かない！
ゴミはきちんと捨てる！
特定区域内での喫煙には、
00円の過料が科されます。

かちゃ
スペース
オムツがえ　お気軽に声をかけて

においがない
ファミリークリーム
ベトつかない・におい
全身どこでも使えるファミリ

幸せを
この一票に
選挙
投票箱

リズムに乗ろう

世界最大の都市である東京は、人工物の最大の集積物でもあるが、東京に住む人々は、この街の自然や文化のリズムのほうにより重きを置いているようだ。物理的なモニュメントはそもそも数が非常に少ないし、人々は時間的モニュメントをより高く評価している。東京の公共交通システムが生み出す日々の鼓動、地域の銭湯に週に一度通って湯に浸かる楽しみ、個性のない、ほとんど数字の繰り返しのような街並み、過ぎてはめぐる季節の方が、歴史的言及よりも意味が深い。東京は石とガラスではなく、脈動と間隔でできている。リズミに乗って、自分の振る舞いを見い出そう。

FOLLOW THE RHYTHM

Although, Tokyo represents the biggest collection of man-made stuff in the world, its inhabitants seem to be more attached to the city's natural and cultural rhythms. More than physical monuments, of which the city has few, residents seem to appreciate the city's more temporal monuments. The daily pulse of Tokyo's public transport system, the joy of a weekly soak in a local bathhouse, the generic and almost metric cityscape, and the recurring seasons seem to be more meaningful than historical references. Tokyo is not made of stone and glass, but of pulsations and intervals. Follow the rhythms and find your bearings.

この部分は建築主・土地所有者
の協力を得て道路として拡幅整備
したものです
中野区

境界

道
禁止

G

境界
八王子市

内幸町交番
8-20

夜間押ボタン式
万引きは犯罪!
昨日の交通事故《都内》
死亡 0 名
負傷 144 名

CITY BEYOND TIME

Naiku, Ise Shrine in Uji-tachi, Japan. The Shrine is rebuilt every 20 years, here you see the new (top) and the old (bottom) shrine next to each other.

日本、伊勢神宮の内宮。伊勢神宮は20年ごとの遷宮で立て直しされる。写真では、新しい内宮（上）と古い内宮（下）が隣り合って並んでいる。

時間を超越した都市

東京は、この20年間経済成長がなく、急速に人口が減少している国の首都である。しかし、憂鬱なデータとは裏腹に、東京の勢いは衰退傾向とはかけはなれている。ポスト経済成長時代にある都市として東京を調査すると、この街のダイナミズムや際立った都市文化をつくりだしているのは、都市の拡大以外のものであることがわかる。しかし、空間の永続性を評価する西洋的な視点を超えて観察すること、空間よりも時間のなかに基礎がメッシュのように織り込まれた街であると捉えることが必要だ。

Joris Berkhout は建築家。2012年以来東京に暮らし、仕事をしている。

Arc de Triomphe de l'Étoile in Paris, France, stands on a historic axis of monuments, starting at the courtyards of the Louvre to the Grande Arche de la Défence.

フランス、パリのエトワール広場にある凱旋門は、ルーブル宮の中庭からラ・デファンスへ至るモニュメントの歴史軸の上に立っている。

Tokyo is the capital of a country that has not seen economic growth in two decades and that is characterized by a rapidly shrinking population. Yet the city immediately confronts us with a contradiction: despite the gloomy data, the city seems far from losing its momentum. It is the prototype of an ever-changing city, a metropolis of consumerism where the old is instantly replaced and the cutting-edge is constantly pushed forward. Deeper investigation into Tokyo reveals a paradox: a post-growth city is not necessarily static; instead it can be, and often has to be, flexible and adaptable.

Tokyo is a city made of many parts but no whole. Its apparent lack of both a structure and a frame of reference makes it confusing and difficult to understand. There are no centers, squares or plazas; streets are usually nameless and seem to lead nowhere in particular: there is a total lack of hierarchy and order in the built environment. However, the structure of Tokyo is not to be found in its physical form. Instead some suggest that another layer, imperceptible but powerful, defines the city. A layer of symbolic meaning, a mythic field that provides coherence in a fractured and ever-changing urban landscape. This field is defined by symbolic elements such as traditions and rituals, local foods, the signs of convenience stores and shops, and the ubiquitous vending machines. Even the falling of leaves and the blossoming of cherry trees have particular cultural value. Similarly, distant mountains that were once visible have become symbols now, existing mainly in people's minds and in the names of places.

Japanese culture consistently values traditions and rituals over built structures. It is, therefore, no surprise that a national or communal identity is not provided by buildings or urbanism. Instead, monumentality is to be found in dynamic processes, which form the mythic field that covers the city. It is this layer that reinforces the identity of its inhabitants and makes Japanese spaces undeniably Japanese. People categorize themselves and their surroundings according to this layer. The mythic field makes it possible to "escape" the physical cityscape. The elements that compose it are temporal rather than permanent, and defined by actions rather than objects. Preference for the temporary over the static relates to an understanding of the fleetingness of time, which is an important aspect of Japanese culture.

In his book *Japan: Cities and Social Bonds*, Augustin Berque illustrates the importance of rituals over static objects in Japanese culture when he describes the shrine at Ise, a shrine that gets rebuilt every 20 years: "At Ise, we are in the presence not of a 'finite object,' but of an 'infinite process' (at least in theory); and this is merely another way of saying that what constitutes the heritage here is as much the subject (the participants in the rite) as it is the object (the temple). This is something radically different from positivist dualism. And this is, indeed, the paradoxical effect produced by temporal forms: by involving subject and object in a single process, they exclude historical objectivization. Like myth, they tend to abolish time."[17] Monumental value is attached not to the built environment but to traditions and rituals. The concept of a building or cityscape as a static monument seems nonexistent. The monumental object or building is replaced through the perpetuation of an action, which then becomes a tradition. By means of this mystification, the ritual defies time—it becomes an infinite process.

Rulers and kings have always sought to defy time and rule for eternity; in Europe, giant stone statues to immortalize power. In Japan, however, rulers did not objectify themselves (there are almost no statues); instead, they tried to become part of the mythic field, positioning themselves beyond time and matter.

In most Western cultures, the planning of the urban environment has been a means of expressing power. The boulevards, squares and architecture for which Paris is famous were introduced over the course of the 19th century by Baron Hausmann. They are the ultimate example of an entity's attempt to enforce its will on the built environment. Power itself is prominently portrayed in the statues and public buildings on grand squares and at the end of wide boulevards.

In Edo-era Japan, even the Shogun was not visibly present in the city; instead he exercised his power indirectly, controlling citizens' daily life through a strict caste society and the danka registration system. He ruled over the people by manipulating the mythic field rather than the physical urban form.

In his essay collection Nurturing Dreams, architect Fumihiko Maki distinguishes two types of cultures: cultures that build towers and those that do not. In tower-building societies (for instance, Western society), it is common to define a center. In Japan, by contrast, no clear center exists. Instead there exists the notion of okusei, or "inwardness", which governs the formation of space in Japan. Important or treasured things tend to be kept hidden and are certainly not showcased, which results in a philosophy of inner space. According to Maki, inner space is "a convenient alternative to the center, devised by a culture that denies absolutes such as centers". The Imperial Palace at Tokyo's heart might seem like a center but is in fact more of a vacuum. There is nothing to be seen. The palace is hidden in a forest on an island.[18]

When one considers the post-growth city, the construction of towers and grand urban plans seems nonsensical. Tokyo provides an interesting case because it is characterized by a lack of urban plans. Owing to the high price of real estate, protection of property ownership, ambivalence concerning urban projects and (more recently) a lack of funds, a masterplan has never actually been implemented in Tokyo. The whole city and its suburbs consist of endless haphazard additions and small alterations. Perhaps the Japanese urban paradigm offers an alternative to grandiose urban designs, which are unsuitable for a post-growth urban society.

The eclectic and chaotic urban fabric of Tokyo, held together by the mythic field, has proven to be very resilient. During the Edo era the urban tissue was deliberately destroyed and then separated into different pieces, to permit control of the population. After the Meiji Restoration, the feudal caste system was abolished and people could operate more freely; the city of Tokyo then grew rapidly. This growth was suspended briefly by the total devastation of the 1923 Kanto Earthquake and that of the Second World War. The city grew so fast and so relentlessly that its structure became stretched to the limit. During the postwar years the construction of metropolitan highways and train-lines ruptured the city once more. As there was no urban ideal to preserve or protect, the city developed unrestrained.

Yet despite all of this it has endured, and the small-scale urban tissue between the highways and railroads has remained especially strong. This strong urban issue has resulted in very lively and thriving neighborhoods, where shops, housing and workspaces coexist.[19] The urban fabric is incredibly flexible: with its focus on the part rather than the whole, the city has been able to transform, through wars and earthquakes, from feudalistic Edo into today's modern Tokyo, while retaining much of its original structure and meaning.

A shrinking population can have a gradual but destructive impact on a city. Tokyo does not suffer as much from a declining population compared to the rural areas, which are currently depopulating. Yet the presence of a mythic field allows the city to remain intact longer than its physical parts, making the city more adaptable to change. Maybe when buildings are not considered heritage, they will be demolished more easily and replaced with nature, preventing urban decay.

The paradox of Tokyo, a stagnant yet ever-changing city, provides important clues for dealing with an emerging post-growth reality. Because of its unique structure and symbolic layer, the urban fabric of Tokyo has proven extremely durable and has withstood destruction. To ask what it means to be a post-growth urban society is to open new avenues for defining what makes a city. Tokyo shows how a mythic field may replace bricks and mortar to provide structure and meaning. It shows how a city can survive without master plans, maintaining an incredible diversity and flexibility, and keeping neighborhoods strong and lively, in the face of many challenges.

KONBINI MORPHOLOGY

コンビニ：流転の形態論

コンビニは絶えず変化している。24時間のサイクルで、棚が補充されるのとほぼ同じスピードで客が棚を空にしていく。しかも、オーナーやフランチャイズ先が変わったり、店自体が完全になくなってしまうこともある。

Gavin H. Whitelaw は日本で生活し、仕事をしている社会文化人類学者。日本のコンビニにおける社会的生活や人間文化的エコロジーを研究しており、フィールドワークとして1年間コンビニで働いた。

The konbini is a hive of perpetual activity and constant flux, conditions that stem from the ceaseless reinvention of the convenience-store model since the opening of Japan's first major chains in the mid-1970s.

Restlessness, you might say, is written into the konbini's manual. Prepared food deliveries occur three times a day. Non-perishables, milk and bread arrive once every 24 hours. Newspapers are dropped off as the sun prepares to rise and set. When customers are not being served, workers focus on restocking, cleaning and refreshing the store. This week's magazines go on the racks; last week's get boxed up and returned. Fresh meals are stacked on the shelves; unsold food gets tossed or quietly consumed. New product banners go up; the old ones are torn down. Store owners rush to place tomorrow's orders, make home deliveries, pay bills, train new staff, receive guidance from service representatives, and remit each yen the store brings in. Sleep is the one activity that there seems to be little patience for.

In Tokyo, there is now one konbini for every 1,860 residents. They are plentiful and recognizable enough to be used as landmarks on maps. But commercial stagnation—poor product turnover, lack of foot traffic, a shortage of workers, or a chain's inability to keep up with industry innovations—remains a nagging concern. This is particularly true for the tens of thousands of families who sign onto 10-year franchise contracts and shoulder much of the risk associated with these round-the-clock businesses. Stagnation can nudge a once-profitable unit into the red. Over successive quarters, losses can accumulate, forcing franchisees into debt, new contracts and store relocation.

Japan's konbini industry is consolidating. Forty predominantly regional chains two decades ago have been whittled down to just twenty today. Within these, three chains—7-Eleven, Lawson, and FamilyMart—account for 70 percent of all stores and nearly 80 percent of industry sales. The rise of this oligopoly has ushered in an era of "scrap and build". Veteran franchisees are aging and many are unlikely to renew their contracts, even if their stores remain profitable. Industry wide, store closures now outpace new shop openings. In 2011, Japan's top five chains created 3,610 new stores while shuttering 2,130 existing establishments. The following year, the same chains opened 2,870 and closed 1,354.

Fierce competition and slimmer margins make owning a konbini—let alone two or three—a hard sell. Nevertheless, chains are promoting the idea. Many companies raised or did away with age-ceilings once placed on ownership contracts. Chain headquarters are also courting new populations of potential franchisees, including datsusara (corporate dropouts), immigrants, and retired members of Japan's self-defense forces. The average age of a Japanese 7-Eleven owner is mid-50s; 35 percent of all 7-Eleven franchisees currently maintain two or more stores.

Snapshots of konbini locations taken over the course of a decade offer further visual clues to the changes underway and to what follows in the wake of these stores closing down. Konbini tend to close quickly and with little warning, save a sign taped to the locked door. Local residents and passersby are left to speculate about what occurred and what may happen next. In some instances, the store will undergo "renewal" and be rebranded as an upscale version of its former self. If the chain is struggling, it might finally succumb to the expansionary appetite of a larger competitor and get "flipped" into a Lawson or a FamilyMart. A poorly positioned store, however, will likely be abandoned. Even if a particular location cannot support a konbini, there may be a fast-food restaurant or a café more than willing to take up residence. Sometimes, the konbini disappears and the site is razed completely. In the empty lot spreads a pay-by-the-hour parking lot or a temporary model-apartment showroom, to generate some income while the property owner waits and weighs various options.

Hacchobori, Chuo-ku, Tokyo 2004

Hacchobori, Chuo-ku, Tokyo 2013

Waseda, Shinjuku, Tokyo 2005

Waseda, Shinjuku, Tokyo 2013

Hacchobori, Chuo-ku, Tokyo 2005

Hacchobori, Chuo-ku, Tokyo 2013

Osawa, Mitaka , Tokyo 2007

Osawa, Mitaka , Tokyo 2013

These images capture changes in Tokyo's konbini landscape over a ten year period.

Shintomicho, Chuo-ku, Tokyo 2005

Shintomicho, Chuo-ku, Tokyo 2013

Osawa, Mitaka , Tokyo 2011

Osawa, Mitaka , Tokyo 2014

Ginza, Chuo-ku, Tokyo 2004

Ginza, Chuo-ku, Tokyo 2013

Iguchi, Mitaka, Tokyo 2007

Iguchi Mitaka, Tokyo 2012

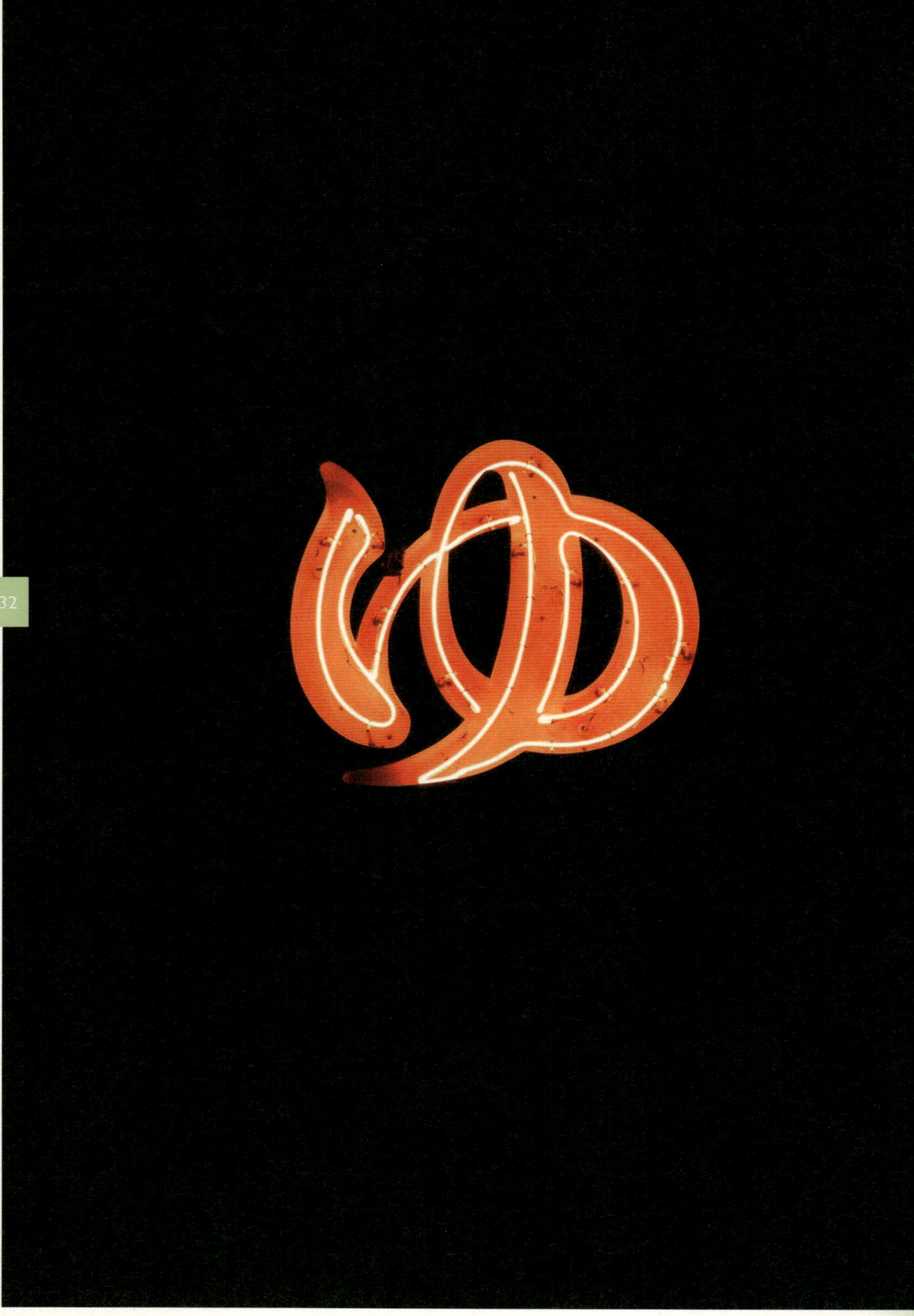

THE NAKED NEIGHBORHOOD: EXPLORING THE METROPOLITAN BATHSCAPE

I am beholden to and dependent on Tokyo's many sento for my sanity in the post-post-postmodern chaos of Tokyo, especially in the freezing winter months. Throughout my two decades of adult life in Japan, I have always been lured to the hot and healing waters of hot springs and public baths throughout the country, and as long as I have lived in Tokyo, I have become a sort of connoisseur, sampling at least one a week. So far, I have been to at least one hundred of these baths in Tokyo alone. It's barely a fraction of the urban bathscape, but I know with certainty that this is a hidden layer of the city that exists in as much complexity as the public transport system—a network of hot water that boils like passionate blood, roaring under the grey concrete skin of the metropolis. And there is more to the Tokyo bathscape than just steaming boiling water. It has profound meaning for how neighborhood and community in this endless metropolis are experienced.

裸のつきあい：東京都心の銭湯

東京で近所の付き合いやコミュニティを体験するということにおいて、東京の銭湯は深い意味をもっている。「裸の付き合い」や「スキンシップ」といった概念は、「裸であること」がもつ、人や物事を平等に捉え、関係性を育む力を強く示している。赤の他人と裸で接することは、絆を強め、ストレスを和らげる体験となる。「湯」を共有することは、コミュニティを結びつける方法である。銭湯は世間から守られた場所であり、日常生活の中でついた塵や汚れと罪を洗い流してくれる場所である。「裸のつきあい」は、東京に暮らす、とてつもない数の、考えの異なる人々を一つにする「社会的接着剤」のようなものである。

Greg Dvorak は一橋大学准教授。太平洋・アジアの歴史と文化を研究している。東京に居住して仕事をしており、「銭湯の達人」を自認している。

吹上湯

ミクロバス
電気風呂

Tokyo baths usually invite passersby to enter via a large, sometimes neon, sign that says "yu" (hot water), written in red, sometimes high on the roof, and rows of shoe lockers near the entrance with wooden keys. The oldest baths, though rare, still even boast a tall chimney extending from their furnaces in the back. They smell of fresh firewood. Proper sento, in their many sizes and varieties, are publicly subsidized and have set prices, still under 500 yen in Tokyo at the time of writing.

More recently, the smaller, older baths have increasingly been eclipsed by "super-sento," which are much bigger baths that can cost much more to use but which usually have a wide range of interesting baths to enjoy. The sento and super-sento are usually sourced with heated, filtered, sometimes softened, tap water, but many super-sento, and sometimes even average neighborhood sento, are fed by onsen natural springs, with wonderfully beneficial minerals. Tokyo-area hot springs can range from the reddish-brown color of tea to the thick blackness of an espresso. Hot springs closer to the sea are salty and high in sodium; others are alkaline and almost sweet in aroma. All of these baths, however, promise a gratifying soak in yu for anyone who desires it and can pay for the privilege.

The word sento, which literally means "money bath," can be traced back to the 15th century. Japan's bath culture is much older, though. The history of communal bathing in Japan dates back to temple-purification rituals that traveled all the way from India along with Buddhism. Commercial bathhouses didn't begin to thrive until the 13th century.

Public bathing was born out of necessity. It was costly and difficult to heat large amounts of water in one's home, and as cities grew bigger, the danger of sparking a big fire was also a serious concern. From pre-modern Edo up to pre-war Tokyo, the luxury of being able to not worry oneself with kindling a fire and to walk down the street to soak in super-hot yu and spacious, overflowing, deep pools became a highly coveted privilege, especially in times of poverty, disaster, and war. Although there are sento located all over Japan, it is said that Tokyo baths are the hottest in the entire country (on average, 46 or 47 degrees), if only because of the tremendous value that people here still ascribe to having ample supplies of hot water, and their pride in being able to tolerate boiling temperatures.[20]

Communal bathing is often portrayed as a fundamental part of popular culture and identity in Japan. Bathing culture and the ritual of cleaning one's body is celebrated so much that sometimes it gets associated with "Japaneseness" itself. The typical mural paintings of Mount Fuji—Japan's national symbol—that adorn the walls of most sento in Tokyo echo this sentiment and earn these baths a reputation as galleries of popular art.[21] Tokyo—and all of Japan—is extremely proud of its bathing culture.

This pride is illustrated poignantly in the award-winning manga comic series Thermae Romae, later adapted into a series of feature films. In the manga series an ancient Roman-bath architect strangely gets sucked through drainpipes between ancient Rome and contemporary Tokyo, where he learns from Japanese bath culture and takes his lessons home. The series humorously and brazenly attributes Roman greatness to its Japanese heritage. It is also worth noting that at the height of Japanese imperialism, Japanese colonists did indeed build baths wherever they went. As symbols of the nation, is no wonder that Japanese communal baths (in the form of typical ofuro deep bathtubs, public sento, and onsen) were found throughout the former Japanese empire, and one can still find these baths, some in ruins and some operational, throughout Asia and Oceania.

In my own research, which deals mainly with postcolonial studies of Japanese and

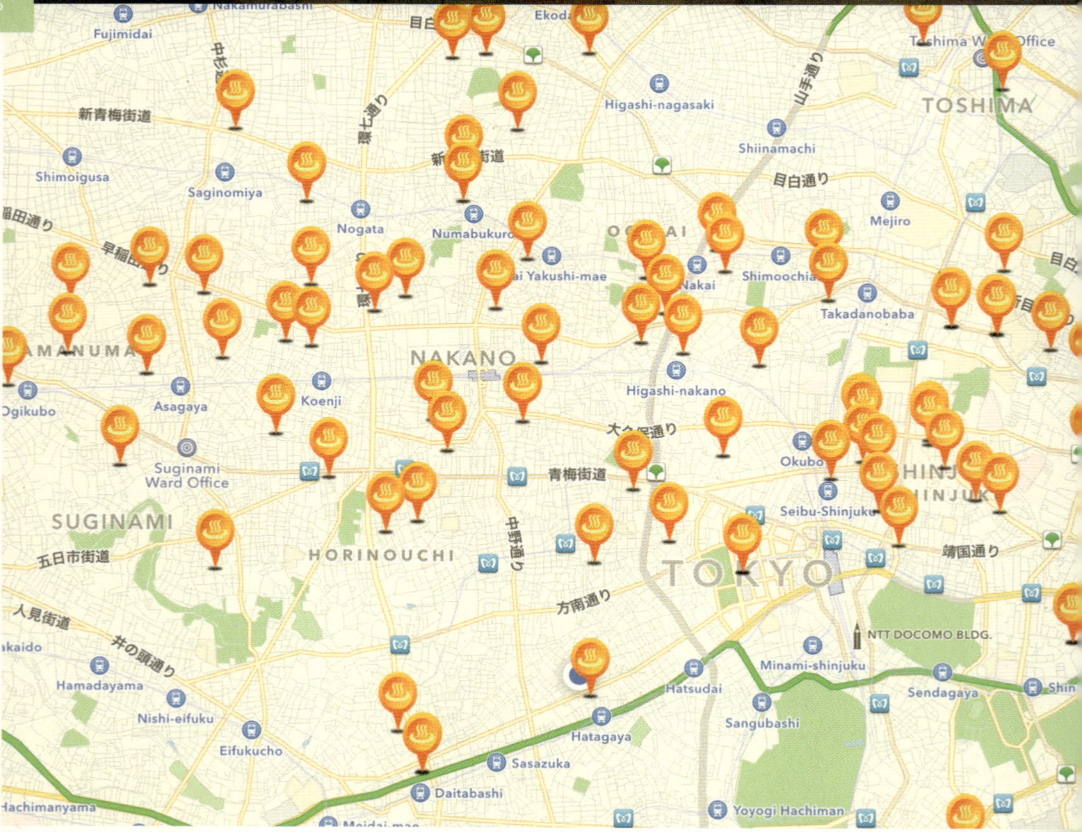
Nakamurabashi
Fujimidai
Ekoda
Toshima Ward Office
TOSHIMA
新青梅街道
環七通り
Higashi-nagasaki
山手通り
Shiinamachi
Shimoigusa
Saginomiya
目白通り
Mejiro
Nogata
Numabukuro
早稲田通り
Shimoochiai
Nakai
Takadanobaba
NAKANO
Higashi-nakano
Ogikubo
Asagaya
Koenji
大久保通り
Okubo
Suginami Ward Office
青梅街道
Seibu-Shinjuku
SUGINAMI
五日市街道
HORINOUCHI
中野通り
TOKYO
靖国通り
人見街道
方南通り
NTT DOCOMO BLDG.
井の頭通り
Hamadayama
Minami-shinjuku
Nishi-eifuku
Hatsudai
Sendagaya
Eifukucho
Hatagaya
Sangubashi
Sasazuka
Daitabashi
Hachimanyama
Yoyogi Hachiman
Meidai-mae

American imperialism in the Pacific Islands, I have often been shocked to find the remains of Japanese baths in seemingly unlikely places. I remember the sense of amazement I felt when I stumbled upon the crumbling bath in the ruins of an old dormitory that Japanese naval pilots used during the Pacific War. The bath was located deep in the jungle of a small, remote island in the middle of the Marshall Islands. Overgrown with vines and covered in graffiti, only local elders who had experienced Japanese colonialism actually knew that it was once filled with hot water. Despite the ugliness of the war, those elders spoke to me fondly about childhood memories of part-time jobs gathering firewood to heat the baths for colonists and soldiers, and how they were also able to partake in a hot bath as part of their reward for the work.

In 21st century Tokyo, public bathing is a relatively sustainable business. Although unfortunately local neighborhood sento are on the decline and many are going out of business year after year, the whole industry of yu simultaneously seems to be experiencing a revival as people of all ages, including increasing numbers of youth, are flocking to new bathing establishments. Even despite the decline, nearly 1,000 businesses belong to the official union of sento, but this number doesn't include the broader list of the countless privately-run and more luxurious super-sento and onsen that proliferate everywhere. There are even iPhone searching applications which use GPS to locate the nearest inner-city sento. For example, the free "Thermae Romae" app, named after the comic series, depicts the neighborhoods around my local train station like this, freckled by an overwhelming number of baths I've never even heard of. Zoom out and Tokyo is completely buried.

Worried by the closure of so many local sento in Tokyo year after year, many businesses are doing their best to come up with new concepts to lure new customers or to awaken a new generation to the joys of bathing. Of all of my experiences sampling all these many bathing innovations, one in particular stands out. Showa Yokujo, otherwise known as "Magic Onsen," near Nakano Station advertises on its website that customers to the bath will be treated to complimentary performances of magic, but I had no idea what this actually meant until I visited the bath myself. The bath itself is a historical treasure, with its old chimney and vintage design, and especially its rendition of Mount Fuji in all its grandeur.

Upon entering the bath, I asked whether it would be possible to see some magic, half expecting that the woman at the counter would laugh at me. Instead she asked, "So, what time would you like your show? After your bath?" Looking at the clock, I could see it was already nearly 11:30 p.m. I was surprised when she proposed that I have a magic show at 1 a.m. No sooner had I finished my bath, gotten dressed, and sat down in the lounge than a peculiar man in bright red pajamas came darting out of the bathing changing area, holding a big black suitcase adorned with circus motifs. His hair was parted down the middle, and although he was probably already in his late fifties, he looked somehow like a little boy who had never grown up, bouncy, impatient, with wide but bloodshot eyes. He was actually somewhat frightening, but fascinating nonetheless. "Hi, I'm Tajimagic," he said, announcing his stage name. As it turned out, Tajimagic is the inheritor and current owner of Showa Yokujo, but he is also an accomplished and renowned magician who compares himself to the biggest celebrity illusionists.

Even without such gimmicks, however, public bathing in Tokyo is a fascinating, entertaining, and comforting space that still serves as a way to connect complete strangers through the shared ritual of nightly ablutions. My local bath, Takenoyu, was one such place for nearly 70 years before it closed down last spring. We may not have known one another's names, but there was a familiarity in seeing the same people there night after night. My friends and

武の湯

I had secret nicknames for the people we encountered there. For instance, there was a guy we referred to as "The Colonel," because of his odd, stiff, disciplined military movements when he washed his body and jumped into the water. Sento etiquette dictates that all bathers must wash their body before entering the communal tubs, achieved by sitting on a low stool in front of a mirror and scrubbing down with soap and a small wash-towel before dousing themselves with hot water, either from one of the yellow plastic basins provided or from the low shower heads. But the Colonel would always begin by hurling cold water all over himself while grunting and spitting, his eyes wide open as if charging into battle. He also would slap his skin vigorously, like an ascetic monk practicing self-flagellation. Once his first cleaning ritual was complete, he would enter the bath, immersing himself and then shouting with a bizarre, surprised sort of howl that always elicited stares from other patrons. He would then submerge himself for at least another minute and emerge again, shouting, gasping with joy. He would repeat his peculiar cleaning ritual of scrubbing and slapping again, only to vigorously dry himself until his skin was nearly red and slap a very strong musky body tonic all over his body when he returned to the changing room.

The Colonel was rivaled by many other regulars. There was "Iguana Man", for instance, who unabashedly strode around with his long legs from pool to pool, diving down into the cold bath, then the hot bath, then the sauna, arching his back so far as he walked that it almost looked as if he were a large lizard walking in reverse. There was the pale white bookish gentleman we called "Kabuki" who always sat in the steam sauna for hours on end. There was "The Wrestler," who probably was in fact a wrestler, who came in with a cohort of other athletes most nights around 10 p.m. There was the punk band who once came in with their hair dyed red and proceeded to wash their hair, resulting in frothy rivulets of bright pink foam that covered the entire floor. There are fathers and sons, old men with wise expressions, young boys chasing each other with buckets, enormously fat people, pencil-thin people; I have no idea what these people do in their everyday lives, or what they might imagine about me. Rarely do we strangers even speak to each other, but in the warm waters we share, we all appreciate, respect, and accept one another's existence.

Aside from the baths themselves and the eccentric patrons who sometimes frequent them, there is a much deeper meaning to the Tokyo bathing culture, with implications for the entire community. Bathing as often as I do, especially in my local neighborhood, I always marvel at the leveling, equalizing power of complete nakedness. There is a term for this in Japanese—hadaka no tsukiai, or "naked relationships"—with the double implication of an unvarnished, honest relationship between friends or family members. It suggests a relationship in which both parties have nothing to hide from each other, as well as the literal implication of being comfortable naked together. When parents bathe with their children, they also emphasize the importance of "skinship" (sukinshippu), a Japanese-invented English word that celebrates a "kinship" nurtured and strengthened through close, physical, skin-to-skin contact between two people. Hot water mediates this contact, like re-entering the womb space, being comforted and healed by the bath and connected by it, all at once.

With strangers, particularly those with familiar faces from one's local area of residence, this nakedness and skinship is significant. For some people, this kind of vulnerability and exposure is terrifying, but for regular bathers, being naked with strangers is a stress-relieving experience. Even though we may never have spoken to each other, I am used to bathing with my local grocer, my postman, the road-construction worker, the old man who fixes shoes, the rebellious youth who works at the convenience store, the obese guy who I always see feeding pigeons in the park, the schoolboys returning from baseball practice, the heavily suntanned gigolo, the muscly athlete, the cop who usually stands in front of the local police station, and the executive who took the last train home after finishing up his work for the day. We may never speak to each other, but we are sustained by the same hot waters. This is our naked neighborhood, and we are equal in our nakedness, even me with my own Caucasian body—sharing the same water, often cramming ourselves into small corners of the same hot bathing pool, sitting only inches from one another.

What is definitely true about public bathing in Japan is not only that it is part of mainstream culture, but also that everyone is naked by default, not by choice. And there are very few Japanese people who find it strange to bathe with others, including strangers. I have been in public-bathing situations with colleagues and superiors. This is simply not considered odd in any respect.

It is in this sense that the naked neighborhood is a way of bringing the community together, for both men and women. As a man I am only aware of what it is like to bathe in the men's bath, the otokoyu. The men's bath is almost always on the left of the bandai counter in the entrance to a bath. Beyond the slitted, blue noren curtain that marks its entrance lies a homosocial world of men. It is a zone of particularized aesthetics that has its own history and trajectory. Aside from its present-day manifestation as a neighborhood retreat, the sento is a space of male fraternization that is also historically associated with the institutionalized, communal bathing reminiscent of all-male student dormitories, male-only capsule hotels, saunas for late-night salarymen who miss their trains, the military (especially during the war), and even organized crime. (Possibly insert Takenoyu 4 or Takenoyu 5 here?)

In disrobing and entering these hot baths, one surrenders oneself to a shared space of manhood that is unparalleled elsewhere. Even if we do not speak to each other, we see one another's bodies. It is, in fact, considered somewhat "unmanly" to hide one's genitals with a towel, and this was especially true during Japan's war years, when militaristic masculinity was so influential. In South Korea, which requires mandatory military service of all young men, it is not even customary in the public bathing areas of jimjilbang saunas to use towels, lest one compromise his proud nudity. In Japan it's a bit more subtle—towels are used for just a trace of modesty, but more teasingly, like the matador tactfully taming the bull with a piece of fabric. Sento and other public-bathing experiences thus reinforce masculinity while they simultaneously disable one's defenses, creating a softening and neutralizing space of vulnerability that transcends and subverts power, bringing everyone together in their shared humanity.

There is also a sense that bath patrons come not only to experience the liberation and equalizing of status that comes with communal nakedness, but also to experience a different kind of nakedness as they take asylum from the outside world. People come to wash away their sins, to scrub off the filth and corruption of the everyday. Contemporary artist Tabaimo, for instance, has immortalized the otokoyu in her hybrid animation/installation of the same title, a work in which she depicts Japanese salarymen and sumo wrestlers in different stages of undressing. Her work also makes reference to the nationalist overtones of bathing and purification in the Shinto faith and the promise of redemption and purity it pretends to deliver. Upon taking off their clothes, these salarymen continue unzipping their skin layer upon layer in vain, their skin falling off like an infinitely unzippable bodysuit, as if to suggest that the corruption of corporate Japan runs so deep that it is impossible to ever achieve true purification or redemption.

Certainly some things cannot be removed with mere nakedness, soap, and hot water. Yakuza gangsters, whose tattoos are like permanent bodysuits, also come to soak away their stress. The upscale super-sentos and almost all onsen have strict rules forbidding anyone with a tattoo to enter. This is their euphemistic way of preventing organized criminals from coming and making trouble for their business. They simply outlaw any and all tattoos, even tiny and innocent fashion tattoos, or that ridiculous Bugs Bunny tattoo one of my friends had, which disqualified him from ever enjoying a decent bath in public. But as public baths that serve taxpayers, local sento businesses in Tokyo (many of whom are built on yakuza-controlled land) place no restrictions on these thuggish men. I actually consider it a thrill to bathe with them. Where else (except maybe in prison) does one have a chance to quietly marvel at the amazing artwork of dragons and giant carp and Japanese gods and goddesses dancing and cavorting across the backs and buttocks of gang members? And my local yakuza are actually quite friendly. Sometimes they even say hello.

And, in this sense, I would argue that this naked neighborhood is not only a place where people come to relax and get clean; it is another dimension, in which the fabric of the community is sustained and replenished, for both men and women, adults and children, Japanese and non-Japanese. No shower or swimming pool, no boring trip to a health spa anywhere else could ever have the same effect. These waterways of yu provide a release for tension, an escape from the everyday, an aesthetic retreat into a space that is at once an art museum and a health spa. They represent an invitation, too, into the heart of a community, an opportunity to connect without the need for the superficiality of social rank, clothing and discourse.

Takenoyu, my local bath, closed its doors on a chilly night at the end of March 2015. I did not expect to see the long queues of patrons that stood waiting to get in all day and night. Inside, the mood was somber and contemplative. Bathers lovingly touched the wall tiles and savored their final moments in the jet massage baths, as if parting with a dear old family home. There were so many customers that there was barely space to fit in the vats of hot water, but everyone still tried to cram in together. And when the clock struck 2 a.m., and the lights dimmed, we all reluctantly walked into the changing room, where, for the first time, I was amazed to see these silent strangers speaking with one another, exchanging names. The Colonel spoke to Iguana Man; Kabuki struck up a conversation with one of the punks. A tough yakuza guy shook his head as he looked at me: "Can you believe this place was in business for 70 years? How long have you been coming here?" he asked. Suddenly, knowing that our water was being cut off, all of us bathers were in a state of grief. Yet in that collective mourning we also realized our ties to one another and to our shared home.

Though more and more of the older sento are closing down year after year, the naked neighborhood is still one kind of social glue that holds this massive and contradictory population together. Tokyo's bathscape still exists right here in the prosaic everydayness of the city, so ubiquitous that it is nearly hidden in plain sight. It may be easy to miss at first, but take a dip and immerse yourself in the naked neighborhood even once, and you will notice that unmistakable scent of soap and steam floating on the Tokyo air wherever you go.

MOMENT IN STILLNESS

静寂の瞬間（とき）

その晩、私は寝付けなかった。彼女が私に、「自殺の名所」青木ヶ原樹海の泥だらけのテントの中で会った男の話をしたせいだ。ドキュメンタリー映画のクルーとともに青木ヶ原に行った彼女は、そのやせ衰えた男に話しかけた。男は物思いにふけっていて、死にたいのかそうでないのかもわからぬようす。テントの中に横たわったまま、生と死の間（はざま）に暮らしていた。

彼女の話に私は驚いた。というのも、同じ夜、やはり生と死の間に暮らす別の男の姿を目にしていたからだ。テレビで、「生きたまま仏になることを目指す」即身仏のことを放送していたのだ。

2人の男が、あれほど長い間、しかも自ら意識的に選んだ生と死の間という場所について、私は考えが止まらなかった。あの晩、私は今日と明日の間を浮遊していた。眠れぬままに。

David Orkand は建築家として4年間東京に暮らし、研究と仕事をした。この短編フィクションのなかで、人が生きようか死のうかと考えているときの時空の変化を探究している。

I had trouble sleeping that night. I felt her movement with every breath. The story she told me just before she fell asleep had sent my mind adrift, passing through other times, other places. She told me of her time in Aokigahara, the suicide forest. She had gone there as part of a team of documentary filmmakers. They brought their cameras to depict the traces of the dead. "Roughly one hundred people go there to commit suicide each year", she said.

I remember looking down upon this forest from the top of Mount Fuji once, where it where it hugs its base. It is dark and quiet. A dense carpet of gnarly evergreens, referred to as Jukai (Sea of Trees) by many locals. It is a primeval forest, sprouting from lava rock and volcanic ash, and resembles the woods that once covered the entirety of what is now called Tokyo. From above, one tree is indistinguishable from the next. A continuous and constant surface. I was left curious as to what lay beneath.

As she and her crew explored Aokigahara, they came across a man in a sullied tent. He remained hidden inside, faint-voiced, answering their inquiries. He said he was fine; he did not want to trouble them; he did not want to be a burden. They let him be, but left with concern.

Weeks later they returned to the tent and found him. An elderly, emaciated man on the brink of death. He had sustained himself solely on liquids over the course of a month. Weak from starvation, he could no longer escape the forest, even if he tried to. He said that he was lost in thought, uncertain whether he wanted to live or to die. Lying there, he inhabited a space between life and death. His indecision was decisive.

As she told me her story, it had startled me. That evening I had been sitting at a local izakaya (drinking establishment), watching the daily news dramatizations. In preparations for the yearly Keiro no Hi (Respect for the Aged Day), Tokyo government officials chose to publicly honor Japans oldest man, Sogen Kato, age 111. After repeated failed attempts to contact him, police were sent to his apartment to investigate. They broke down his door, finding his mummified remains, dressed in pajamas, lying in bed. Kato's family was being interviewed. They told investigators that he was a stubborn man, locking himself in his room over 30 years ago, declaring that he was not to be disturbed; he was to become a "living Buddha", he said, referring to a practice of elevating oneself to this state through ritualistic self-mummification.

To mummify a body in a living state is a long, painful process, requiring years of disciplined asceticism. Normally a corpse will decompose rapidly, as the organs' toxins are released and the fat and watery tissue decay. The body of a monk is first emaciated through years of consuming solely forest nuts and soba (buckwheat) dough. Then come years of ingesting small amounts of bark and pine-tree root, just enough to sustain prayer and mantric chant. A tea made from the toxic sap of the Urushi tree, normally used as a varnish, is then drunk. Literally embalming the monk in a state of meditative suspension, prolonging and preserving his near-death moment on the path to enlightenment.

After she told me her story, I wanted to tell her mine, but she dosed off and I was left with my thoughts, unable to sleep. Thinking about the place between life and death that both these men had dwelled in for so long, and so consciously. The sun would soon rise. It felt eerily still, somewhere between today and tomorrow.

DOCUMEN-TARIANS OF CHANGE

A SHORT HISTORY OF STREET FASHION IN TOKYO

This is the story of two street documentarians: Wajiro Kon and Shoichi Aoki. Kon and Aoki memorialized Tokyo street fashion in post-quake Ginza and recession-era Harajuku respectively. Kon and Aoki are responsible for creating some of the most important images of dress culture in Tokyo. Kon illustrated the Westernization of Ginza in the 1920s and Aoki photographed the bricolage of Harajuku street fashion worn by the disillusioned youth during the recession of the 1990s.[22,23] The cultural changes these areas were experiencing at the time materialized in the way people dressed in the streets and on other surfaces of non-verbal communication that were conducive to visual documentation.

Wajiro Kon (1888-1973) was an ethnographic documentarian who, through illustrations and writing, researched changes in Ginza after the 1923 Great Kanto Earthquake. His illustrations and textual observations of material desires and human interaction with space, during that time, are now part of the national identity of Japan, and are used as a historical record of Tokyo's then-contemporary material culture.[24] After the earthquake, he conducted numerous studies in fashion and housing in which he witnessed young men and women with disposable incomes dressing increasingly in Western clothing. At that time, they were thought of as hedonistic, delinquent youths—manifestations of modernity and the Westernization of Japanese culture during the Showa period—and given the titles "moga" ("modern girls") or "mobo" ("modern boys").[25,26] His findings helped establish Ginza as a significant district for cultural formation—a district that continues to influence fashion trends to this day.

Kon's illustration juxtaposing Western and Eastern dress culture (National Museum of Ethnology 2011).

今和次郎のイラスト。西洋と東洋の服飾文化を並べて比較している。

変化をめぐるドキュメンタリー ー 東京のストリートファッション 小史

1920年代、今和次郎はモボ・モガの姿を記録した。モボ・モガとは、日本の伝統的な着物ではなくモダンな洋装を身につけ、銀座を闊歩したモダンな男女のことだ。今和次郎のおよそ80年後、写真家の青木正一は、1990年代の原宿のファッションの変遷を写真に記録した。この2つの記録（ドキュメンタリー）は、それぞれ、日本のストリートファッションの集合的想像力に貢献した。しかし、今と青木は変化を記録しただけではない。変化に貢献した可能性もある。青木が撮影するストリートファッションスナップ雑誌FRUiTは、ある種の着こなしを正当化し、それを広める舞台となった。モボ・モガも90年代の原宿ファッションも今は廃れてしまったが、それらが残したものは今も、原宿の小道や銀座の目抜き通りにしっかりと染みこんでいる。この論文は、当時の社会的変化の中で二人のドキュメンタリストがそれぞれに果たした役割を比較している。

Daphne Mohajer Va Pesaran は東京に暮らし、仕事をしているファッションデザイナー、フォトグラファー、研究者。フォトグラファーとしての仕事の傍ら、『FRUiT』の創刊者であり編集長である青木正一の英語の窓口として仕事をしている。

In 1996, almost 80 years after Kon studied Ginza, magazine publisher and photographer Shoichi Aoki would document changes in dress on the streets of Harajuku. He has created a body of work that may be considered as culturally significant as Kon's for having defined a new category of dress culture in Tokyo. Aoki's visual documentation has greatly affected the collective memory of Harajuku. But unlike Kon, whose documentation of Ginza was informed by quantitative and qualitative sociological research methods, Aoki was more involved: his subjects were selected based on his personal emotional response to what he calls an "aura" (an ironic reference to Walter Benjamin's description of a quality retained by artworks that were made before the age of mechanical reproduction).[27] Aoki sees his subjects as living sculptures who exist in a specific time and space.[28]

As far back as 1949, Harajuku was distinct among Tokyo districts. Post-war Harajuku was rebuilt as an American Army base for soldiers and their families; Japanese citizens were not allowed to enter. Owing to its foreign residents and imports, low-cost rent and car-free Sundays (which began in 1977 on one of its main roads, and acted as a means for young people to congregate), Harajuku would earn a reputation as a place of counter-culture and rebellion, facilitating youth-led subcultures, art and fashion design (notably the work of Rei Kawakubo and Yohji Yamamoto).[29] The area would become one that allowed young people to experiment with various dress styles and transform themselves during their formative years. Some individuals would go so far as to change their outfits to something that was more appropriate to the district before exiting Harajuku train station.[30]

In the mid-1990s, Aoki noticed a new trend in self-styling surfacing among young people in Harajuku and began photographing those he considered influential in this new mode of dress. In June 1996, he began publishing these images in a monthly magazine titled Fruits, created during what economists would call the "lost decade" (the decline following the prosperous bubble economy of the 1980s).[31] It was a time in which Japanese youth felt helpless and unsure of their future, leading them to mistrust traditional establishments and to seek alternative modes of consumption.[32] The changes after the consumption-driven culture of postmodernity in the 1970s and 1980s stimulated growth in art and creative cultures in Japan. At the beginning of the 1990s, young creative people had started to search locally for the means and materials to create their own culture. This introspection was concurrent with a move away from the conspicuous, import-driven consumption of the 1980s and toward a trend of local-brand consumption. This resulted in tighter bonds between local consumers and producers of fashion items, and thus facilitated the birth of a unique location-specific dress culture.[33]

The resulting dress culture was identified as a bricolage that challenged established rules of garment usage: participants traded ideas and challenged one another on the street during social interaction. It is this moment in time that Harajuku is now known for, and Aoki's memorializing photographs of crowds gathered along the district's Omotesando Street on car-free Sundays during the 1990s were instrumental in generating this association.[34, 35, 36]

Through actively selecting people from street crowds to appear under his Fruits label, Aoki acted as a participant-observer in the formation of this new mode of self-styling.[37] While Aoki claims that he never styled or posed his subjects, he affected his subjects simply by categorizing them. Through naming and classifying subjects chosen from the streets, he catalyzed an aspiration to appear in his magazine. In effect, his publications acted as a vehicle for the legitimization of this mode of self-styling that appeared in Harajuku. Aspiring subjects

The cover of issue No.1 of Fruits Magazine (Aoki 1996).

『Fruits』の創刊号の表紙。

would do what was called "Aoki-machi": they would emulate the manner of dress seen in Fruits magazine and wait for Aoki in areas he frequented. Ostensibly this would enable the documentarian to historicize them in his magazine; in reality, however, the subjects affected themselves in a manner that made it difficult for the documentarian to authentically represent cultural shifts.[38] Once a category has been established—when a movement is named—can new participants become part of the movement or are they considered followers, simulating the original members of the group?

Perhaps Maurice Halbwachs (1877-1945)—the French philosopher who developed the concept of "collective memory"—can provide some insight into the relationship between a group and the milieu in which it forms its material culture: "A group not only transforms the space into which it has inserted itself, but also yields and adapts to its physical surroundings. It becomes enclosed within the framework it has built. The group's image of its external milieu and its stable relationships with this environment becomes paramount in the idea it forms of itself, permeating every element of its consciousness, moderating and governing its evolution. This image of surrounding objects shares their inertia. It is the group, not the isolated individual but the individual as a group member, that is subject in this matter to material nature and shares its fixity."[39]

According to Halbwachs, a space retains something from each of its inhabitants over time. By situating themselves in Harajuku, a neighborhood with a reputation for creative culture formation and experimentation, participants in this new dress culture were subjecting themselves to alteration by the space; in the meantime they imprinted on the space their own actions, which were then memorialized in Fruits magazine. Today—though the architecture, pavement, trees and shops have changed—Harajuku maintains its identity as a place for culture creation and consumption. Not even the arrival of foreign fast-fashion retailers like H&M and Forever 21 has interrupted the ability of Harajuku to act as a place that exerts an influence on fashion trends, so long as its permanent fixtures (for example, streets and signage) exist.[40]

Though Aoki's moment has passed, his images remain as representations of an alternate space: one that doesn't really exist, but appears when one thinks of Harajuku.

Kon and Aoki were in the right place and time to witness societal changes that materialized on surfaces in the streets. Stimulated by intuition, these street-fashion documentarians went on to create some of the most important images of Tokyo dress culture. The images they created of pivotal moments in Ginza and Harajuku became records of an alternate space—an authentic, subjective telling of a moment in time. Access to these spaces was easy; they were available to consumers through purchase of the magazines in which they were published. The proliferation of these publications and images would legitimize members and affect the direction taken by the new culture that was being documented.

Modern-day Ginza and Harajuku are very different to what they were when Kon and Aoki first examined them. However, the identities of both districts as places of cultural influence endure. Designed by Rei Kawakubo of Comme Des Garcons in 2006, Dover Street Market opened a branch of its avant-garde high-end department stores in the back-alleys of Ginza, while in Harajuku artists like Sebastian Masuda and Kyari Pamyu Pamyu carry on the legacy of colorful bricolage and youth-led resistance to the adult establishment in Harajuku.[41] Their numerous appearances in media continue to have a strong impact on the modern aesthetic image of Japan.

An inside image of issue No.1 of Fruits Magazine (Aoki 1996).

『Fruits』の創刊号

TIME IN THE CITY OF TEMPORAL MONUMENTS

The current of the flowing river does not cease, and yet the water is not the same water as before. The foam that floats on stagnant pools, now vanishing, now forming, never stays the same for long. So, too, it is with the people and dwellings of the world.

Kamo no Chomei. *Hôjôki 1212.*

The average age of buildings in Tokyo is 26 years. The average age of residents of Tokyo is 44 years.[42] Tokyo is a city in which the people are, on average, older than the buildings.

Tokyo is often said to be a city without monuments—stable, enduring artefacts that provide a tangible connection to earlier times and past generations. But what the comparison of the average ages of buildings and people suggests is that the true monuments in Tokyo are its people, particularly its older citizens. Rather than lining up in front of a crumbling old stone pile (of which few examples exist anyway), it makes more sense for visitors to Tokyo taking holiday snaps for the family album to bunch up in toothy enthusiasm around the nearest old man or woman. For it is his or her eyes that have borne most durable witness to the dramatic energies that remake the city every couple of decades, and his or her skin that has touched the stones and timbers of buildings long since gone.

Monuments are to urban space what photographs are to daily life. They pluck a moment—ideally one bearing pith and precision—out of the flow of life and suspend it in motionless counterpoint to that ever-moving river. These moments may be static but they are not passive: they bear upon the flow of life, diverting and channeling it, provide markers and datums for its gauging and measurement. In cities whose monuments are made of durable matter, these effects of focus and calibration happen in the great spaces of public gathering, the squares and parks and boulevards that shape populations and give them visible representational form.

But what happens to this conception when the monuments are themselves embedded in the flow of experience, as are the living monuments of Tokyo? Here the spaces of the city lose their categorical, pre-existing character, and become malleable, defined by social phenomena, varying with situation and occasion. Monuments no longer stand in some sense against or outside of time, but incorporate temporality within themselves. They become more akin to events than artifacts.

I suggest that in such a city, it is *rhythm* that becomes the crucial element in establishing such "temporal monumentality". Instead of spaces that are clearly defined and understood as "public", we can consider the notion of *public rhythms* as establishing the basic armature that structures the urban space-time continuum, the datums by which growth and change are registered, and through which collectivities are gathered and rendered visible. This insight could be extended to describe a layering of diverse rhythms, of varying pitch and intensity, amounting to a cartography of temporal monuments as intricate as that of any urban map.

Rhythm is defined by repetition at regular intervals, and so has an intrinsically cyclical or seasonal character. It emphasizes internal metabolic energies over externally directed motion. Growth is not *expansive*, but *intensive*. This makes it a potentially rich avenue of investigation in considering what a "dynamic stillness" might entail for a contemporary urbanism.

"Each epoch not only dreams the next, but also, in dreaming, strives towards the moment of waking," wrote Walter Benjamin in his *Paris, Capital of the Nineteenth Century*.[43] Benjamin conceived of a temporality in which time is not linear but is folded upon itself. Time becomes a matrix in which shiny flecks of times past and times future are embedded in the inert grey mortar of the present. Under such temporality, "progress" does not involve the logical advancement to a hitherto unexperienced level of existence, but involves a cumulative process of encounter between these "flecks" in vivid flashes of similitude and recognition.

What these thoughts are gradually unveiling is an urban historical imagination that sees a layered, rhythmic urban space-time fired by vivid encounters between images and ideas, cycled through its matrix by the slow churn of the great gears that are the city's temporal monuments.

時のモニュメントの街における「時間」

モニュメントと都市空間の関係は、写真と日常生活の関係に通じている。瞬間を―理想的には正確にその真髄を―、一生の流れの中から切り取り、一時停止させて、永遠の時の流れに対する不動状態を対位法で提示する。耐久性のあるモニュメントをつくる都市においては、モニュメントのもつ焦点化と較正(キャリブレーション)の効果は、人々が集まる大きな空間、広場や公園、あるいは人々が行き交う大通りにおいて発揮され、モニュメントには可視的な表象としてのフォルムが与えられている。しかし、こうしたモニュメントが体験の流れの中に根ざすとしたら、この概念はどうなるのだろうか?もはやモニュメントは時に抗うものでも、時の外部にあるのでもなく、モニュメントそのものの内部に時間を組み込み、物体というよりはイベントに近い存在になる。
都市では、こうした「一時的なモニュメント性」を確立する非常に重要な要素はリズムである、と私は考える。「パブリックなもの」として明確に定義・理解される空間の代わりに、パブリックなリズムという概念を、都市の時空の連続性を構成する基本要素としてとらえることができる。

Julian Worrallは建築家、都市計画家、研究者、批評家。2000年から日本で研究し、生活し、仕事をしている。

BELOW 1.30

Ground level. A spatial outcast permanently short of attention and rarely left with good words. Especially in a city such as Tokyo that inundates you with exotic images. One would hardly dare to stare at one's feet when strolling through all those captivating environments. Yet down below, there are things to see. In that lower slice of the city, different behaviors reign. Different organizations, rules and classes are at work, deviating from the upper realm, which is dominated by the business of functioning. This construction of the city depicts people who are cast away from capitalist or mainstream considerations. For a moment, a while, some time, or indefinitely, they adopt the lower posture that makes them unfit to be pro-active citizens.

The eye level of an average person sitting on the ground, of a child or a person in a wheelchair, is taken as the limit for observation. In situ photographical documentation, fictive personas, numerical facts, and snippets of Western media are juggled together in a collage that opens up a world we could only see if we were to look at it through our bellybuttons.

1.30メートル以下の世界

地面のレベル。顧みられることもなければ、美辞麗句で語られることもまずない、常に空間の中ののけもの的存在。しかし、そこまで身を低くすると、見えてくるものがある。それは、都市の低い部分であり、異なる法則と行動様式が支配する領域である。

人間にとって、地面に座ったときの目の高さが、観察の限界となる。写真ドキュメンタリー、虚構のペルソナ、数値、西洋メディアの断片を合わせてコラージュにしてみると、へその高さよりも低い位置からしか見えない世界が目の前に開けてくる。

Thekla Boven、Bastian Boss、David Bauer は、2012年から2013年にかけて東京で建築のリサーチをしている間に知り合った。

DIARY OF THE BIKE ORGANIZER

bike
bike
bike
bike
bike
bike
bike
bike[A]
motorbike
cone
cone[B]
drunkard[C]
cone.

[A] **Wikipedia.org:** "5S is the name of a workplace organization method that uses a list of five Japanese words: seiri, seiton, seiso, seiketsu, and shitsuke. Transliterated into English, they all start with the letter "S". The list describes how to organize a work space for efficiency and effectiveness by identifying and storing the items used, maintaining the area and items, and sustaining the new order."

[B] **Wikitravel.org:** "Japan is usually perceived as a very expensive country to visit [...] Perhaps the biggest way of massively cutting down your expenses is to do urban camping."

[C] **Canadian Medical Association:** "Sixty percent of problem drinkers are salaried businessmen who claim that getting drunk with clients or coworkers is part of their job and a mark of company loyalty. To refuse a drink from the boss is a terrible insult that can damage a career. And although alcohol consumption is now decreasing in most industrialized countries, it has quadrupled in Japan since 1960."

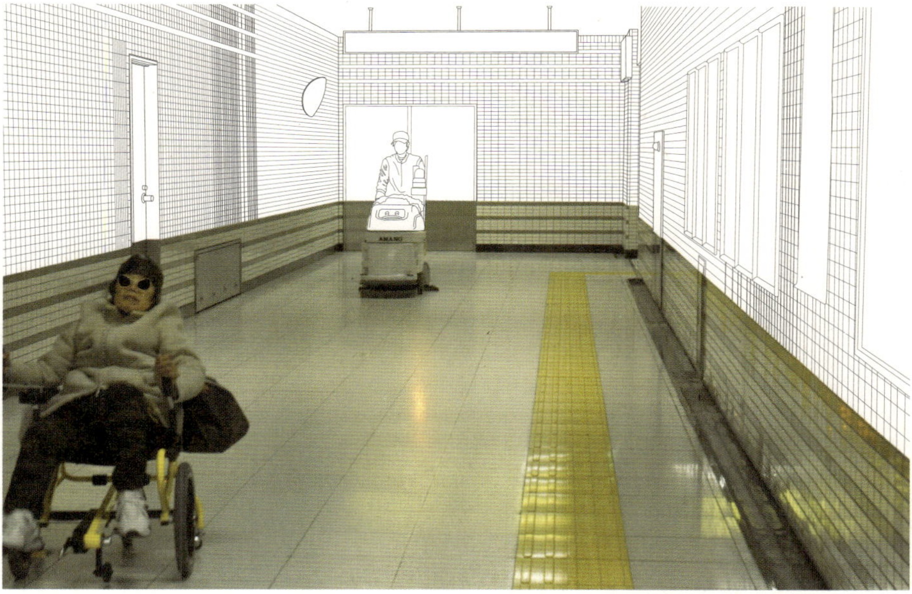

UBASUTE[A]

Out of my way fool![B]
Oh—the pilot hag[C], again.
Wuhahahahaha
Hey I am working here[D] you know
What a waste of time
Some grow crazy
Some grow old![E]

[A] **Wikipedia.org:** "Ubasute (literally 'abandoning an old woman') refers to the custom allegedly performed in Japan in the distant past, whereby an infirm or elderly relative was carried to a mountain, or some other remote, desolate place, and left there to die, either by dehydration, starvation, or exposure."

[B] **Telegraph.co.uk:** "[M]any elderly people have abandoned politeness and understanding—values for which the Japanese are renown—and are now rude, demanding and threatening. 'I watched this man shouting at a member of staff in a supermarket and then he went into the bank and did exactly the same thing again...'"

[C] **Telegraph.co.uk:** "The Japanese government is spending ¥8.3 billlion on constructing 3 new prison wards that are specifically designed to cater to the rising number of elderly inmates. Many are repeat offenders who commit another minor crime shortly after their release simply to get back into a community where they are comfortable, warm, fed and have friends of their own age."

[D] **Japantimes.co.jp:** "[S]tudents are expected to devote all their time to study, so traditional cleaning jobs, such as hotel housekeeping, have been filled by middle-class housewives and retirees, usually on a part-time basis."

[E] **Businessweek.com:** "Though Japan's retirement age stands at 60, more than 5.7 million Japanese have continued to work past 65, either because they can't afford to stop working or they're looking to get out of the house."

FROM A TOURIST GAZE[A]

I saw a girl picking leaves[B] in the streets of
Tokyo and everything made sense.
This is what it is all about!
You have to become water.
Go with the flow.[C]
Empty your mind![D]

[A] **Wikipedia.org:** Victoria and Albert Museum: "Eastern Exoticism: The myth of the exotic East has always been a potent one in the West [...] Both the Chinese and the Japanese were considered to be a nation of children [...] The Japanese were not seen just as picturesque, they were seen as a literal embodiment of their art. The adventurer Isabel Bird, when she arrived, felt that she had seen them all before, 'so were they like their pictures on the trays and the fans and teapots'."

[B] **Wa-pedia.com:** "For a Westerner this might be unbelievable, but Japanese believe that their country is somehow unique for having four distinct seasons."

[C] **Japan-guide.com:** "To mix things up: A survey showed that Christian style weddings are clearly most popular (46%) among Japanese, followed by Shinto style weddings (18%). Even among Shintoists, Christian style weddings are more popular (50%) with many people expressing their wish to combine the two styles in their wedding ceremony."

[D] **Wiki.answers.com:** "'Do all Japanese perform Zen?' No. Most Japanese are secular people (84% of the Japanese claim no personal religion, less than 15 percent reported any formal religious, 64% do not believe in God, 55% do not believe in Buddha) using religious rites only for ceremonial events."

"ALL CHILDREN, EXCEPT ONE, GROW UP"*

Why stop dreaming when you wake up?[A]
Come with me, where dreams are born and time is never planned.
Come, sit and listen to me[B] at Shimokitazawa, South exit.
You know, at that place between sleep and awake.[C]
That place where you can still remember dreaming.
That is where I'll be waiting.[D]

[A] **Wikipedia.org:** "Escapism is mental diversion by means of entertainment or recreation, as an 'escape' from the perceived unpleasant or banal aspects of daily life."

[B] **The LA Times:** "[K]amishibai, a popular pastime during Depression-era Japan. Kamishibai means 'street theater using painted illustrations' [...] Storytellers would travel from town to town with their butai (miniature stage) on the back of a bike. The set-up was reminiscent of a 'Punch and Judy' show, but instead of puppets the narrator would slide a series of poster boards with water color illustrations in and out of the box. He would act out the script, which was written on cards placed on the back of a board."

[C] **App-store:** "Manga-Camera, Tokyo Otaku Mode: phone app that converts your regular image into a frame from a manga comic."

[D] **Christian Comics International:** "In 1995 of all the books and magazines sold in Japan, 40% were manga (comics). That amounts to 15 copies for every man, woman and child in Japan."

**Peter Pan, J. M. Barrie*

TO LICK SOMEONE'S SHOE

All I ever wanted...[A]
was to touch people's heart with my songs and own the stage with my guitar.
But, [B]
all that they let me have[C] is a spot to shine their shoes[D] and make them sleek.
If only I could stand up.[E]

[A] **Ministry of Foreign Affairs:** 1986: the "Equal Employment Opportunities" law for men and women went into effect. 2010: the average monthly salary for women in 2010 remained at about 69.3% of that of men.

[B] **Factsanddetails.com:** "According to the Organization for Economic Cooperation and Development (OECD) the underemployment of well-educated women in Japan is a 'considerable waste of valuable human resources.' Japanese women are among the best educated in the world. In 2005, 42.5 percent of them had at least some post-secondary education. The gender pay gap at median earnings is the second highest in the OECD."

[C] **Factsanddetails.com:** "In the 1990s, thanks to a recent deal with Disney, stewardesses at Japan Airlines were ask by their employers to wear Mickey Mouse ears on the job. Though women complained, it was decided that the flight attendants will decide if there are enough children on the plane justify wearing the ears."

[D] **BBC (2014):** "Shinzo Abe wants 30% of all managers in Japanese companies to be women by the end of this decade."

CHELLY BURASSAMU

Handing out leaflets[A] is not my thing either.
They have a nice color though.[B]

Cherry blossom in evening.
Ah well, today also belongs to the past.*

Fuck it.
I'll get a job at Docomo.[C]

[A] **Urbandictionary.com:** "A freeter in Japanese refers to someone in their 20's who is moving from job to job, often part time and with small wage."

[B] **Independent.co.uk:** "Japanese males are transforming into 'grass-eaters' (shoshoku danshi).
Japan's twenty-thirty males seem disinterested in careers and apathetic about the rituals of dating, sex and marriage. They live with their mums and sit down on the toilet when they pee. Some have even been known to wear bras. 'What is happening to the nation's manhood?'"

[C] **Web-japan.org:** "The Japan Institute of Labor [...] published the results of an interview survey of 97 freeters in 2000 [...] The report classifies freeters into three types. One is the 'moratorium' type (where freeters put off taking a regular job until they know what they want to do). Another is the 'dream pursuing' type, and the third is the 'no alternative' type."

**Kobayashi Issa (1763–1828)*

やわらかとんかつサンド
やわらかいとんかつをサンドしました
110円(税込)
おかか
コシヒカリ使用
新潟
コシヒカリ
おにぎり
おにぎり屋
瀬戸備前にがり塩
焼さけ
ハラミ
168円

ITADAKIMASU: DIGESTING THE KONBINI'S MANY MENUS

Konbini put you at ease. I live in Tokyo and see them as refrigerators. There is one right in front of my apartment. I buy something every time I pass by. My fridge at home is always empty.

Tokyo salaryman, age 48

Food—whether in the form of bottled barley tea, soy-sauce-flavored crackers, or a grilled salmon lunch—is the cornerstone of Japan's konbini economy. Food is where the Japanese radically parted ways with the American convenience-store manual and where, for the last 40 years, they have competed among domestic rivals on variety, taste and product design. Chains, with names like Lawson, Daily Yamazaki, 7-Eleven, Sunkus and Seikomart, team up with food makers to invent such staples as onigiri (rice balls), obento (box lunches), and oden (savory stew). They are also responsible for introducing new flavors and choices into what people eat every day: dairy-based dessert drinks and steamed pizza buns; yakisoba sandwiches and wakame (kelp) salads; pickled celery and mango flavored softserve. Within the next 24 hours, roughly 40 million people—one third of Japan's population—will stop at a konbini to buy something: food items will constitute two-thirds of their purchases.

いただきます：コンビニに並ぶたくさんのメニューを消化する

24時間以内に、日本の人口の3分の1がコンビニに立ち寄って買い物をする。最も多いのは食べ物だ。だが、コンビニが提供するメニューから、彼らは何を選ぶのだろう？　おにぎりや焼きそば、サンドイッチ、コンビニ弁当は、人々の生活のどんな場所を征服したのだろうか？　そして、24時間または36時間という陳列時間が終了すると、こうした食べ物は実際のところ、どうなるのだろうか？

Gavin H. Whitelaw は日本で生活し、仕事をしている社会文化人類学者。日本のコンビニにおける社会的生活や人間文化的エコロジーを研究しており、フィールドワークとして1年間コンビニで働いた。

Tokyo-based journalist and self-professed konbini denizen Torigoe Shuntaro sees the konbini as "paradise within walking distance". Born in rural Fukuoka on the eve of Pearl Harbor, he has childhood memories of hunger and deprivation. In the late 1940s, lunch for him meant gleaning yams from harvested fields or frying locusts in soy sauce for protein. For some people, the konbini truly is a heaven that satiates young appetites, fulfills the wants of weekday wage-earners, and brings comfort to Japan's growing population of seniors who may be weary of cooking for themselves or who may lack the momentum required to visit a crowded supermarket. The konbini's modest bounty of ready-made and easy-to-consume foods offers familiar staples, new treats, and a modicum of social contact at a relatively small cost.

While konbini cuisine has its fans, its critics also exist. Concerned parents, nutritionists and environmental activists take store menus to task for the amount of additives, preservatives, fat, salt and sugar they skillfully blend into Japanese diets. In his book *Dangerous Konbini Foods* (1999), Yamada Hiroshi tastes subterfuge and collusion even in the humble rice ball. Savory ingredients, he reports, expertly mask the presence of agricultural toxins and genetic modification. Ingenious packaging wraps each bite in endocrine disruptors and adds to consumerism's expanding carbon footprint. At this end of the food-discourse spectrum, the konbini is a true weapon of mass consumption and food is the well-crafted delivery device deployed by governments and corporations that place profit and power above public health, safety and general welfare.

Somewhere between visions of heaven and hell lie the palates and purchasing habits of most people—women like Okamura Akiko, a retired middle-school nurse from Tohoku. Okamura enjoys cooking and takes pride in preparing meals that are delicious, nutritious and economical. But with her three daughters now married and living away from home, she occasional turns to the chilled cases of the 7-Eleven up the street to find a side dish and a can of Asahi Super Dry to accompany the leftovers she and her husband are having for dinner. "Konbini food has become tastier," she says, adding, "I wouldn't want it to be my only choice, however." Sugiyama Keiko is in her mid-50s and dishes out curried rice, tonjiru (miso soup with pork) and handmade onigiri at a lunch counter near Tokyo's Tsukiji fish market. She uses konbini when she travels. For her, konbini-ben (konbini boxed lunches) and onigiri provide predictability and ease when on the road. "I didn't really appreciate konbini until I was away from home," she says.

The relationship that konbini forge with the popular stomach is undeniable: it has nestled into the psyche. Customers now expect konbini to be stocked with food. Due to space limitations and a reputation for freshness, the stores can only carry a limited amount of any given item and must depend on three, just-in-time food deliveries each day to keep their shelves filled. Lack of a particular food at one store can drive customers to the competitor across the street. Barren store shelves following a disaster amplify public anxiety and induce panic buying. On March 11, 2011, Tokyo largely escaped the destruction caused by the massive earthquake and tsunami along Japan's northeastern Pacific coast. Many of the konbini's regional production centers were damaged, however, and food distribution temporarily ground to a halt. Tokyo's empty konbini shelves were among the first images to circulate in popular media about the toll the disaster was having on the city's sense of normalcy and security.

The weight resting on konbini owners' shoulders is great. On a daily basis, they must be sure to keep food shelves sufficiently supplied while not ordering more than will sell in a 24- to 36-hour period (the typical shelf life of many of these perishable products). Invariably, though, some items do not get sold by the consume-by date (shohikigen) and require immediate disposal in accordance with strict industry regulations. In a 2003 report issued by the Japanese Ministry of Agriculture, convenience stores and supermarkets annually produce 600,000 tons of food waste, enough food to nutritionally maintain a city of 3 million people for an entire year.

But in numerous stores, unsold food has an afterlife. Although significant volumes of old konbini food are tossed in the bin each day, practices in individual stores frequently deviate from what chains stipulate in their manuals and training courses. Food that is past its consume-by date is regularly gathered by workers and taken into the store's backroom, or backyard. There it gets recast as "loss" (rosu) and may be served as meals or snacks for the store owners and workers, or gifted to friends, associates, and sometimes even the homeless. In interviews, people with konbini work experience often mention that their employer's attitude toward unsold food was an important factor in their selection of a workplace. One college student said that a classmate advised him to look for a job where the owners let workers eat loss.

Aoki Isamu and his wife, Emi, live in Tokyo's shitamachi (low town) district and have run a konbini for over 20 years. They regularly give unsold snacks to deliverymen and former clerks who occasionally drop in to say hello. Expired obento, dairy products, bread, oden, and fried foods go into shopping bags and are casually ferried up to the couple's second-floor apartment. In her kitchen, Emi turns what did not sell into lunches and dinners for the couple and their staff. Aoki inherited his business from his father, a former egg distributor. Instilled from an early age with a respect for food, Aoki feels uncomfortable wasting something that can still be eaten. Turning the store's losses into meals comes naturally to him and his wife. "The one thing about the job that part-timers remember are the meals," Aoki says.

A kitchen is not always essential for transforming food waste into sustenance. Sometimes just the store's microwave oven or some hot water will suffice. Watanabe Ken likes to make ochazuke at around 2 a.m. on his night shift at Daily Yamazaki. Ochazuke is a popular late-night pub food consisting of a bowl of rice with hot green tea poured on top. The ingredients Wanatabe uses are all close at hand: an onigiri, loose tea, and hot water. He keeps his equipment in a knotted plastic bag at the back of a store locker. The bag contains a bowl, chopsticks, and a small canister of loose genmaicha (green tea containing toasted rice) that he purchased from a 100-yen shop on his way to work that night. He borrows a small Japanese tea pot from a desk drawer, adds a heaped spoonful of loose tea, then fills the pot with boiling water from the carafe at the end of the store counter that customers use for instant noodles. As the tea steeps, Watanabe plucks an onigiri from a basket of expired food on the floor. He unwraps the rice ball and removes the nori (seaweed) that comes with it. The bare onigiri goes in the bowl; the nori gets crushed and sprinkled on the top. The best ochazuke is made from the simplest onigiri, Watanabe explains. Grilled salmon and pickled plum are his favorite; "sea chicken" (tuna with mayonnaise) is best avoided. The final step is to pour the hot tea over the rice. The tea dissolves the seaweed and the onigri begins to collapse. Watanabe helps things along with prods from his chopsticks. He inhales the steam rising from the bowl. "Itadakimasu," he says, then gingerly slurps his first piping mouthful.

都市を見出そう

訪問者も住人も、東京に対して同じように戸惑いを覚える。モダンで未来的でありながら、歴史と伝統にも未だに強く結びついた大都市だ。エチケットや役割を演じること、期待通りの行動が求められる都市でもある。自分の役割がわかっていないと、関わりのある他の演者全員にとって混乱の種となる。だから、その点の一貫性に多大な関心が払われる。東京を前にすると、人々はアート、イデオロギー、経済、政治といったあらゆる種類の解釈を試みたくなる。あなたはこの都市をどんなふうに解釈できるだろうか？　あなたが見たいと思うのはどんな都市なのだろうか？

CHOOSE YOUR CITY

Tokyo confounds visitors and inhabitants alike. It's a modern, even futuristic, metropolis that is still very much attached to its history and traditions. It's also a governmental city of etiquette, role-playing and behavioral expectations. If you don't know your role in the play, it becomes a confused piece, for all actors involved. So there is a lot of interest in keeping it coherent. Tokyo inspires people to make all kinds of artistic, ideological, economic or political interpretations. How can you interpret the city? Which city do you choose to see?

専用

VIEW FROM NIHONBASHI, TOKYO
ムヲ望リ越三

IN THE ARENA OF ALTERNATIVE MODERNITIES

To a 20th-century gaze, Japan represents a conundrum: modern, but not Western; technologically advanced, yet deeply traditional; unashamedly artificial while acutely sensitized to nature. Japan seemed to offer a space to view modernity from outside itself. This essay explores how Japan has been seen as an alternative modernity, and asks what imaginative potentials this interpretation can offer us today.

What is modernity? Modernity is a term for a particular kind of historical imagination. At its core is a sense of temporality. In Baudelaire's formulation: "Modernity is the transient, the fleeting, the contingent; it is one half of art, the other being the eternal and the immovable."[44] Here there is change, movement, the ephemeral, but the aspect of temporality that is specific to modernity is the notion that it is directed, linear, progressive. This reflects a sense of the perfectibility of man through rationality. Progress is its watchword. Progress of knowledge, of technology, of wealth, of consciousness. This movement forms the impetus for the narrative of history.

もうひとつのモダニティのアリーナの中で

20世紀を俯瞰してみると、日本はひとつの謎に見えてくる。モダンでありながら非西洋的。先進技術を備えながら、深く伝統に根ざしている。恥じらいはないのかと思わせるほど表層的でありながら、自然に対する鋭敏な感性を備えている。日本は、モダニティの内側にいながら、モダニティを外から見る場を提供しているように見える。このエッセイは、日本がいかにしてモダニティのもうひとつの可能性としてとらえられるようになったのかを考察し、この解釈が今日の私たちに提供してくれる想像の可能性を問う。

Julian Worrallは建築家、都市計画家、研究者、批評家。2000年から日本で研究し、生活し、仕事をしている。

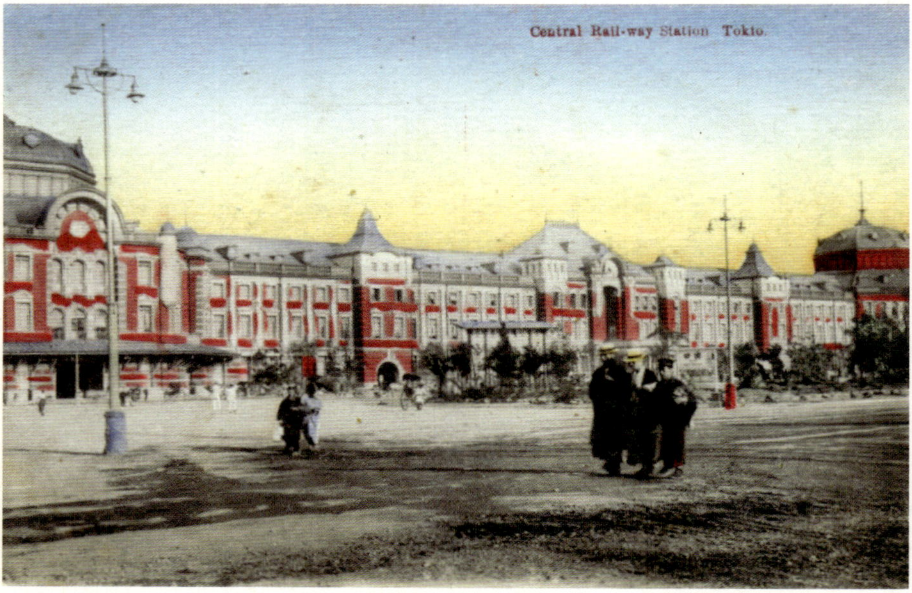

Tokyo Station, Tokyo 1918.
1918年の東京駅

Modernity also describes a particular relation to the world. In Marx's poetic words: "All fixed, fast frozen relations...are swept away. All that is solid melts into air, all that is holy is profaned".[45] Nature and human beings become a "standing reserve", ready be measured, evaluated, and applied to production. Matter is transformed into usable goods through material production. Objects and relations are rendered exchangeable and fungible. Modernity is a relation to the world that dissolves places into spaces. This is the spatial dimension of modernity.

"Modernity" so described has its origin in historical time and geographical space (even as it has transformed these categories). As the above quotes suggest, historically it is located in the 19th century, and geographically in Western Europe. Its character and experience were most vividly felt in the great metropolises: London, Paris, Vienna, Berlin. Each of these sites of modernity had their individual flavor, and the concept diversified further with the distinctive experience of the frontier of North America and the other European colonial territories. But modernity was Western. At the end of the 19th century, the terms were virtually synonymous.

Japan complicates this story. After some initial prompting, Japan modernizes on its own terms. Japan industrializes. Japan builds its own empire. Japan becomes the Eastern West, the non-modern Modern. It becomes an "alternative modern".

Over the course of Japan's modern history, this alternative modernity has acquired various forms and manifestations. Some external observers have found in Japan a model of an alternative configuration that they can use to critique or contrast their own local context, an exemplar of a harmonious society or a coherent culture. Others have seen in Japan a temporal displacement of a familiar world, typically into the future. Another approach uses Japan as a figure with which to exemplify a theory or an ideal. Each of these external representations has a specific distance to our own space and time. They have also intersected with Japan's own self-conception and representation. This range of interpretations is traced historically below.

Ho-o-den, Japan pavilion at the Chicago World Fair of 1893.
1893年のシカゴ万博の日本パビリオン「鳳凰殿」

THE PARADE OF ALTERNATIVE MODERNITIES

The history of Japan since the latter part of the 19th century can be seen as a parade through an arena of alternate modernities. In reviewing this parade we gain a clearer view of which aspects of our present view of Japan cast fresh light, and which reflect light cast from older sources.

We can identify four major periods in this parade of modernities, each of which finds its physical distillation in an architectural form. The first develops in the later 19th century, during the urgent modernization of the Japan of the Meiji period (1868-1912). Across the full sweep of society—including government, law, education, the military, industry, art, architecture and city planning, even food and dress—Western models were studied and applied, while pre-existing native approaches were shunned or abandoned. The Japanese word for this period and attitude is kindai-shugi. The architectural emblem of kindai-shugi is Tokyo Railway Station, a monumental structure in stone and red brick, completed in 1914 and designed in a faithful British style by Japanese architect Tatsuno Kingo. Symmetrically disposed around the main road to the Imperial Palace, the building was the figurative center and origin of all journeys across the growing Japanese empire, and managed to represent the mastery that the newly modern Japanese had achieved over technology and territory, while simultaneously revealing the dependency of this mastery upon Western sources and models.

Meanwhile, Western visitors to Japan were enthusiastically reporting back to their own publics on the qualities of Japanese prints, artefacts, dress, and buildings, generating a wave of "Japonisme" in European and American cities.* A young Frank Lloyd Wright was enraptured on viewing the Japan pavilion at the Chicago World Fair of 1893, and the simplicity and nobility of the space and the construction of traditional Japanese timber architecture became a recurrent touchstone for the architect of an idealized relation to art and nature. The art historian Okakura

*Examples include the British designer Christopher Dresser; the American scientist Edward Morse; and the American art historian Earnest Fenellosa.

Expo Tower, designed by Kiyonori Kikutake for Expo '70, Osaka. Realised in 1969.
菊竹清訓が1970年の大阪万博のために設計したエキスポタワー

Kakuzo was a key player in bringing the Japanese pavilion to Chicago. Okakura's writings expressed the idea that native Japanese culture (and, in his own interpretation, "Asiatic ideals") offered a coherent, meaningful alternative to Western extravagance and bombast. "The history of Japanese art is the history of Asiatic ideals," writes Okakura, "the beach where each successive wave of Eastern thought has left its sand-ripple as it beats against the national consciousness."[46] In this account, Japan becomes the safety deposit box for the precious inheritance of a vital Oriental culture threatened by a rapacious Western modernity.

Okakura's reading finds resonance several decades later in another influential foreign reading of the Japanese tradition, that of German architect Bruno Taut in the 1930s. Taut was a modernist; he had taught at the Bauhaus, and by the time he visited Japan from 1933 to 1936, he was an exile from Hitler's Germany. His account of the 17th-century Katsura Villa in Kyoto finds it a paragon of all the qualities that the modernists had been striving for: "Its principle is absolutely modern, and of complete validity for contemporary architecture."[47] However, in contrast to Okakura's image of Japan as an Oriental redoubt stoutly defending itself against Western modernity, in Taut's account, the Japanese exemplar prefigures and anticipates the aesthetic developments of Western modernity, in the case of Katsura, by as much as 300 years. Japan, in short, was already modern.

This represents the second act in the parade of modernities—that of "overcoming modernity". It is not far from Taut's reading to the idea that Japan has superseded or overcome Western modernity, and it was this idea that fired the romantic idealists who supported Japan's aggressive expansionism across the East Asian hemisphere in the 1930s and 40s. In 1942, the Japanese government sponsored an academic conference entitled "Overcoming Modernity", attended by the most respected philosophers and cultural authorities of the day, with the aim of clarifying what alternative (and superior) set of principles and values to Western

Blade Runner, directed by Ridley Scott, 1982.
1982年に公開された、リドリー・スコット監督の映画「ブレードランナー」

modernity might be implemented by a victorious Japan. The architectural image that perhaps best captures the sensibility of the era was by the young Kenzo Tange, with his competition proposal for the "Monument to the East Asia Co-prosperity Sphere", executed in the same year as the conference. The conference ended inconclusively, and it was followed three years later by the more conclusive end of the war itself. Japan's experiment in overcoming modernity was a failure…for the time being, at least.

With the prospect of instantiating an alternative modernity in the geopolitical sphere foreclosed, Japan's energies turned to the economic sphere. Between the end of the American-led occupation in 1952 and the oil crisis of 1973, Japan underwent a frenzy of industrialization and urbanization at historically unprecedented rates. By the end of this period, Japanese postwar modernity, although growing from the same seeds as that of Western countries, seemed to exhibit amplified proportions and intensified energies. The architectural and urban experiments of the Metabolists, commencing with the Tokyo Bay Plan of 1960 and culminating in the Osaka Expo of 1970, gave physical expression to this sense of amplification. In this view, Japan's modernization had been accelerated, providing a window to an alternative modernity positioned now in a bright technological future rather than a luminous aesthetic past. This constitutes the third act in the parade—that of the "accelerated modern". Japan became, in the words of cyberpunk novelist William Gibson, "the global imagination's default setting for the future".[48] Rather than the Katsura palace and the tea ceremony, it was its robots, its automation and its miniaturization that become the emblems of the Japanese modern. Atmospherically and urbanistically, the shoji-screen serenity of Kyoto was replaced by the neon-screen intensity of Tokyo. The settings of Ridley Scott's 1982 film Bladerunner, set in the Los Angeles of 2019, were inspired by the streets of Shinjuku circa 1980. Japan presaged a future in which technology became embedded, immanent, the advanced machines within our primitive ghosts.

Fundamentally, such futurism still relies on a modern teleology of linear progress, a bounded track along which different societies are traveling at different speeds, where they can overtake or be overtaken, but where they are all heading towards the same destination. But from the 1970s onwards, this view has intersected with readings that position Japan entirely outside of or beyond this modernist frame. This configuration can be identified as the Japanese postmodern, the fourth act in the parade of alternative modernities, in which the meaning of the prefix "post-" oscillates between temporal and spatial senses, between "after" and "beyond" modernity. The hallmark of this interpretation is the interweaving of ideas drawn from traditional Japanese sources with contemporary theories, conditions and phenomena circulating globally. The writing and work of architect Arata Isozaki is emblematic of this approach, so that an elaboration of the Japanese spatio-temporal concept of "ma" (interval, spacing, gap) could also constitute a contribution to the postmodern conversation around aesthetics and philosophy.[49] The most brilliant of such interpretations was that of Roland Barthes, who in his The Empire of Signs of 1970 set out to "isolate somewhere in the world (faraway) a certain number of features…and out of these features deliberately form a system. It is this system which I shall call: Japan." Here Japan becomes a "fictive nation" with a "reserve of features…whose invented interplay" affords Barthes the delicious opportunity to explore the prospect of an "unheard-of symbolic system, one altogether detached from our own," in which signs and signifiers do not carry meanings or signifieds but are rather "empty".[50] In readings such as these, "Japan" becomes not just the site of an alternative modernity, but an occasion for an alternative thinking.

DYNAMIC STILLNESS: TOWARDS AN ALTERNATIVE TEMPORALITY

Reviewing the alternative modernities encountered in this parade, we can identify each as characterized by a particular relation to a dominant modernity: imitation; overcoming; acceleration; and transcendence. If our present condition remains defined by a modernity in thrall to the telos of progress and the instrumental exploitation of resources both human and natural, what imaginative possibilities might be found in a reading of Japan, or more narrowly of Tokyo, today? My approach to this question is guided by the idea that at the heart of modernity lies the temporal project we name progress or growth, a project that is illuminated by Walter Benjamin's evocative conception of history as a fluid spatial matrix structured by shifting "constellations of recognition", linking past, present and future. For Benjamin, "the past can be seized only as an image which flashes up at the instant when it can be recognized and is never seen again", and history is not a linear sequence but a field "shot through with chips of Messianic time."[51]

Under such a temporal imagination, a view of historical change as the progressive unfolding and flourishing of rationality becomes untenable. Social and cultural dynamism may longer require progress but could instead be all about rhythm. Energy could involve motion without necessarily implying movement. Growth could be intensive rather than expansive. Equipped with such a consciousness, we could find in Tokyo—in the coruscating kaleidoscope of its fashions; in the endless churn of its building sites; in the urban metronome of its train timetable; in its diurnal round of morning sobriety and nocturnal exuberance; in the annual exultation of spring sakura and the summer matsuri; in its April inductions and December big cleans; and in the slow soft toll of the New Year's bell—the rhythms of an alternative modernity, one whose procession is nothing other than an eternal perambulation around the arena of history.

STILL POWER: SARTORIAL SURVEILLANCE AND THE UNDER-CITY

静かなる権力

東京では、しばしば権力は堕落する。堕落するときは激しく、底まで落ちる。その底が山谷だ。山谷は、東京の社会的階層の最下層となる、日雇い労働者の町だ。今日、山谷ではゆっくりとジェントリフィケーションが進んでいる。この変化の世話役たちが、交番からあたりを覗いている。身分証の提示を求められるのは、前科者であることが明白にわかる場合や犯罪の危険が迫っているときだけだ。しかし、髪を脱色して金髪にしたこの女性に対して、そうした配慮はなされない。警察は彼女に身分証の提示を求めた。彼女は拒否した。そして、権力はさらに堕落した。拒否したことで、疑わしいと判断したのだ。彼女の行動を止められると思っているから、こうした権力の濫用が行われる。

Jonathan M. Hall はカリフォルニア州クレアモントにあるポモナ大学助教(メディア・スタディーズ)。長年に渡り何度も東京に滞在している。

ザッ
ザッ
ザッ

NOT SHOWING US YOUR ID MAKES YOU A PERSON OF SUSPICIOUS CONDUCT.
I DON'T NEED TO SHOW YOU ANYTHING.
WHAT ARE YOU HIDING UNDER YOUR JACKET? REMOVE IT NOW!

I HAVE NOTHING TO HIDE. JUST LEAVE ME ALONE!
スタ スタ

ぴ〜ぷ〜
ぴ〜ぷ〜
POLICE
ぴ〜ぷ〜
明治通り左折
車検
安心の全国チェーン
出入口

ハタ
ハタ
LET ME GO!
I'M CALLING THE PO.... !?!?!????
YOU CAN HAVE MY ID!
I'LL SHOW IT!
YOU TRIED TO CROSS THE STREET ON A RED LIGHT. WE CAN ARREST YOU NOW.

CAN I GO NOW?
OK.
SHE'LL KNOW BETTER FROM NOW ON.
プーン
プーン
完

In a city of Tokyo's unbearable weight and ceaseless energies, power is always at hand. Fixing power and holding it is impossible, and when its minor lords attempt so, it grows recalcitrant. Reified and stilled, power thus falls hard—and to the bottom.

That bottom has long been Sanya, once the bustling district for day laborers at the lowest rungs of the social ladder: Tokyo's Under-City. These days, Sanya's cheap boarding houses are being traded up for uninventive apartment blocks with white lobbies and autolock doors. The grubby stalls along the freight yard, with their unusual pairing of strong liquor and instant ramen, are now tidied up into the mundane menus of Mos Burger and Mr. Donuts. Silent stewards to the neoliberal gentrification, peering out from their police boxes, Tokyo's avatars of justice act with deliberate restraint. Dispassionate faces tired of giving directions, they itch for something besides friendliness.

I am often in Sanya, so it was no surprise to see still power again in its petty play. The avatars of justice—the law tells us—can reason. And only when there is reasonable judgment of a past or impending crime may they demand identification. Yet for this woman whose bleach-blond hair matched her unusual persistence, the subtleties of their judgments would make no difference. No code violated except for her unconventional look, the avatars demanded she perform. For them, it was law—for her, its most sloppy interpretation.

She refused.

Silent, reified power lowered itself further into Sanya's back alleys.

And the city began to stop.

In the next, common turn of the constabulary screw, the refusal became her suspicious nature, their intrusion the very reason they could stop her. Now, she was an indentured actor, forced to perform in their costume drama, with a clumsy Sanya dance added as special act. "Not showing us your ID makes you a person of suspicious conduct." "What are you hiding under your jacket? Remove it now!" Circling her, they wrestled the coat off her back, each avatar of justice fastidiously careful never to touch her body: the bride was stripped bare by bachelors more interested in sartorial surveillance than flesh or body.

東京では、しばしば権力は堕落する。堕落するときは激しく、底まで落ちる。その底が山谷だ。山谷は、東京の社会的階層の最下層となる、日雇い労働者の町だ。今日、山谷ではゆっくりとジェントリフィケーションが進んでいる。この変化の世話役たちが、交番からあたりを覗いている。身分証の提示を求められるのは、前科者であることが明白にわかる場合や犯罪の危険が迫っ

When I brought 104 still images I had shot of this scene to Chinese artist Zhang Yi, Zhang suggested using Japanese manga as a means to return motion to the stilling power of that early November afternoon. Zhang didn't know it, but Sanya was an important setting for Kajiwara Ikki's *Ashita no Joe* (Tomorrow's Joe), the long serialized mid-20th century manga about a boxing underdog. From the same era, Japanese gekiga, or action manga, trace roots to the radical, counter-establishment politics of the 1960s and 1970s, combining dramatic visualizations of action with careful social commentary. Shirato Sampei and other contributors to the magazine *Garo* emphasized the political, educational function of their gekiga. With Zhang's adaptation of the afternoon events to gekiga's action format, the shaky, blurry nature of my images began to better reveal the social forces at play.

Pinned against the wall, stripped of her jacket, and surrounded by justice's avatars, this woman became invisible to a small crowd that had assembled. Still, we could tell she was there. The drama's climax began. Her tormented voice instinctually called for justice above the fray: "Let me go, I'm calling the po..." Just as she began to speak that final word, the nature of the avatars' power dawned on her. She couldn't finish, her voice falling back into the mass. Then, the dance picked up again. A dozen avatars would shuffle in unison left, then in unison right, left, right, left— clearly in tandem with her tiny step invisible within.

It was her one step forward that was the fatal flaw. Given the commotion, I'm sure she couldn't tell it was a red light. The battalion of avatars and the assembled crowd must have blinded her to the importance of traffic safety. She pushed forward—away from the wall she had been pinned against. Mere centimeters from it and surrounded finally by dozens, she made her one step ahead when others had the right of way. Little kept her now from arrest for this violation.

She showed her ID, the drama ended, and the Sanya afternoon turned to evening. Cruelly harnessed from the moving megalopolis that was backdrop to us all, the Undercity's relentless energies cast even longer shadows at our feet.

ているときだけだ。しかし、髪を脱色して金髪にしたこの女性に対して、そうした配慮はなされない。警察は彼女に身分証の提示を求めた。彼女は拒否した。そして、権力はさらに堕落した。拒否したことで、疑わしいと判断したのだ。彼女の行動を止められると思っているから、こうした権力の濫用が行われる。

A MACHINE FOR LIVING

Le Corbusier posed that "the house is a machine for living". In his 1923 book *Towards a New Architecture*, he explains how architects should look at how cars are designed and engineered. How with each new model they approach perfection in function and beauty through standardization. Just as the perfect harmony of the ancient Greek temples is the product of a careful selection of standards that evolved over the ages.

Flipping through a Japanese magazine less than a century later, Corbusier would see his recommendation realized. Side by side are the advertisements for machines for living and driving. Features pointed out, prices for options, payment plans, tax benefits and discounts explained. After consumption their value decreases and they'll be disposed of. For a car, a second life usually starts after 7 or 8 years; for a Tokyo house, life ends when on average 26 years have passed.

住むための機械

ル・コルビュジエは、「住宅とは住む機械である」という理念を掲げた。1923年の『建築をめざして』の中で、建築家は自動車のデザインや設計のあり方に目を向けるべきだ、と説いている。自動車は、新モデルを打ち出すたびに、機能の完成に近づき、標準化を通して美に近づいていく。ギリシャの寺院が、長年にわたって生み出されてきた標準型を注意深く選択することでできあがった成果であることを思い出させる。

以来100年も経っていないが、もしコルビュジエが日本の雑誌をぱらぱらとめくってみたなら、彼のヴィジョンが実現されたことがわかるだろう。住むための機械と運転するための機械の広告が並んでいるのだ。特長、オプションの価格、支払い計画、税制優遇、割引の説明も掲載されている。

Joris Berkhout は建築家。2012年以来東京に暮らし、仕事をしている。**Thijs Middeldorp** はPartizan Publikのパートナー。2012年11月に日本に滞在。Partizan Publikはもっと勇敢でサステナブルで包括的な社会をつくるための活動を展開している。

134 TOWARDS A NEW ARCHITECTURE

PAESTUM, 600–550 B.C.

When once a standard is established, competition comes at once and violently into play. It is a fight; in order to win you must do better than your rival *in every minute point*, in

HUMBER, 1907

SUPER LEGAL BUILDINGS

When I returned to Japan in 2001 after residing in the Netherlands for two years, I felt extremely at odds with Tokyo's streetscapes, which had once been familiar to me. The city center was densely populated by an array of small-detached houses, the façades of large buildings had been cut off to have unreasonable inclinations, and even the various attached fittings such as balconies and stairs appeared somewhat awkward.

In Tokyo, 16 million people use the railways every day to commute to school and to work, approximately 8,000 tons* of waste is produced daily, and near 7,000 convenience stores provide over 3,000 items that can be purchased 24 hours a day. The reality that architecture is part of this haphazard urban landscape and at the same time performs as a highly functional vessel for civic life seemed at the time like a complete contradiction.

In my mind the following hypothesis emerged: "The seemingly haphazard architecture and cityscape of Tokyo is in fact not haphazard at all." Accordingly, I decided to do fieldwork with my students. My objective was to seek out credible circumstances that resulted in Tokyo's buildings appearing to express a "so-what" attitude towards their apparent haphazardness. I had come to realize that behind these ostensibly peculiar-looking buildings was a series of specific legal corroborations. These buildings had acquired their unique forms through an attempt to circumvent laws and regulations, or as a result of excessively respecting them. I decided to collectively refer to examples pertaining to both cases as "Super Legal Buildings." The results of our fieldwork were collected and accompanied by a series of images that illustrate the invisible guidelines that are designated by the law. These were eventually transformed into the book: Super Legal Buildings Guide.

** The total amount of waste produced by Tokyo's 23 wards in 2013 was 2,816,809 tons/year (7,717 tons/day). Furthermore, the amount of waste produced per person each day is 857 grams. (The population of Tokyo's 23 wards in October 2013 was 9,008,9990 people.)*

吉村靖孝は、東京を拠点に国内外を問わず広く活動する建築家。ダイナミックに変容する市場、法、規範をデザインの契機と捉え、次世代の建築／都市の姿を模索している。

超合法建築

2年間のオランダ滞在を終え2001年に日本へ戻った際、見慣れていたはずの東京の街並みに猛烈な違和感を覚えた。都心部にも小さな戸建て住宅が密集して建ち、大きな建物の壁は理不尽な斜面でえぐり取られ、バルコニーや階段などの付属物もどこかぎこちない。にもかかわらず東京では、毎日1,600万人が鉄道を利用者して学校や会社に通い、1日に東京都で約8,000t*のゴミを排出し、約7,000軒のコンビニエンスストアで24時間いつでも3,000品目が手に入る。建築がデタラメな都市景観の構成要素になっている現実と、市民生活の器として高度に機能している現実が、まったく乖離しているように見えたのだ。そこで思い至ったのが、「一見デタラメに見える東京の建築や都市は、実のところデタラメではない」という仮説だった。

そこで私は、学生を連れてフィールドワークに出ることにした。デタラメ上等と居直ったかのような東京の建物の、やむにやまれぬ成立条件を嗅ぎ取るために、、、。そしてほどなく気がついたのは、一見奇妙に見える建物の背後に、ことごとく法規的な裏付けがあるということであった。あるものは法規の網をかいくぐるように、またあるものは法規を過剰に尊重するようにしてその特異な形状を手にしていたが、私はその両方をまとめて「超合法建築」と呼ぶことにした。このフィールドワークの成果を集め、法による見えない補助線をイラスト化して添えた図版集が、やがて1冊の本になった。それが「超合法建築図鑑」である。

*平成25年度における東京23区のゴミ量2,816,809t／年（7,717t／日）。なお、1人が1日に出すゴミの量は約857g（平成25年10月時点での東京23区の人口：9,008,990人）。

Reprinted in this volume with the courtesy of Shokokusha Publishing
本頁イラストの出典：『超合法建築図鑑』（彰国社、2006）

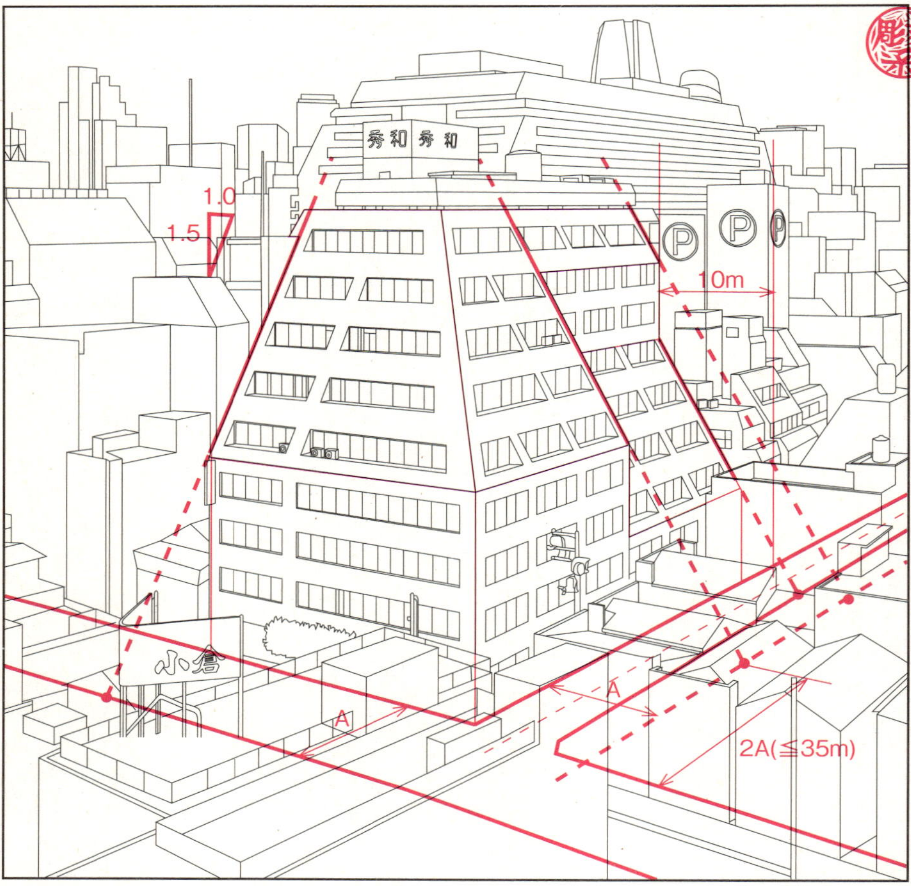

SNOWSLIDE BUILDING / 雪崩ビル

When a building faces onto two or more roads with different widths, the narrower road is considered to have the same width as that of the wider road, and as a result the height restriction from the road is relaxed for a portion of the building. This relaxation is applicable for the portion that lies within twice the width of the wider road measured from the intersection (this must simultaneously be less than 35m), and the portion that exceeds a distance of 10 meter from the centerline of the narrower road. The unevenness created in the boundary of such regulations, produces a form that appears as if a part of the building has collapsed.

幅の異なる2本以上の道路に面している場合、狭い道路側に広い道路と同じ幅員があるとみなして道路からの高さ制限が緩和される部分がある。緩和を受けることができる範囲は、交差点から広い道路幅の2倍以内でかつ35m以下の部分で、狭い道路の中心線から10mを超えた部分。境界にできる段差はまるで建物の一部分が崩れ落ちたような造形を生み出す。

BALCONY EYES / 複眼バルコニー

For a balcony to be considered valid for evacuation, hatches must be provided to ensure an escape route to the ground. To prevent risks of falls, the hatches must not be positioned in line with the hatch on the floor directly beneath. The way in which the circular hatches waver from the right and to the left on the circular balconies, look like numerous eyeballs constantly shifting their gaze.

避難上有効なバルコニーには、ハッチを設けて地面までたどりつけるように計画しなければならない。転落の危険を防止するため、ハッチの位置は、直下階のハッチと同一平面上にはつけられない。丸いバルコニーに空いた丸いハッチが左右に揺れる様は、まるでたくさんの目玉が視線を泳がせているかのよう。

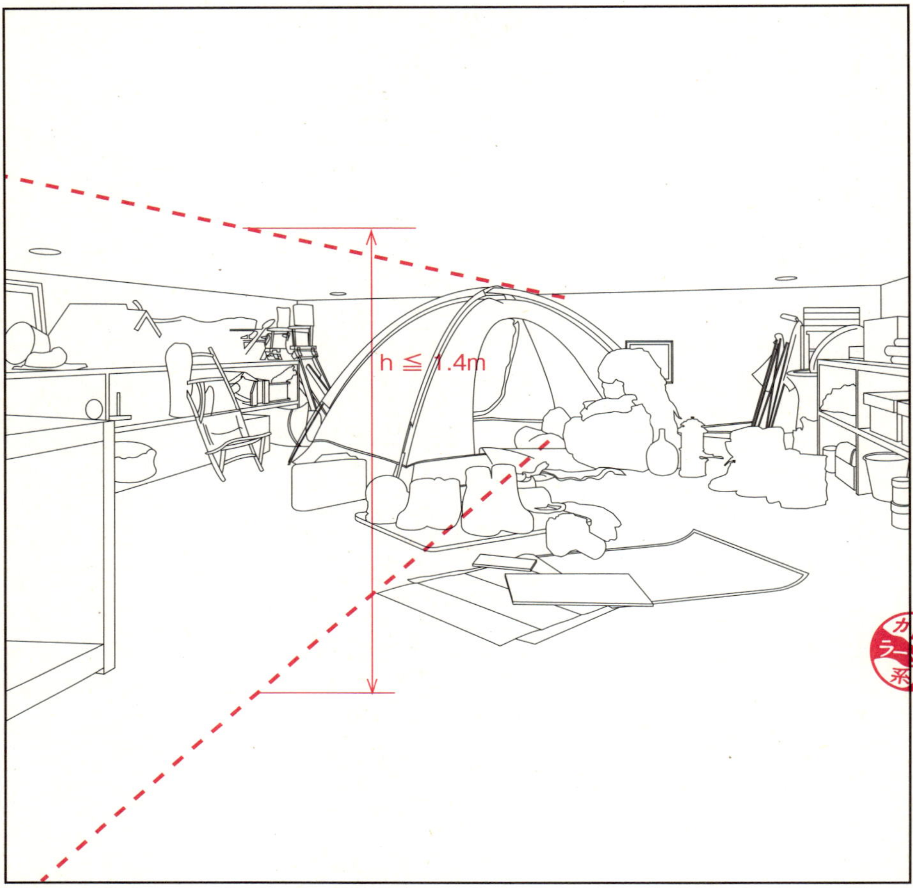

HALF STORY / 1/2階

Storage areas that utilize attics and loft spaces with ceiling heights of less than 1.4m and meet the condition of having an area of less than 1/2 of a story are not treated as an official floor. The drawing is of the interior of a commercialized residence that utilizes this regulation as one of its sales attributes. I find great appeal in there being another space beneath the floor or above the ceiling.

小屋裏や天井裏などを利用した物置のうち、天井高が1.4m以下で、かつ面積がその階の1/2以下など条件を満たした場合、そこは階として扱われない。写真はその法律の活用を売りにした商品化住宅の内観。床や天井の裏側にもうひとつ空間があるなんて男心をくすぐります。

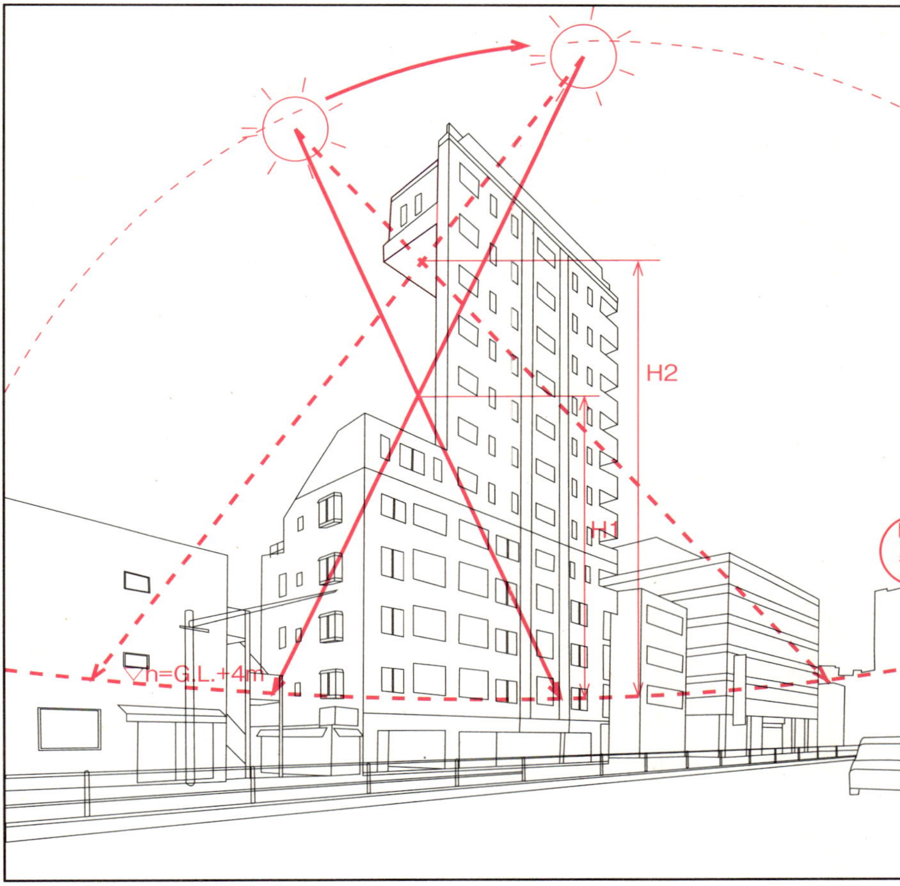

GIRAFFE BUILDING / キリン・ビル

Sun-shadow regulations exist in order to prevent the shadows caused by mid- to high-rise buildings from disrupting the surrounding environment. The basis of evaluation is not the extent of the area that the shadows affect, but rather the time that it remains in a certain place. The shadows caused by the higher section of the building move faster than those caused by the lower section, thus it is more lucrative to distribute the volume of a building to its higher section. Top-heavy buildings as shown in the drawing, can be found in various areas of the city.

中高層建築物によって生じる陰が周辺環境を悪化させぬよう日影規制がある。その評価方法は、影の落とす範囲ではなく影が留まる時間。高層部分の影は、低層部分の影に比べ早く動くため、同じ容積なら高層部へ振り分けた方が有利と言うことである。写真のような頭でっかちのビルは、都内各所で見ることができる。

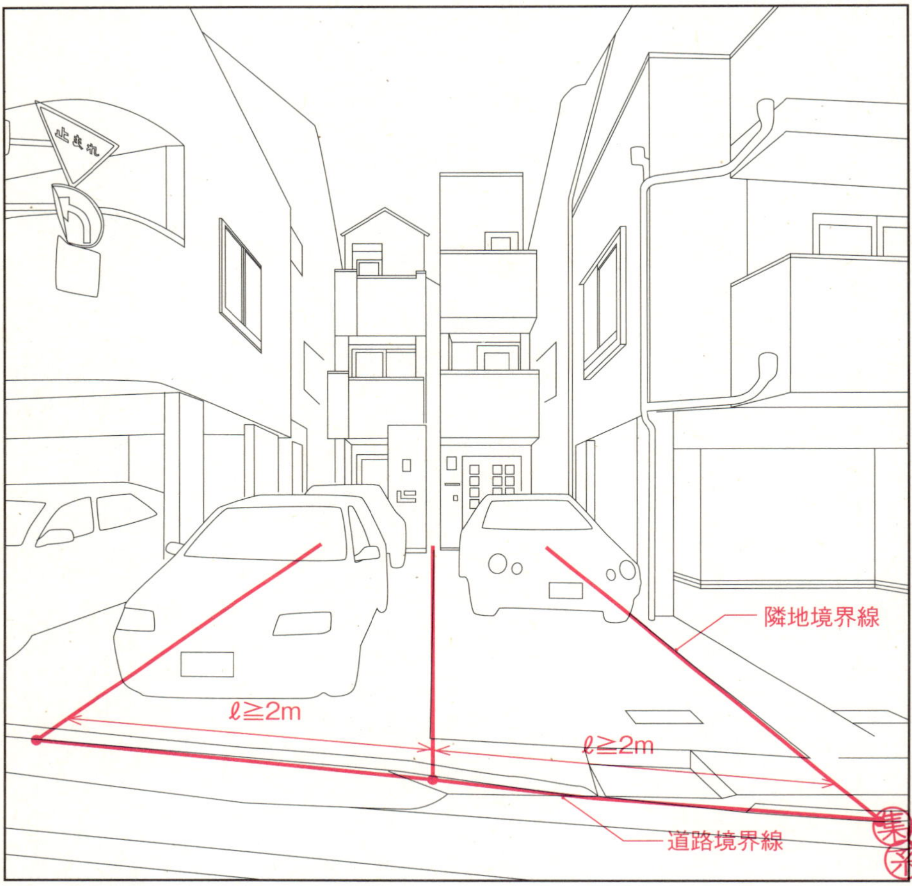

ENTRANCE HOUSE / 玄関ハウス

Individual plots in Tokyo are becoming smaller and smaller due to the division of land caused by the high inheritance tax. Where sites come into contact with the road they need to have a width of 2 meter or more, and thus plots are often flagpole shaped where the pole portion connects to the road and the site widens in the back. The drawing shows a more extreme case, a pole-without-a-flag plot with a three-story residence no wider than its entrance.

相続による分割で、東京の土地はどんどん小さくなっている。しかし敷地は道路に幅2m以上接していなければならず、旗竿の竿の部分のみ道路に接する独特の地割りが生まれた。写真は、その竿の部分まで住宅がはみ出してきたような事例で、玄関の幅のまま3階建てになっている。

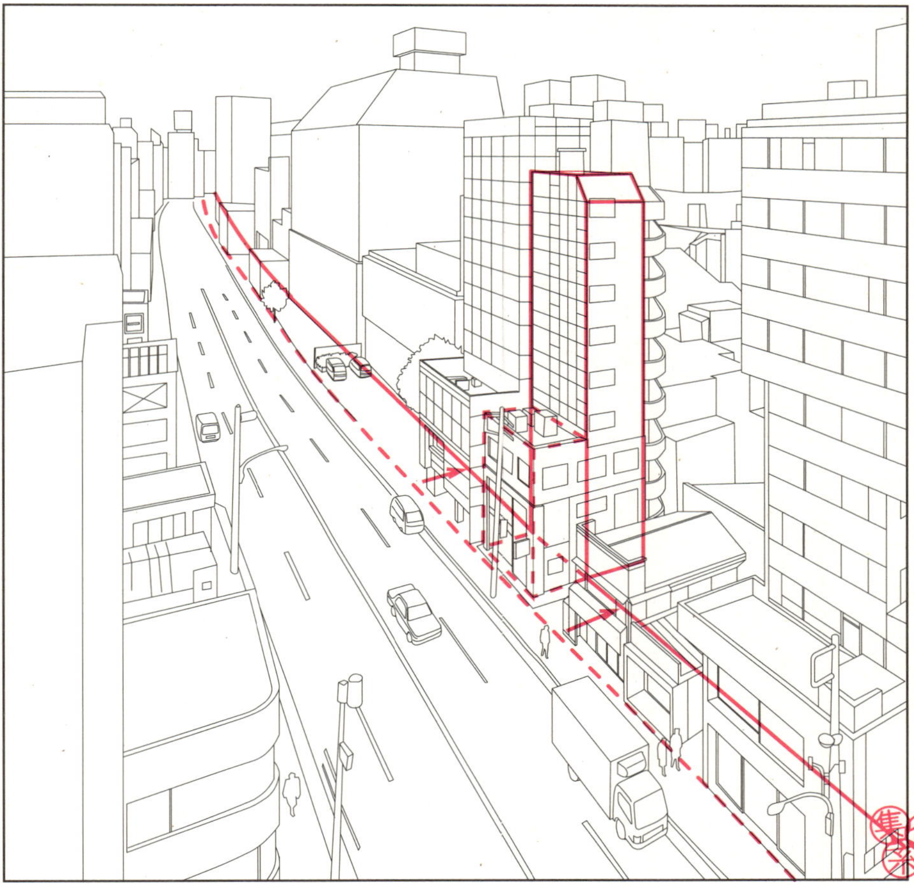

BOOTS STREET / 長靴通り

If the widening of a road is anticipated, the architecture that can be built along this road is subjected to certain restrictions regarding its size and structure. The manner in which these buildings align to the road, being lower in the front and higher in the back, almost seems like a row of boots neatly placed along the road. The lower front section gives rise to a moderate sense of scale that is optimal for stores. Typically one will find such buildings on relatively busy streets.

道路の拡幅が予定されている場合、その部分に建てることのできる建築は、規模や構造の制限を受ける。手前が低く背後が高い建物が道路に沿って並ぶ様子は、まるで長靴がつま先を揃えているかのよう。手前の低層部分が適度なスケール感を生み出し、店舗としての利用もしやすいことから、比較的賑やかな通りに多いのも特徴。

へら絞り

北嶋絞製作所は大田区京浜島にある絞り部品加工企業だ。会長の北嶋實は、この同族会社の三代目である。地元の神社に飾る銅の鈴から、国際的航空機産業に納品するユニークなハイテクロケットの先端部まで、さまざまな製品を手がけている。工作機械を扱うには、身につけた技と才のすべてを注ぎ込む必要がある。そのため、従業員たちは若くして引退するし、週5日、週に8時間以上は働かな

HERA SHIBORI

Fritzi Ponse はライター、デザイン研究者、教師。彼女は2012年11月に東京を訪れた。

い。手作業はなくてはならないものだ。必要なスキルをすべて身につけるには10年かかる。北嶋によれば、従業員は「職人」だから、良い仕事のためにその身を捧げているという。ときには、不可能と思われる仕事も引き受ける。きっと新しい方法を編み出すことができるという自信があるからだ。この自信は、経験が鍵となる金属曲面づくりを、長年かけて培ってきたことから生まれているのだ。

TAKIZWA
モーターカーボン
ペンチ
ニッパープライヤー
ベアリング
刻印
超硬ロール
救急箱
スパーク

It takes about an hour to get from eclectic Shinjuku to Keihinjima in Ota-ku, an industrial area in southwestern Tokyo where there once was sea. The wharves, the viaducts, the sky and the ocean seem to blend in an endless grey palette, disturbed only on occasion by bright, multicolored sea-containers. Here you won't see flashing neon lights scattered above your head, billboards or shopping malls. Here there are only traffic lights, signs, low-rise concrete buildings, lots of trucks and, sporadically placed, beverage vending machines on street corners.

The smell of greasy rain mixed with tobacco fills the bus. The passengers look different from those who frequent the Tokyo subway system. No one wears a suit. It could very well be that one of our fellow passengers in this public-transport bus makes parts for the smartphones they are all busy with. This is the area of the machi koba (Japanese for "small- to medium-sized town factories"). These factories produce all kinds of low- and high-tech products and parts for different types of national and international industries. It is here that you enter the base—or engine—of the Japanese economy. I am with my friend and translator Reiko Kageyama. We are here to visit Kitajima Shibori Seisakusho, a metal-spinning company. We are looking for contemporary craftsmanship: people who work with their hands, know a skill and make contemporary products.

A few days ago I met design researcher Eizo Okada in his spotless design office downtown. When I told him I was looking for present-day craftsmanship—people who work with their hands, know a skill and make contemporary products—he suggested that I go to Ota-ku. He explained that, although relatively unknown, machi koba are as representative of Japanese economy as giant firms like Toyota and Canon. In fact, they were (and are still) crucial to the industrialization and modernization of postwar Japan.

I understood from Okada that machi koba typically employ between 10 and 300 people and that they form the engine of the so-called Toyota system—a system of efficient and lean production that focuses on just-in-time delivery in order to eliminate waste and inconsistencies. At the turn of the 21st century there were almost 5 million machi koba, accounting for no less than 99 percent of the total number of Japanese enterprises. Little is known, however, about these grassroots town factories. This is partly because they form the base of a pyramid-like hierarchical structure of subcontractor networks (as is the case with Toyota City and Hitachi City), and partly because machi koba are located in the backwaters of modern Japan, far from the inner-city corporate headquarters. Though it was once thought that they delayed the process of modernization, today they are considered among the most innovative and flexible work environments in Japan.[52]

Okada told me about metal-spinning craftsmen who produce not only pots and pans for local households, but also the noses for Japanese bullet trains and the casings for NASA's rocket engines; they do it all by hand too, assisted by homemade machinery. I got curious. I wanted to meet these "high-tech craftsmen". I wanted to see how they worked, how they combined manual skills and home-made-machinery to produce not just cutlery but vital parts for smartphones, satellites and high-speed trains as well.

Entering the office building of Kitajima Shibori Seisakusho (established in 1947) is like entering a potpourri of glimmering, abstract metal objects. They are displayed everywhere: on the floor; on the steps that bring you to the office; in display cabinets. Some of the objects are recognizable as household items—bowls, cups, kettles and pans—but with most it is impossible to tell what they are and what they are for.

The secretary is busy answering phone calls. She's standing behind a desk cluttered with papers and old computers. She won't sit for a second. She brings us tea and tells us to sit in the

large dark leather fauteuils at the window and wait for the company president. The office and meeting room are adorned with office furniture from the 1950s. I glance at pictures of giant rocket engines and tiny young women standing next to them; pictures of men in overalls, who pose with seemingly important persons in suits; and at a painting of a waterfall. Rain beats on the window.

After a while a man in his fifties enters the room. He has on worn green overalls. He introduces himself as Minoru Kitajima, the company president. He tells us that he represents the third generation of his family to run the enterprise. When he sees us looking at all the unfamiliar objects he smiles. Though the objects have a three-dimensional, cylindrical shape in common, we learn that their purposes vary greatly, as do the clients for whom they are made: some are made for religious purposes (a huge copper bell for a Shinto Shrine); some are decorative (a casing for a giant Seiko clock, made to hang in a shopping mall, or a small turquoise-colored side table). But there are also mechanical parts for cars, as well as for air- and spacecraft industries.

Reiko and I follow Kitajima downstairs to the plant. Kitajima, who has a humble demeanor, admits that he spends most of his time working on the factory floor, where he blends in with his staff. The company employs 30 metal-spinning craftsmen, ranging from 30 to 56 in age.

Kitajima demonstrates one of the manual manufacturing processes. He manipulates an aluminum plate over a mandrel by pressing a spoon-like tool, while the plate and mandrel are spinning on a lathe. In no more than five minutes, Kitajima produces a perfectly finished aluminum bowl. It is a rather simple product to make, he tells us; making one would take a newcomer a week of practice, perhaps. At the other end of the learning curve are the complex parts for the spacecraft industry, for which a skilled craftsman can produce shapes that are accurate to within 0.1 millimeter. In Kitajima's company manual labor is indispensable: no pressing machine is able to produce as precisely or accurately as the human body. They have computer-programmed pressing machines, but these only make sense for high-volume production runs that don't require high precision.

Becoming a hera shibori crafter involves the passing down of skills from veterans. There is no instruction manual or school. According to Kitajima, you need to learn how to communicate with the materials by doing. Your body is your main tool, as the essence of the work depends on tactility. Some materials need a delicate, but evenly exerted force, while thicker and heavier metals require more strenuous power. It takes about ten years to fully master the skillset, which includes not only producing the objects themselves, but also the designing and making of mandrels, the spoon-like tools, and the many other instruments. I ask what makes these men craftsmen. Kitajima thinks about it and says that it probably has something to do with dedication to doing good work for the sake of doing good work.

On the factory floor we meet Abiko. Akibo is 30 years old, and the youngest employee of Kitajima Shibori Seisakusyo, which only welcomes a newcomer once every few years. Abiko is still an apprentice. Though he has master's degrees in physics and engineering, he realized he wasn't going to be happy if he couldn't work with his hands. His parents were surprised when he chose to work in this metal-spinning factory, but he's happy now. Kitajima tells us that his oldest employee, who is 56, is about to retire, though it is likely that he will stay a little longer. They always do.

People who work in machi koba usually retire relatively young, for one needs all of one's wits when working with heavy machinery. This also means that working hours in machi koba are—especially by Japanese standards—very reasonable. In Kitajima Shibori Seisakusho people work five days a week, eight hours a day—including the president.

The merit of doing a job for its own sake is often overlooked these days. According to sociologist Richard Sennett, who wrote a book titled The Craftsman, "craftsmanship" is defined by a state of engagement, and therefore transcends materiality and instrumentality. The better his skills are developed, the busier a craftsman is with getting things to work, and the more capable he is at feeling and thinking deeply about what he is doing.[53] This also seems to be the case with the people who work at Kitajima Shibori Seisakusho. Kitajima tells us that they sometimes accept jobs that at first glance seem impossible. They take the job anyway because they feel confident that they are capable of inventing new approaches to creating objects that have never been created before.

Through a decades-long process of experimentation and trial and error the craftsmen succeed in ways that go beyond metal spinning. There seems to be a sort of creative and resilient material consciousness at play here. Perhaps this is also the reason this factory operates successfully without a sales force and was hardly affected by the economic crisis. The products sell themselves, Kitajima says dryly. I have a feeling this might not be the case; perhaps it's not just because the products sell themselves, but because of the craftsmen and their complete engagement.

Lately there has been a certain amount of attention paid to machi koba in Japanese media. Popular TV shows feature different factories that compete against one another using their specific skills and products. Reiko gives an impromptu impression: "Person 1: 'My concrete wall is indestructible!' Person 2: 'Well, wait till you see my wrecking ball!'" And so the action begins. Kitajima laughs. According to him the shows help popularize this type of industrial work. Kitajima too has had some TV exposure, which helps attract new people. "It works better than advertising in the local papers." According to Kitajima this attention derives from renewed interest in technique and craft in Japan and from the fear that these industries are disappearing. Kitajima is not afraid. He has plenty of work and he doesn't think that machines can or will ever take over his handiwork.

Walking around the factory floor I can't shake the feeling that modern society doesn't think to highly of manual skills—skills that are driven not just by competition but by a deepening personal knowledge and the creation of quality. Kitajima clearly takes pride in his work. He also seems eager to share this knowledge.

I ask president Kitajima to pick his favorite tool. He starts rummaging in a large barrel filled with strange instruments. The tools look like nothing I have seen before: large iron bars with curvature and a rubber skateboard wheel on the top. With a cheerful movement Kitajima grabs one. There's only one reason this is his favorite spoon, he says: "I made it myself, so it fits perfectly."

SATURATION POINTS

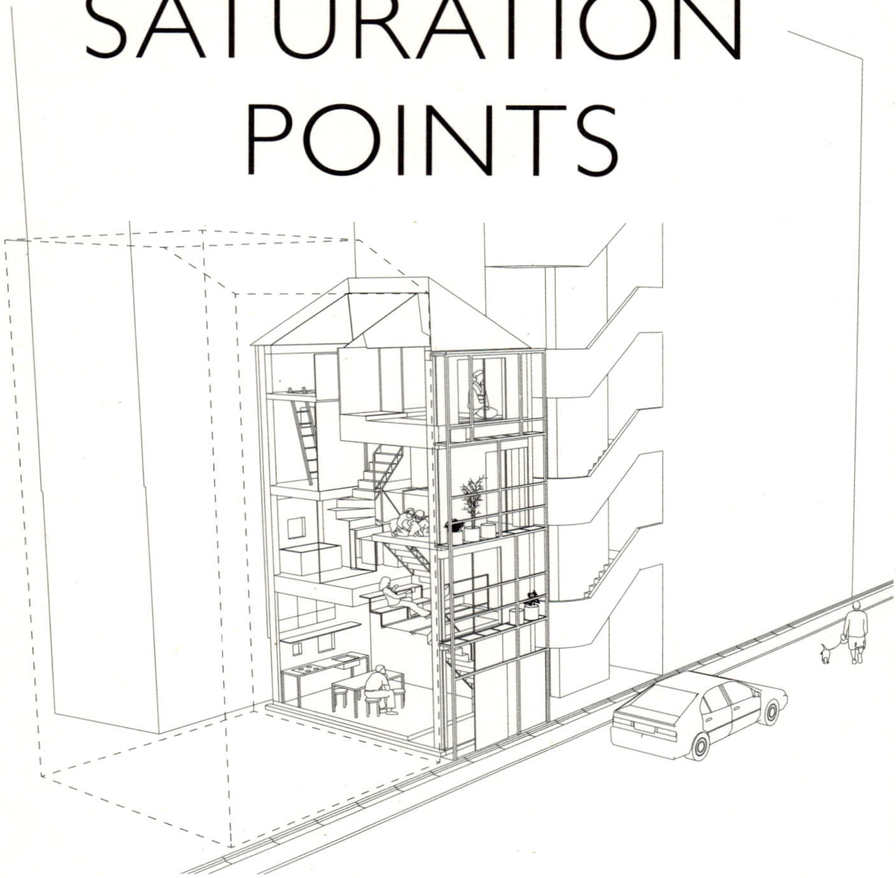

SATURATION POINT 1: TOWER MACHIYA, ATELIER BOW-WOW.
Today, in Tokyo, it seems that a single parking lot is all the space you need for a house.

飽和点その1: アトリエ・ワン「タワーまちや」
今日の東京では、家を建てるのに必要なスペースは、車1台分の駐車スペースだ。

飽和点

建築家や都市計画家が都市の強度や規模を語る場合、たいていは、密度——土地1平方メートルあたりの人口や床面積——に言及する。しかし、東京という都市の建築的環境に限っては、密度だけでは物事の半分しか語れない。もう半分は、飽和度だ。飽和とは、あるものに溶解・吸収されうる最大量を示し、通常はパーセンテージで表現する。都市というコンテクストにおいては、あるエリアの土地にどれだけの建物を建てうるか、ということになるだろう。あるいは、1軒の住宅を建てうる最小の敷地、ということになるだろう。

Gabriel Verret はパリと東京で建築を学んだ。

SATURATION POINT 2: GARDEN & HOUSE, RYUE NISHIZAWA.
A house rises from a four-meter breach in the street facade.

飽和点その2：西沢立衛「Garden & House」
通りに面した4メートル幅の隙間に家が立っている。

Usually when architects and urbanists talk about the intensity and size of urban areas, they refer to its density: the amount of people or floorspace per square meter of land. But in qualifying Tokyo's urban built environment, density is but half the story. The other half is saturation. Saturation is the degree to which something is dissolved or absorbed in proportion to the maximum possible absorption, usually expressed as a percentage. In an urban context this would refer to the maximum amount of buildings one could fit into a certain area of land. Or, in other words: what is the smallest plot you can still build a house on?

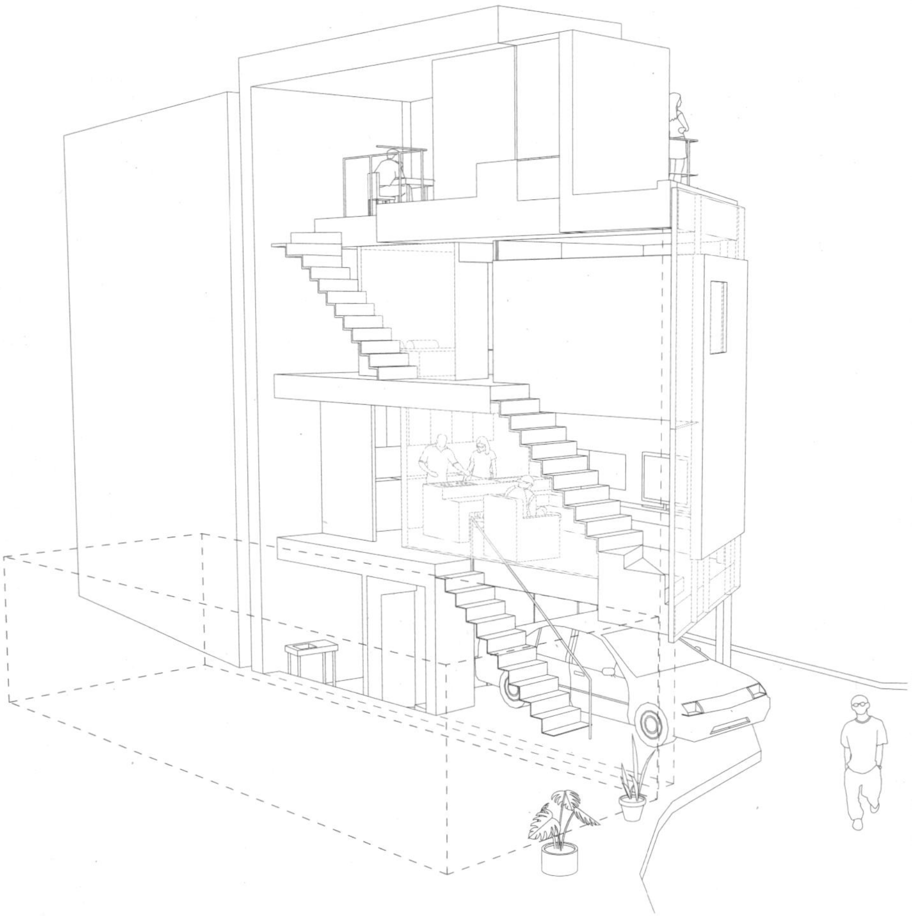

SATURATION POINT 3: HOUSE IN NAKAMEGURO, YORITAKA HAYASHI
This compact house emerges in a fascinating way out of a challenging site that has been shaped by the numerous subdivisions of the original parcel.

飽和点その3：林順孝「中目黒の家」
1つの土地を何度も分割してできた難しい敷地から導き出された、魅力的なコンパクトハウス。

In postwar Japan, the city expanded as if no limit existed, but soon the city reached its physical boundaries: mountains and sea. Unable to grow any further, it needed to optimize space within its borders by filling every urban gap available.

For a saturating city, no site is too small for occupation. In the past decades the combination of rising land prices and inheritance taxes have forced generations of land owners to divide their plots and sell pieces they could not afford. As a result, low-rise residential areas in the

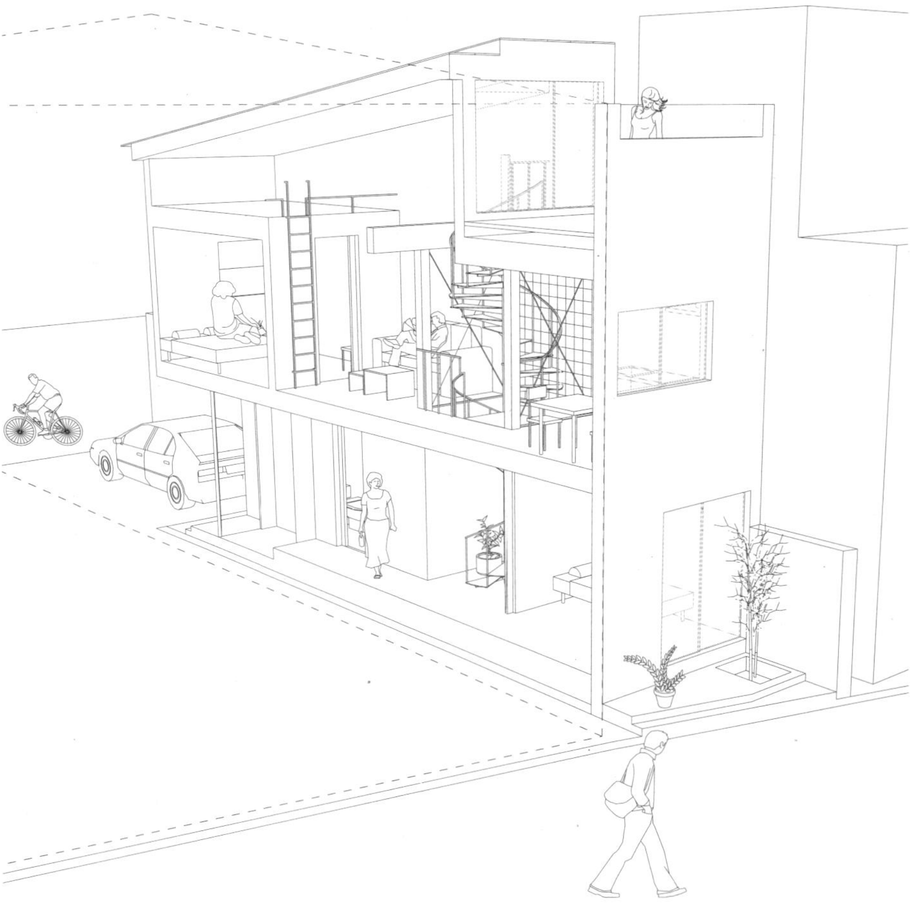

SATURATION POINT 4: MICHINOIE, TAKAFUMI MATSUNAGA
On what used to be a three-meter-wide alleyway, a comfortable house now stands.
This narrow site is as good a point of reference as any for saturation!

飽和点その4：松永隆文「ミチノイエ」
元は間口3メートルの小さな通りだったところに、快適な家が立っている。
この細長い敷地に立つ住宅は、飽和点の好例だ。

center of Tokyo have seen a proliferation of pocket-sized plots just wide enough to build on.

As the value of these miniature sites rise, they are becoming increasingly desirable for use. A great number of Japanese architects have managed to turn these peculiar environments into opportunities to make daring work that shows how one can inhabit the micro-scale. For the urban wanderer with a watchful eye, these tailor-made houses are a recurrent phenomenon throughout Tokyo's urban fabric. Look and you will find!

TRACING THE PAST IN THE CITY OF THE FUTURE

Old buildings and historical monuments are scarce in this city. Through a perpetual cycle of demolishing and rebuilding, either by human or natural forces, Tokyo has emerged as an ultra-modern cityscape. History, as it is represented in bricks and mortar, seems to be completely wiped out in this often very generic urban landscape. For visitors from Europe this can be very confusing, especially for someone who has made a professional practice out of writing and advising about urban heritage.

When I arrived in Tokyo I noticed myself looking in vain for visual reference points to Tokyo's urban heritage. I realized that I couldn't "read" the city. Cities are many things but for me they are also historical "texts"—archaeological sites that were never abandoned and that are still in full swing. In Amsterdam, my hometown, you can tell from the buildings which period they were built in. Buildings are not easily demolished there. Each building, whether it originates from the Renaissance or the Art Deco period, tells you something of its respective age—what the dominant ideologies were at that time and how people lived. Walking along the streets of Tokyo, you can deduce almost none of these things just by looking at the cityscape. It made me wonder how exactly Tokyoites are reminded of their history, how they relate to the past and how the past is present in the now.

未来の街の過去をたどる

東京は古い建物や歴史的記念碑がほとんどない、ウルトラモダンな街並みを生み出してきた。東京の建物は、平均26年という非常に短い寿命で建て替えられていく。地震、津波、火事に見舞われてきた歴史を考えれば、古いものをどんどん新しいものに置き換えていくのも理解できる。しかし、東京という都市は、その歴史的なナラティブ（語り）やパターンも数多く保持している。東京の都市遺産は、アイデンティティ、機能、プログラムの連続性、ある種の建物、街、パブリックスペースの連続性の中で経験される。東京においては、都市の真髄は、レンガや石造りの建物や街並みではなく、そこに住む人々や彼らの活動の中にある。

Jephta Dullaart は都市遺産の専門家。2012年に東京を訪れた。

Sake Store Museum Old Yoshida-ya near Yanaka Cemetery.
谷中霊園近くにある旧吉田屋酒店

Science fiction writer William Gibson once said that Japan represents "the global imagination default setting of the future", and his point is especially true for its capital. Tokyo is often portrayed as the city of the future, a place where new technologies rule and social change is constant. Tokyo's buildings have a remarkably short life-span, averaging 26 years. Looking at the many skyscrapers in this wealthy city one can easily blame economic forces. And although economics without a doubt plays a large role in overriding concerns of preservation and historic urban appearance, I also stumbled upon socio-cultural attitudes that seem to promote continuous urban renewal.

In Japanese society it is apparently not uncommon to demolish your parents' house the moment you inherit it in order to build a new one, accommodating the ever-changing living needs and circumstances of a new generation. In Japan the family history, I discovered, is more rooted in the soil, in the family's owned land, then it is in the preservation of wood, stone or brick. During my walks trough the older residential neighborhoods of Tokyo, I encountered a hotchpotch of old, rundown houses made from wood or brick, mostly inhabited by elderly people. Next to these houses were brand new ones, made from concrete, glass and steel, in which the younger generation seems to have found a home. Restoring or renovating traditional houses is an exception, and mainly seen in specific areas that are generally considered "historic neighborhoods", such as the small district of Yanaka.

When I think about the geographical condition of Japan and its history of devastating earthquakes, tsunamis and fires, I'm beginning to understand the ease with which Tokyoites replace the old with the new. It is no surprise that the ideas of Metabolism, a post-war architectural movement, sprung from this seismologic unstable soil. The Metabolist architects, of whom Kenzo Tange is the most well-known representative, believed in the continuous renewal of the city, identical to the organic growth of natural organisms.

Ironically, the icon of Metabolism—the beautiful Nakagin Capsule Tower, a building now considered a monument of world architectural heritage—will soon be demolished and replaced

Zojo-ji Temple with Tokyo Tower in the background.
東京タワーを背後にして立つ増上寺

by a new 14-storey tower. Probably Kenzo Tange and his peers wouldn't have minded, but an international group of architects tried in vain to save the building. The majority of the apartment owners are, however, completely in favor of renewal, in line with Metabolist principles.

So it goes in Tokyo.

In my quest to find Tokyo's heritage, it occurred to me that the city has still preserved a lot of its historical narratives and patterns. These narratives are not manifested in monuments but in the soft urban tissue and in neighborhood identities. Tokyo's urban heritage cannot be experienced in the typical European way, by walking through quaint cobble-stoned streets, lined with beautifully restored historic townhouses. Instead it is often experienced by the continuation of the function or program of a certain location, building, or public space. The building may have been demolished but the program of the space seemed to have been maintained over time.

Neighborhoods like Harajuka and Akihabara have changed greatly in their appearance, but its present day function is a continuation of the historical narrative of the neighborhood. Harajuku, for example, has always been a place where young people flocked together to look for new things and encounter the "exotic". This part of town, close to Roppongi and the Olympic Park, was always a place where foreigners lived and hung out in cafes and shops. Here, Tokyoites had a chance to see international movie stars promenading the broad, Western, boulevard-style streets. It was a place to see and be seen. Many Tokyo teenagers still go to Harajuku to see and be seen, although not to spot Westerners; they go to spot their peers wearing extravagant fashion items. The same is true of Akihabara, where teenagers buy new cell phones or computer games, just as their grandparents in the 1950s went there to buy new radios or other electric appliances. In Akihabara it is still common to negotiate with the vendors about their prices.

Standing in front of Zojo-ji Temple one fine morning, with the Tokyo Tower in the background, I realize that Tokyo has indeed a very different approach towards urban heritage preservation.

Reuse of urban heritage: the Scai Bathhouse in Yanaka transformed into an art gallery.
都市遺産の再利用例。銭湯を現代美術ギャラリーに転用したSCAI THE BATHHOUSE

This understanding turns my notion of urban heritage and the historical narratives of a city upside down. What looks old in Tokyo is not old and what looks new is already outdated, and will probably not last long. Zojo-ji Temple was built in 1974 and Tokyo Tower was erected in 1958. After building the new and much taller Tokyo Sky Tree, the old tower has lost its prime function. How much longer will it stand?

And although the temples and shrines in Tokyo are not centuries old, like the churches in Europe, they are reconstructed in the same spot every 50 to 100 years. So, even though the building is new, the Temple grounds have been the site of consecutive incarnations of the Zojo-ji Temple for more than 400 years. And before that the Zojo-ji Temple stood in Tokyo's Hibiya neighborhood. The history of the Zojo-ji Temple goes back more then a thousand years.

So what, then, is the value of old stones in this city? Is the understanding of historical continuity enough? Is my gaze too Romantic?

Tracing Tokyo's urban heritage has also made me think about the approach to preservation and heritage issues in my own country. In the Netherlands we value original outer form much more than original inner function and usage. We are refurbishing historic churches as new apartments, office buildings or department stores. Are we not making empty shells of our historic streets and monuments? The historic cityscape still largely exists in Amsterdam but does this make Amsterdam a more authentic and therefore historic city than Tokyo? What neighborhood in Amsterdam has kept more or less the same commercial function for over 50 years? Is there a neighborhood or street where my grandfather shopped for a certain product, and where I can still go to buy the same product? I can't name any.

What makes a city "authentic"? Is it bricks and stones or is it the people? In Tokyo it's definitely the people.

(In that sense, perhaps one can even make the case that Tokyo, with its inner continuity, is more a city of the past then it is one of the future. But it would probably be wise to leave this particular claim to others.)

LOVE OF NATURE

Anna Berkhof は社会科学者、建築・景観史家。2012年10月から2013年10月まで東京で調査を行い、東京の路地の庭における家と自然の捉えられ方を研究した。

Both Japanese and Western scholarly discourse suggest the Japanese have a profound love for nature and a great appreciation of natural beauty.[54] This image is idealized and does not necessarily correspond with reality. It has, however, been repeated so often that to a certain degree it has become a self-fulfilling prophecy.

自然を愛する心

日本と西洋の学術研究の多くが、日本人は自然を深く愛すると主張している。このイメージは理想化されたものであり、必ずしも現実に即してはいない。

The idea of Japanese closeness to nature took hold during the Meiji period (1868-1912), when Japan tried to define its identity in relation to the west. Western orientalist imagery was appropriated by the Japanese. Characteristics that were meant to suggest the weakness of Eastern people were redefined as strengths.[55] Westerners had supposedly become alienated from nature, whereas the Japanese had stayed true to their close relation with it. The love of nature was presented as the nature of the Japanese.

現代の日本人が持つ自然への親近感は、明治時代につくられた。オリエンタリスト的イメージが当てはめられたのである。東洋人の短所とされた特徴が、長所として再定義されたのだった。

In Japan, nature is not viewed as the opposite of culture. Instead it is seen as oscillating between two extremes. On the one side of the spectrum there is raw or uncooked nature; on the other side lies cooked or wrapped nature. Artificial things can also be categorized as "nature".[56]

日本において、自然は文化に対立するものとはとらえられていない。料理においても、生のものと火を通したものまで、振れ幅がある。人工物でも自然としてとらえられるものがある。

When nature and culture are not opposed, it changes the value put on "raw" or wild nature.[57] Despite the alleged Japanese closeness to nature, the way they treat the environment does not always reflect this affection. The nature that is out there, far away, is easily forgotten.

自然と文化が対立しないので、荒々しい自然のもつ価値も変化する。

The nature that is most appreciated is the so-called cooked nature. This means that the idea of nature is closely linked to smallness, symbolism and traditional Japanese aesthetics. An appropriation, or translation, of nature through the shape of a bonsai, ikebana, image, flavor or ritual is still considered part of nature.

料理された自然が最も高く評価される。自然という概念は、小さいこと、象徴性、伝統的な日本の美意識と深く結びついている。

During the Edo period (1603-1868), scenic spots from the countryside were replicated in Tokyo gardens so lords didn't have to travel home. Gardens were used as microcosms of Japan's view of the world. A miniature is the transformation of wild nature into an idealized shape, and can be symbolic of another place.

江戸時代には、田舎の美しい風景が、東京の庭園で再現されていた。これは、荒々しい自然の理想化である。

In Tokyo nature is far away, and there aren't a lot of parks. Inhabitants of the city create makeshift gardens in front of their door. Nature is present in the many potted gardens you see throughout the city.

東京では、街のいたるところに、鉢植えの並んだ路地庭がある。

The Japanese climate is characterized by a very equal division of the seasons. Rituals to mark the passing of the seasons are a way to strengthen the experience of nature, especially in a city where the 'real thing' is so far away. Often these rituals take place at a local shrine, but they are also visible in the street, where yard decorations tell you the time of year.

季節の移り変わりを示す儀式は、自然をしっかりと体験するための一方法である。

PLANT UNIFORM

プラント・ユニフォーム

u·ni·form
/ˈyo͞onəˌfôrm/

ユニフォーム

Adjective
- Not changing in form or character; remaining the same in all cases and at all times: “a uniform decline in fertility”.

【形容詞】
形や性質に変化がなく常に一様または画一であること。「繁殖力の一様な衰退」

Noun
- The distinctive clothing worn by members of the same organization or body or by children attending certain schools.

- A code word representing the letter U, used in radio communication.

【名詞】
同じ組織や集団の成員やある種の学校に通う子供たちが着用する特定の衣服

無線通信においてアルファベットのUを伝えるときに使う言葉。

Verb
- Make uniform.

【動詞】
画一化する

Synonyms
Adjective: even - equable - homogeneous - same - equal – steady
Noun: regimentals

【類義語】
形容詞：同じ、同量の、
均質的な、同質の、
一定の

Definition ‘uniform’ from the Oxford Dictionary of English
オックスフォード英語辞典によるuniformという単語の定義

Anna Berkhofは社会科学者にして建築史・景観史研究者。Cameron Allan McKeanはジャーナリスト、写真家、空想的地理学者であり、ファッションデザイナーで研究者のDaphne Mohajer Va Pesaranとともに東京に暮らしている。ふたりは2012年に出会い、自然、社会、服飾文化、サイエンス・フィクションを織り交ぜて推論するアート作品を共作してきた。

銀行
SEVEN

THE SEA WE WOULD LIKE TO SEE

私たちが見たい海

東京で電車に乗ったり街を歩いたりしていると、東京が海辺にあることを忘れてしまうのはたやすい。東京とは、常に大海原と関わりをもってきた島国文化を持つ国の首都であることを。魚を食べたり、災害を恐れるときに、思い出すことはあるかもしれない。また、東京の住民たちは、伝統文化を守るための砦を築くかのように、新しい人口島を建設している。しかし、メタボリストなど、中には、完全なる浮遊都市を構想した人たちもいる。この推論は、日本の過去と未来における想像の領域としての海を考察する。

Manar Moursi は建築、都市計画、アート、デザインを研究している。ユートピア的な現実逃避を思わせる東京のカラフルなプラスティックボックスや、カイロのストリートファニチャーなど、日常的なるものに関心をもっている。2012年11月に東京に滞在した。

Renders by Rowan Kandil

If the center of a city is connected to its past and sheds light on its history, a city's edge is equally revealing; it defines the outline of the city's present, its growth and its relationship to its hinterlands. Tokyo's map presents an intimidating and thick web of metro lines. This, combined with the seemingly endless multitude at its heart, provoked a strong urge in me to etch myself into one of those bold-colored lines in an attempt to reach the edge of this town.

How does this endless city end? How soft or hard are its edges?

Taking the Odayku line westward, all the way to its last stop, Tokyo fades from dense metropolis to American dream. From glitzy scrapers to pitched-roof single family dwellings in suburbs with strip malls and amusement parks. Like pendular movement, this exploration of the inland edges prompted me to think of Tokyo's other boundaries: the sea and the bay on which it sits. Formerly known as Edo, which means bay entrance or estuary, Tokyo's industry and harbor areas mostly block its seashore. Wandering the streets of the city today, one hardly sees its watery edge. Even facades of buildings on the waterfront turn their back to the sea. And yet, this edge has so powerfully defined the city and the country as a whole.

Surrounded by the ocean, Japan as an island has always honored the blessing of the sea. The ocean is the bearer of bounties. But the sea is also the generator of catastrophes. In recent years, with rising sea levels, the ocean has betrayed the Japanese with tsunamis that have swallowed entire towns. Though the ocean has often played a catastrophic role, looking back one finds an almost continuous thread of artificial island projects. From Edo times to today. Each telling a different story of the city's relationship with the sea.

The earliest of these projects were the artificial islands that were built with the intention of defending a vulnerable Japan against Western intrusions. A series of five island fortresses, called Odaiba, was constructed in 1853 by Egawa Hidetatsu for the Tokugawa shogunate, to protect Tokyo from attack by sea. Of the five fortresses, only two survived to today.

What we today know as Odaiba began as landfill no. 13: a vast new piece of land in the middle of the bay. In the early 1990s, Tokyo governor Shunichi Suzuki made plans to redevelop this land into what he called "Tokyo Teleport Town." It was to be a showcase for futuristic living, for a population of over 100,000. When the housing bubble burst, the plan was put on hold. But in the late 90s Odaiba saw a comeback as a tourist and leisure zone, complete with several large hotels, shopping malls and a giant Ferris wheel.

Artificial islands were not only constructed for protection and pleasure. In April 1958 an extreme solution to the Tokyo Metropolis' land shortage was proposed by the Japan Housing Corporation (JHC). The JHC's plan, laid out in the Kuro Kano proposal, was to fill and polder the entire east side of Tokyo Bay, from the Tsukiji District to the Boso peninsula. The proposal was conceived as the ultimate solution for the exceptional urban growth Tokyo was experiencing. It was met with severe criticism, due to the damage it was projected to cause to the ecology.

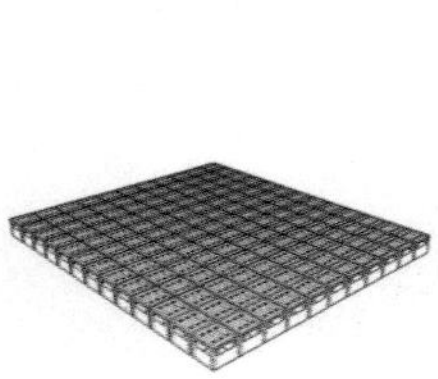

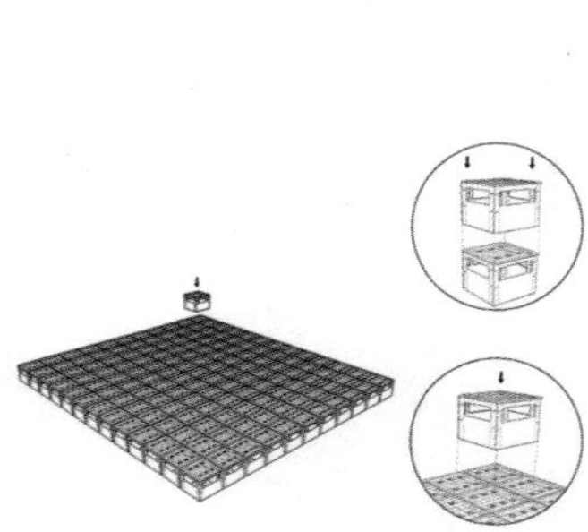

Marine City, 1958.
Designed by Kiyonori Kikutake.
菊竹清訓「海上都市」プロジェクト（1958年）

Two months after the Kano plan was announced, architects Masato Otaka and Kiyonori Kikutake of the Metabolist Movement made their respective counter-proposals, "Neo-Tokyo Plan: City on the Sea" and "Marine City", which were schemes for new marine urban habitats on floating offshore islands. Their proposals were largely accepted by the government, which was seeking solutions to the dramatic growth that Japanese cities were experiencing. Creating new "land" in the sea was less costly than redeveloping the inner cities.

For the Metabolists, though, building floating cities in the ocean was about more than just a search for additional land. Architectural historian Kenneth Frampton explains: "[When] the Metabolists looked to the sea as the locus of a new civilization, they looked to the one element which had always been deeply linked to the spiritual and material survival of Japan."[58] They

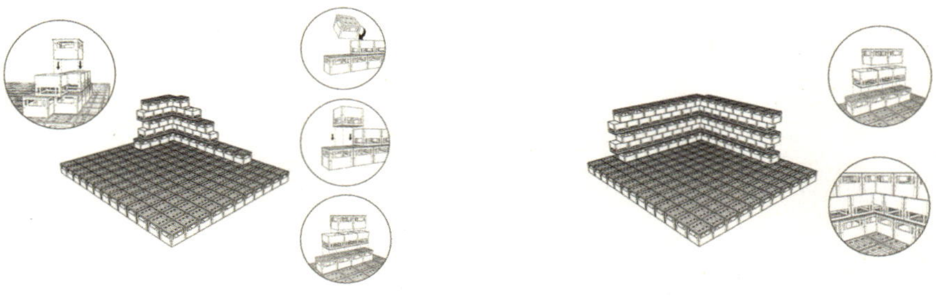

felt their projects were models for the future that could be universally adopted. They were convinced that a brand new civilization would emerge once people were brave enough to reject the chaos, danger and misery of "continent civilization" and turn to the sea. Kikutake declared that "The civilization of continents was an accumulation of bloody struggles of human relations established in limited land, so it was a history of endless wars". The Marine City, he claimed, "will be a unit of human community, not the individual life."

While the fortress islands built during the Edo era were created to protect and stabilize an older order, the Metabolists thought of their proposed islands as vessels heading towards a new world. Kikutake's vision was futuristic, technocratic and romantic. In his floating city designs, the city was radically nomadic, modular and metabolic—not anchored at any fixed point. All or part of it was able to cruise to new moorings if necessary or desired. And at the end of its useful life, the floating city was to be sunk to the ocean floor where it would be re-territorialized as a reef for marine life. With science and technology as their tools, the Metabolists tried to define new relationships between nature and human beings. Land did not belong to any individual. The foremost objective was to eventually liberate the land through people choosing to live on artificial islands. Land could then become public property and restore itself to its natural state.

Kikutake elaborated his vision of nomadic, organically adaptable human habitats in the sea by building a dramatic Aquapolis as a prototype, for the government's Expo '75 in Okinawa. It had a futuristic marine theme: The Sea We Would Like to See. For Kikutake, the Expo was a platform to build and showcase his ideas. A 100-by-100-meter floating city block containing accommodation, a banquet hall and offices was built in Hiroshima and then towed to Okinawa.

But the mood changed shortly afterward. Expo '70 was critiqued as a dystopia far removed from reality, and the 1973 energy crisis exposed Japan's reliance on imported oil. Thus, the floating-cities projects were shelved and the utopian spirit lost its momentum.

In the context of a post-war Japan, the Metabolists' floating-city solution can be read as a way of questioning Japan's cultural identity. The Metabolists linked the ultra-modern concepts of nuclear physics and biological growth with traditional Buddhist thought on regeneration. A marriage of two visions of the world—scientific and spiritual—gave birth to a utopia whose core concepts are still applicable today. With rising sea levels and a desire to create flexible, modular and responsive housing solutions, the Metabolists' floating-city ideas seem to be in tune with the needs of our times.

To me, floating cities imply a resilience and a conviction on the part of humanity to survive even the deepest disasters and create novel solutions. Liberated from the restrictions of the land and the soil (and nationalism) that we are born into, new self-built islands endow their builders with a Godly control, beyond the power that architecture alone can provide. From above, I see new lines drawn in the vast ocean that can overlap, interlace or be erased completely, generation after generation—defining somehow a new humanity that is resilient, but that at the same time embraces more willingly the transience of things and believes always in the possibility of newness and renewal.

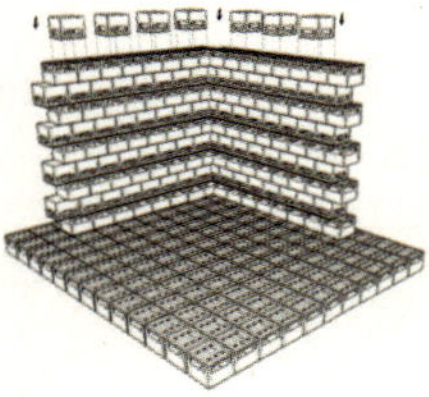

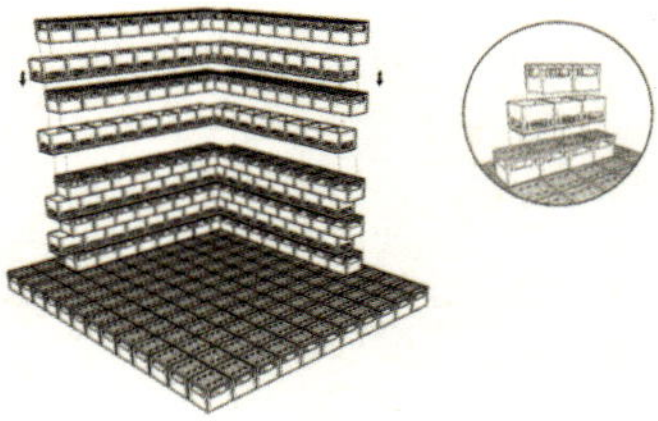

Aquapolis, 1975.
Designed by Kiyonori Kikutake.

菊竹清訓が設計した「アクアポリス（1972年）」

The island is like a tiny star
that Space doesn't see and mutely crushes
as it grinds on fearfully ignorant…

it tries to go on blindly, on its own
self-invented course, outside the scheme
of the planets, suns and systems.

Rainer Maria Rilke

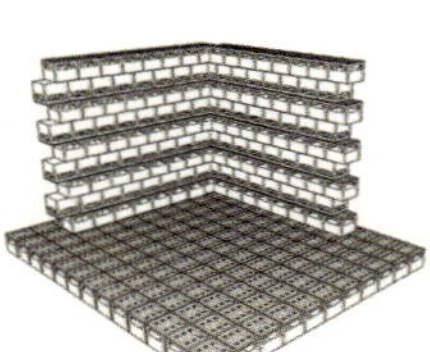

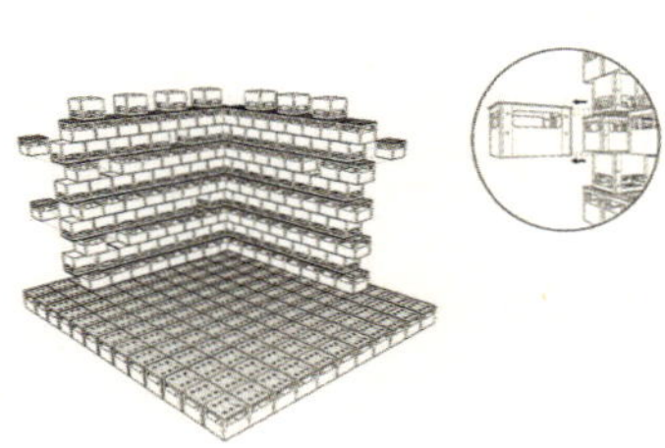

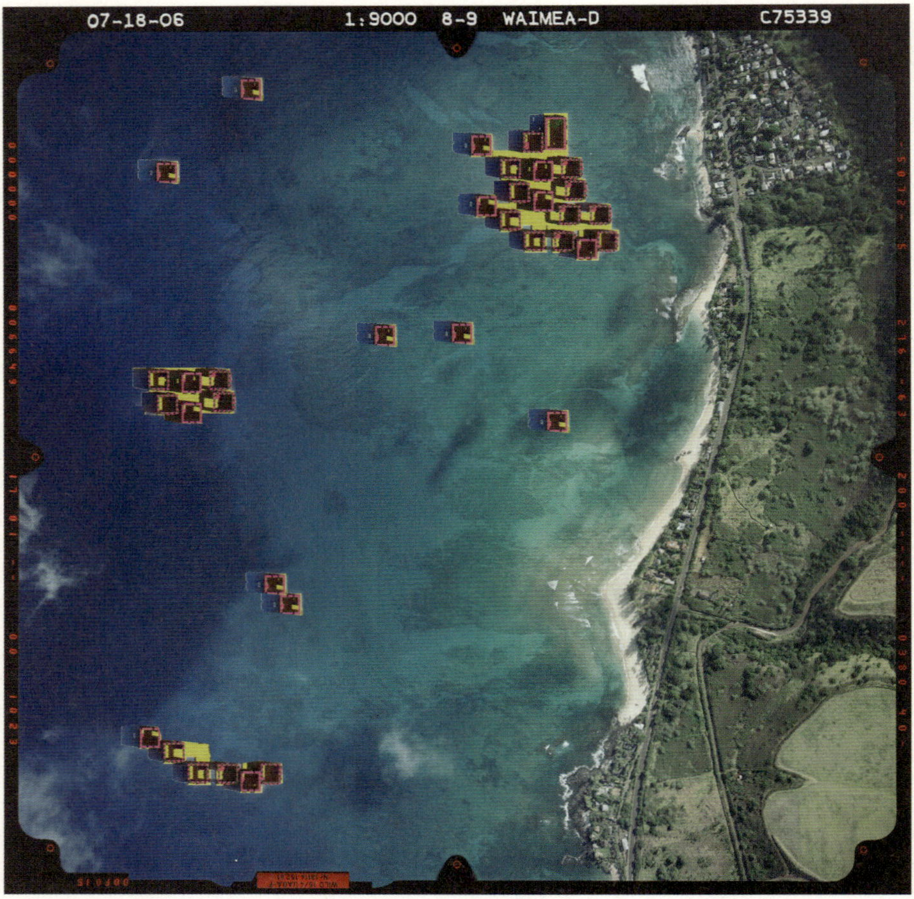
07-18-06
1:9000 8-9 WAIMEA-D
C75339

D.I.Y. METABOLISM — A UTOPIAN SURVIVAL GUIDE

"The sea is awaiting a new discovery which will promise true happiness for human beings. It is just a matter of time that the civilization of continents hands over its part to the prospective civilization of the sea…Just as life originally came from the ocean, so will the metabolism of the city be given the opportunity to develop in a smoother manner by floating on the ocean."

Kiyonori Kikutake, 1964[59]

In a future of climate change and with the threat of rising sea levels, the words of Japanese Metabolist Kiyonori Kikutake seem prophetic. The context of this quote is a post-war Japan that had failed to expand its territory through the conquests of war, and was now searching for new sites to accommodate future growth.

Today, we have indeed colonized the ocean. Possibly the only human relic in a world with risen sea levels will be non-biodegradable artificial plastic.

Will we be there? Living on plastic islands in the sea? On utopian floating cities?

The ubiquitous plastic crates of Tokyo may offer a hint to what life in the future might look like. These readily available modular units can easily be configured to create inexpensive floating habitats and reefs, providing the building blocks for a second chance for humanity. Flexible ad-hoc networks of mini-islands, structured and governed by the laws of the sea, and the standardized dimensions of crates.

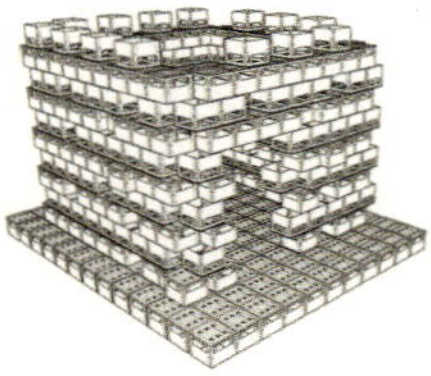

くつろごう

世界最大の都市において、東京人たちはどんなふうにくつろいでいるのだろるか？どんなふうに通りや近所、地下鉄網を動きまわるのだろうか？東京の都市環境をどんなふうに理解しているのだろうか？プライベートとパブリック、あるいは内と外の間の障壁をどんなふうに体験しているのだろうか？そして、東京への期待とどうにもならない現実の間の折り合いをどうつけているのだろうか？「家」という概念の探究は、この街でくつろぎを手に入れる助けになるかもしれない。

MAKE YOURSELF AT HOME

How do Tokyoites make themselves at home in the largest metropolis in the world? How do they navigate the streets, neighborhoods and subway systems? How do they make sense of their urban surroundings? How do they experience the barrier between private and public, or between inside and outside? And how do they navigate between their aspirations and Tokyo's sticky uncompromising reality? An exploration of the notion of home in Tokyo might help you to make yourself at home in the city.

中野中央四丁目店
FamilyMart

歩行者自転車専用
ELEVEN
酒
ATM

sunkus
串カツ

Asahi CALPIS
100円
WONDA

ヨーロピアン

Otsuka

FIRE

FEELING AT HOME IN TOKYO

Overlooking the city, one of the main characters in *Tokyo Story*, Yasujiro Ozu's 1953 cinematic masterpiece, says to her husband: "Look how big Tokyo is. If we get lost, we'd never find each other again." The film tells the story of an elderly couple visiting their children in the expanding metropolis that is 1950s Tokyo. Today, more then sixty years later, Tokyo has grown roughly five times in size since then. The Tokyo Metropolitan Area, with its 37 million inhabitants, is considered the biggest urban conglomeration in the world. Getting lost has gotten much easier.

Tokyo has a dissociated and fragmented nature, with no center to give you a sense of direction. Add to this the sheer size of the city, the generic quality of the built environment, the fact that the main way of getting from one place to another is underground, and the fact that the average lifespan of a building is roughly 27 years, and it becomes clear that Tokyo is a city that can easily make you feel lost. For an outside visitor, the city provides few reference points for navigation. But how does this work for a seasoned Tokyoite? How do Tokyoites feel at home in this dense and dynamic megalopolis? How do they relate to the city and navigate its seemingly endless complexity?

A concept that may help us to understand how Tokyoites feel at home is the duality of "uchi" and "soto". Uchi means inside, soto means outside, and the dual concept is often associated with the creation of a sense of self in Japan. It is a cultural notion that distinguishes between us—uchi—versus others—soto, and it's therefore a bit different from the Western duality of

東京でくつろぎを感じる

東京で迷子になるのは簡単だ。東京には、訪問者のための道案内がとても少ない。でも、東京人にとってはどうなのだろうか?　東京人のくつろぎを理解する手助けとなる概念は、「内」と「外」の二元性だ。片方を「内側」あるいは「くつろぎ」、反対方向を「外側」あるいは「場違いな感じ」としたグラフで理解できる概念である。職場から地下鉄や電車の駅を通り、よく知る人々の顔や場所がある地元の街に帰る道のりの間に、所属するということのさまざまな体験がある。「内」の基本となる自宅の中でも、内と外の二元性を示すものを見つけることができる。

Anna Berkhof は社会科学者、建築・景観史家。2012年10月から2013年10月まで東京で調査を行い、東京の路地の庭における家と自然の捉えられ方を研究した。

the individual versus the rest of the world. Uchi connotes not the individual but the closest group around the individual: the community. The key inside group is, of course, the family, but the word is also transferred to broader groups, like neighbors, schoolmates, colleagues, and even nationality.[60]

In a certain manner, uchi and soto can be compared with the Western concepts of private and public. Both dualities have intimate, emotional connotations and more political connotations. One difference is that uchi and soto are more flexible concepts, less well defined. They're understood in context. What in a certain context can be defined as uchi can in another be defined as soto. Space that seems public to the Western eye can, in certain situations, be part of an uchi realm. Sometimes certain places and situations can be felt as inside, in contrast to a larger outside, and sometimes these same places are marked as outside, in contrast to a smaller inside. Sometimes the neighbors are outside, compared to the nuclear family; sometimes they are inside, compared to a person's anonymity in Tokyo's massive public-transport system.

Uchi and soto are therefore more interesting, perhaps, when one understands them as a spectrum, with feeling "inside" or "at home" on the one end, and feeling "outside" or "out of place" on the other.

In Ozu's *Tokyo Story* the parents arrive in the city by train. Today, the train is still the first space you encounter when you enter Tokyo as a visitor. Getting out of the plane at Narita airport, for instance, you take a train to Shibuya or Shinjuku, the main train stations of the city, only to transfer to another train or subway towards the place where you are staying.

The subway is the most public space that you can find in Tokyo. People from all over the city and from all walks of life come together in the tubes. The atmosphere on the subway is different depending on the time of day. In the morning everyone is very quiet; you could hear a pin drop. Later in the day there is more chatter; friends and colleagues sit close together and talk in soft voices. At any given time, there is minimal contact between strangers, and little to no eye contact. Everyone is in his/her own little bubble, reading a book, looking at his/her Smartphone, or falling asleep and leaning over and getting dangerously close to his/her neighbor. The subway is a place where you are confronted with a lot of strangers. During rush hour you are crammed together, invading one another's private space. Within the Tokyo context, the subway experience is probably the furthest away from feeling at home. From here you go to a familiar workplace or return to your own neighborhood.

The train is perhaps the closest thing to a non-place, an outside, that Tokyo has to offer. But, then again, when a tourist from Tokyo rides the unfamiliar London tube, and is confronted with different behavior to what he/she is used to, he/she might use the word "uchi" in relation to the subways in Tokyo.

When you get off the train and step on solid ground, the train continues on its journey, and you have arrived. The subway stations in Tokyo are quite non-descript. If you removed the nameplate, many of them would be recognizable only to the trained eye. They do, however, have their own personal tunes that play when the train enters and exits the station, some of which are pretty elaborate and worth listening to. I would not be surprised if, when hearing the tune of your neighborhood station, you enter a more inner ring of uchi. The train station is a central place in your neighborhood. It is its entry point. You probably see some familiar faces. From here everyone starts his/her journey into the increasingly smaller spaces of the neighborhood.

Tokyo's has 23 inner wards: ku, which are divided into districts; machi, which are divided into neighborhoods about the size of a city block; and chome. Where most Western cities are structured by linear streets, in Japan cities consist of areas. The chome is home to an everyday community of neighbors and familiar faces.[61]

The train stations are the hubs of the urban fabric. They provide access at the level of the machi or the chome. These train stations are placed on large streets, with a lot of traffic going through them. This is the image most people have of Tokyo: a bustling metropolis with billboards, neon signs and many tall buildings. On these streets, a lot of offices are situated. It is the natural habitat of the city's office workers, the so-called salarymen, whom you can see walking and eating in formation during their lunch break.

Many office workers are apparently comfortable enough (or tired enough), whether in a restaurant or on the subway, to take a re-energizing nap. The extent to which people feel safe in the public spaces of Tokyo is quite astounding. You might be sitting in Ueno Park, when a man at the table next to you leaves his MacBook, iPad and iPhone unattended for fifteen minutes or so, to go for a leisurely stroll. It's no big deal. Even in big streets or parks, where you are completely anonymous, there is a sense of social control, and correct social behavior. And to remind people of what constitutes correct social behavior, all through the city you can find stickers with two eyes looking at you plastered on walls and vans. It seems that there is always someone watching, and making sure you behave yourself.

The city feels so safe and familiar that it is almost like an indoor space. For some, the uchi seems to pervade even the most public of places.

When you leave the large street with the metro hub, via one of the side streets on your left or right, you enter a completely different world. Instead of the metropolitan atmosphere with its high-rise buildings, dense traffic, armies of office workers and high-end street shops, you find yourself enjoying a village vibe in narrow streets and alleyways—an intimate space with lots of residential housing, pot gardens, neighborhood eateries, shrines and temples, small supermarkets, workshops and konbini.

In Tokyo the larger streets form a kind of border around these more intimate neighborhoods. They call it the egg-and-shell pattern. Low-rise residential areas, eggs, are surrounded by a shell of high-rise buildings facing the larger streets on the edge of the chome. In this way, Tokyo is, despite the more than 3 million cars registered in the city, a city of pedestrians and bicycles. In the security offered by the egg-and-shell pattern, autonomous neighborhoods have a chance to bloom. The neighborhood as uchi is quite well defined. This urban structure has its roots in the time when Tokyo was still called Edo and was divided into the high city, with its feudal garden settings, and the low city, which was home to the commoners.

Looking back, Edo's spaces were divided into a network of multi-layered urban districts whose scale became more refined and more human as they grew closer to the daily lives of its inhabitants. This complex structure was deemed necessary for the defense of the castle town, the seat of the shogunal government.

Back then, city space was partitioned both functionally and visually. High wooden gates separated neighborhoods from one another. The gates closed at night, to ensure a tight reign on the commoner population. This was integral to the establishment of feudal order under the shogunal regime, but also produced a spatial unity within a confined area, binding residents of each block into a coherent social organization. Since Edo, the city has been modernized and rebuilt after countless disasters—but, apart from street broadening, the original urban layout has been preserved with every restructuring.[62]

This neighborhood in Minamiaoyama is a good example of the egg-and-shell pattern. Low-rise residential areas, eggs, are surrounded by a shell of high-rise buildings facing the larger streets on the edge of the chome.

南青山は「卵と殻パターン」の好例。街区の境界にある大通り沿いにある高層ビル（殻）が低層住宅地区（卵）を取り囲んでいる。

In the neighborhood, you can still find the hierarchy of increasingly smaller spaces that was established during Edo. The largest street is the shotengai, which is often located in close proximity to the train station, and which functions as the main shopping street of the neighborhood. Usually a soundtrack is playing from boxes strung up every few meters, and the street is often decorated with seasonal props hanging from the lantern poles. Here the neighborhood inhabitants do their shopping, in walking distance from their home in one of the side streets.

Neighborhoods often resemble villages, in a physical and metaphysical sense. The small-scale residential areas are vernacular in their architecture and home to low-rise, detached houses, with restaurants, small workshops, groceries, temples and shrines scattered between them. Walking around, you pass through streets lined with bicycles, potted gardens and unsupervised umbrellas. The space of the street is appropriated for personal use, such as keeping a garden or parking a bike. You might even get the feeling that you are invading someone's private space, and that you're not supposed to be there. The streets sometimes feel like an extension of the home, as if the key uchi, the family inner circle, colonized the street.[63]

The home forms the base of the uchi, which in addition to the societal meaning of the word also signifies the home itself. In the house you find physical markers of the uchi/soto dichotomy, shaped as boundaries to regulate the distinction between the two. Traditional Japanese architecture consists of transitory units. When you visit a Japanese home, the first space you enter is the genkan. The genkan is situated a step lower than the rest of the house. It is the first transitory unit between the street and the home. Here you take off your shoes and leave them—and the outside world with them—behind as you enter the living space.[64]

In the traditional house, during the Tokugawa period, the largest part of the house was reserved for entertaining.[65] The inner uchi at this time included the family, but also the servants, the concubines and the apprentices: they were all part of the household.[66] It seems to have had a less private character than later on, during the Meiji period, when the focus was on the smallest possible uchi, including only the conjugal family. During the Meiji area, influenced by European culture, the home was redefined as an intimate space set apart from society, focused on parents and children. The Japanese family, and with it the home, became more private, more sheltered from the outside.

More recently, developers have started catering to the single workingman, and the single workingwoman as well. It is uncommon in Japan to live with non-family. This means that there are a lot of very small, individual homes in Tokyo. This individualization of space leads to an increasing sensitivity to privacy.[67] Many homes have steel doors and window shutters. The Tokyo home has indeed become a very private place.[68] When you walk around the city it is impossible to look into someone's house. All windows and doors are visually blocked, so you can only guess what the inside might look like.

The small homes and apartments are supported by Tokyo's impeccable infrastructure. Here the konbini, the convenience store, plays the star role. In the konbini you can do everything you would normally do in your living room or study. In many ways, it's an extension of your house. It is not uncommon to see local residents do a last-minute errand in their pajamas. You can make a photocopy, get money and pay your bills. You can do your regular groceries, buy ready-made meals, or go for something more exciting like glitter nail polish or a handkerchief decorated with a print of Mount Fuji. Since the konbini documents the spending habits of its customers, it caters perfectly to the specific needs of the urban dwellers around it.

In modern-day Tokyo, uchi is more private than it traditionally was, as the home is only used by its inhabitant, but it is also more public, as many functions that traditionally took place inside the safe realm of the home have been moved outside, into the street and konbini. Social activities with friends or family usually take place outside of the home as well, in public spaces like restaurants or coffee shops. The neighborhood sento, or communal bathhouse, is another popular place for many local residents: it unites them in hot water and nakedness. In many ways the neighborhood can be described as more uchi then soto, and even outside the neighborhood you can feel the reach of the uchi.

While travelling from the large scale of the rail network to the small spaces and private homes of Tokyoites, the spectrum of soto and uchi is not always apparent. The subway is a hyper-public space, and the home has become a very private space, but in between these two extremes people can be found sharing intimate space in the most unexpected locations. This makes Tokyo, if one dares to look beyond the surface spectacle, a surprisingly comfortable and intimate city where the configuration of the urban fabric actually helps make you feel at home.

DRAWING / ドローイング

私は横川さん一家の家を訪ね、このドローイングを描いた。この家は東京の都心から電車1.5時間ほどのところ、越谷駅の近くにある。25年前は田んぼばかりだった場所が、東京の郊外にのみこまれてしまった。

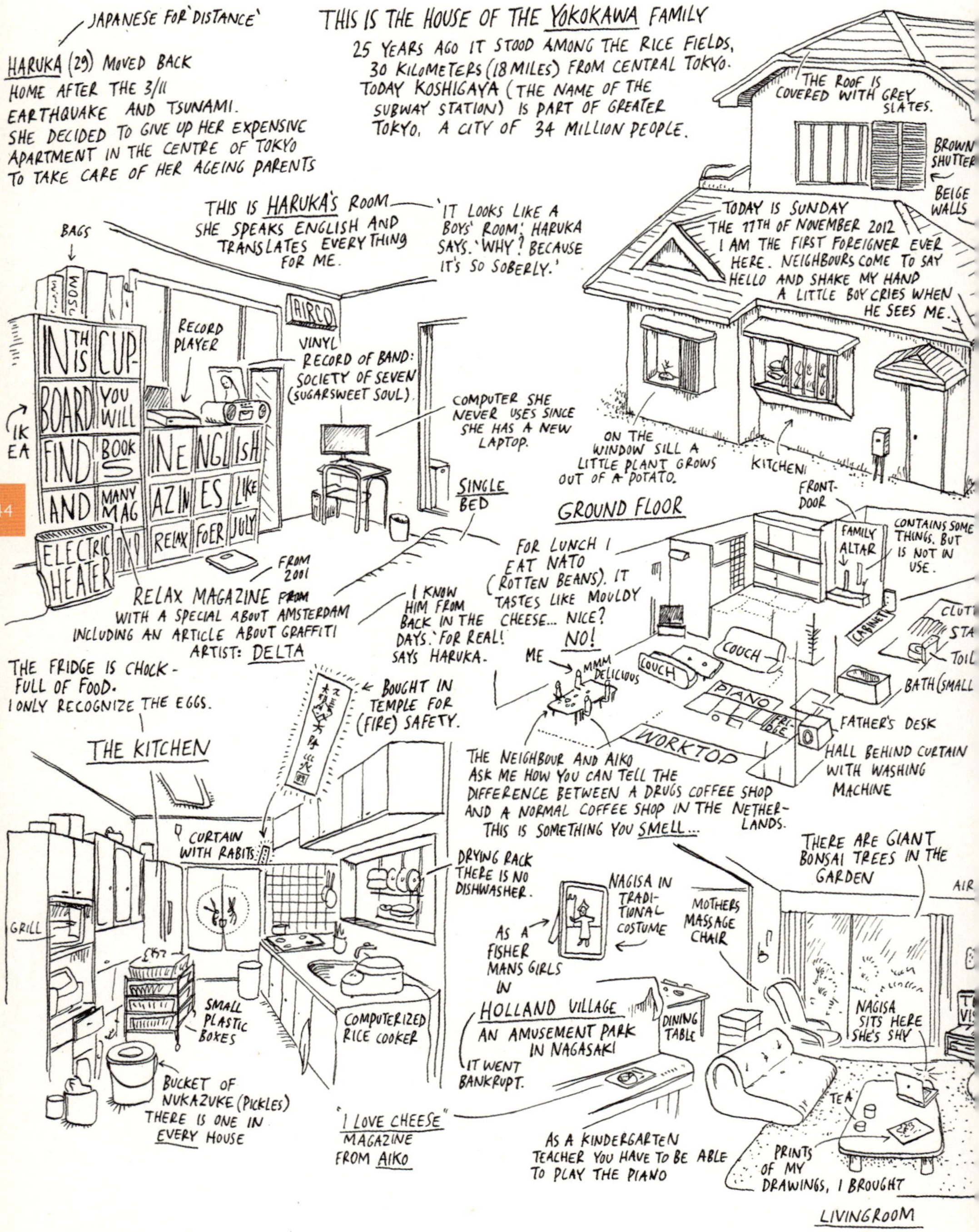

JAN ROTHUIZEN

Jan Rothuizen はヴィジュアルアーティスト。2012年に東京を訪問した。ドローイングの中に世界をマッピングし、個人的だがフィクションではなく、ときにジャーナリスティックだがよりドキュメンタリー性の強い作風で、常に見るものを驚かせる。

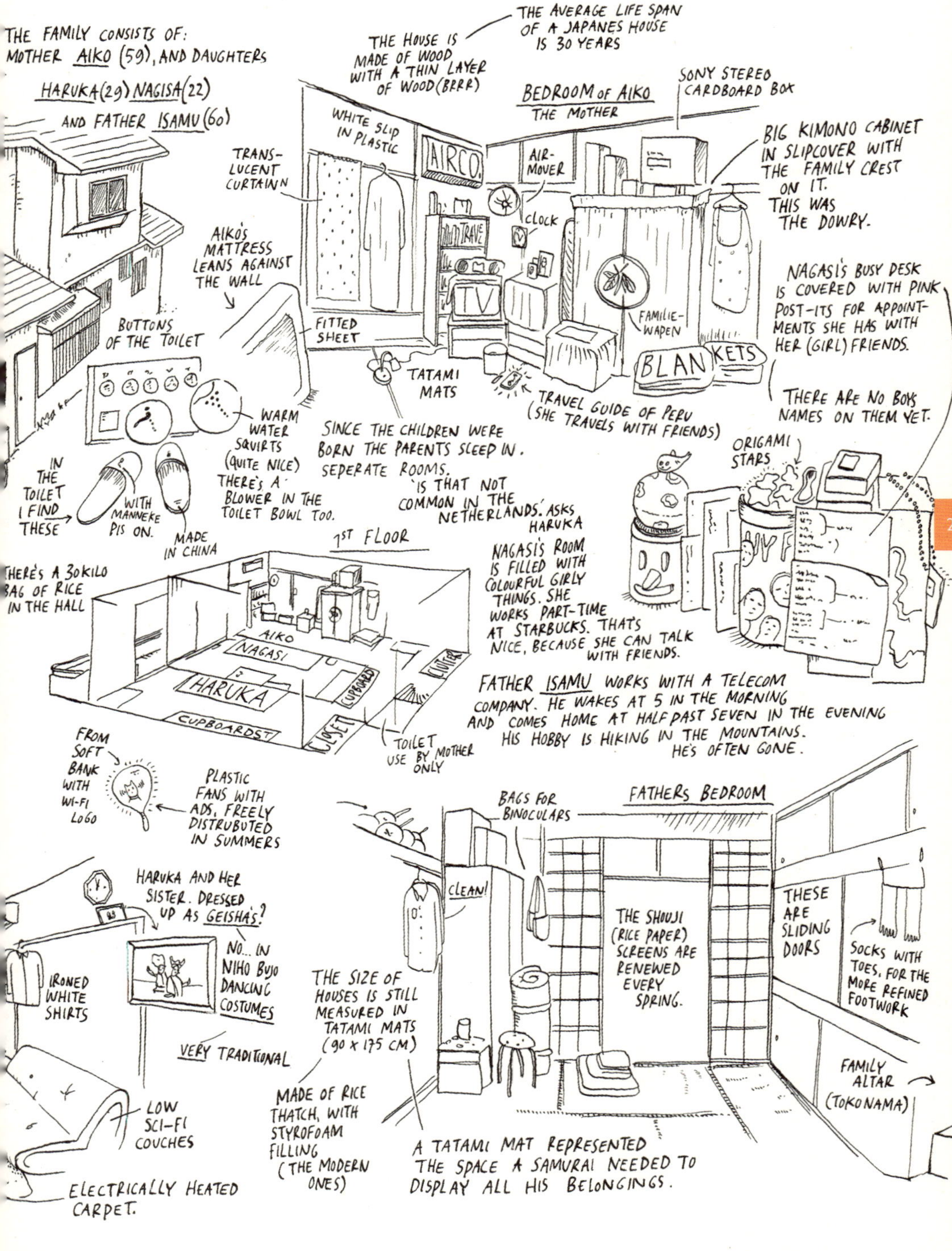

OMOIYARI

I grew up in a mixed family. A Spanish father and a Japanese mother produced my brother and me, two of the thousands of hafus (mixed Japanese people) around the world. Every summer, after the school year was over in Spain, we used to go to Japan to visit our relatives and, study the language and the culture of my mother's homeland.

This is a story of one of those summer mornings. The first few days after the arrival, I would wake up at 5 a.m. The temperature was already around 25 degrees, with a 90 percent humidity. My 130-centimeter figure moved slowly through the wooden corridors that creaked with each step. I went down the stairs and turned left into the engawa, the passageway facing the Japanese garden. On the other side of the window: a perfectly designed and pruned courtyard lit by the summer sun. Finally I was home.

I continued my route to the kitchen. There, in front of the stove, a tall twiggy man welcomed me. He turned around and without being at all surprised by the little visitor he said "good morning" and continued his work. His movements were harmonious. He handled the tools with the skill that only routine use can give you.

思いやり

食べ物とは、栄養があるとか美味しいということだけに価値があるわけではない。食べ物がどのようにつくられ、どのように出されるかによって、優しさの伝わり方が変わり、受け取った人が心地よく感じたり癒やされたりする。食べ方やお箸の置き方で、料理をつくった人へ、感謝や喜び、あるいは悲しい気持ちを伝えることができる。食べ物は、気持ちや記憶を共有するための強力な媒体になる。一膳のご飯と納豆は、私にとって家庭的な暖かさの象徴だ。ある特定の味が、私を子供時代へ、つまり、私の記憶の中にある、気楽さと代わり映えのしない日常ゆえの魅力を持っていた、穏やかな街だった頃の東京へと連れ戻してくれるのだ。

Maiko Arrieta Aoki はスペインと日本で育ち、東京で料理人になる修行をした。東京で育った頃の記憶と、いかに食べ物が記憶を呼び起こすのかについて書いてくれた。

Manhattan

My grandfather had prepared his breakfast like this every morning since he was widowed. After 30 years he could complete this task with his eyes closed: an apple salad, miso soup and umeboshi with rice. It was his way to wake up in the morning.

When I arrived in the kitchen, still in my pajamas, this ceremony was almost completed. Far from giving him a hand, I would sit at the table waiting for the dreamy Japanese breakfast that I couldn't enjoy during the rest of the year. My menu wasn't the same as his; it consisted of natto (fermented soybeans) and a bowl of rice. A basic and insufficient meal that later would be completed when the rest of the family woke up.

My grandfather would place my little chopsticks and my tiny rice bowl to his right side. It was his quiet invitation to share this moment. Once we sat down to eat I would chat non-stop, telling him about my daily adventures: something that had happened at school or gossip about my brother's bad behavior. He always listened to me, nodding his head and asking questions about my childhood stories. When the breakfast was over I used to remain seated while he did the dishes. This was our shared moment, intimate and unique, while everybody else was still asleep. I was very conscious, even as a kid, about the importance of these times. That's why I used to tiptoe down to the kitchen very often during the summer, making the most of a conversation I couldn't delight in during the rest of the year in Spain.

Nowadays, when I go back to Tokyo, I have the same breakfast, but without my grandfather. A bowl of rice and natto represents homey warmness to me. A particular taste that makes me travel back to my childhood, when Tokyo was, as I remember it, a calm city that had a charm that came from an easy and routine-based life. This was a Tokyo where we used to pass our time chatting, seated on the entrance steps, encouraging the neighbors to come in and share a glass of iced tea. Our seimon (front door) was always open.

This idealized Tokyo of my childhood is not there any more and the wooden seimons have been changed to intercoms with security codes. As in any other big city in the world, neighbors don't know one another and the traditional grocery stores have been replaced by practical convenience stores (konbini). When I visit Japan now, during the first few days I often feel some nostalgia and sadness thinking about all the lovely things that have disappeared over the years. It is a "happiness lost" feeling.

Absorbed by these tragic thoughts I normally go to an izakaya, a little family-run Japanese restaurant where people go to eat and drink. At the izakaya, I drown my sorrows in food, much like the main characters in such Japanese gourmet dramas as *Kodokuno Gurume* (The Solitary Gourmet) and *Shinya Shokudo* (Midnight Restaurant). Some of these izakayas are places that might not pass a sanitary inspection in Europe. Despite this, they are the preferred meeting places for groups of friends, salarymen at the end of the work day, or people like me just looking for a comfortable place to be.

Once inside, I usually sit at the counter and, like most clients, carefully read the menus hanging on the walls. Finally I ask for the daily recommendations, and choose one of them. While the food is being prepared, I enjoy watching the other clients, listening to the conversations between the regulars and the restaurant owner. It is delightful to be part of this familiar mood, watching how different people join in or leave these easy discussions. The topics are not important; it's about sharing a moment.

Food here is not sophisticated or fancy. There is no sushi or scrupulously presented dishes. Most dishes consist of simple home-made plates that the owners recommend to their clients depending on the season and on the available products in the marketplace. Oden in winter, edamame in summer, and rice with chestnuts in autumn.

ALASKA
'89 7 23

The most important thing at the izakaya, even more important than the food, is that clients feel as comfortable as they would in their own homes. It is a place to relax. Good izakaya owners work hard to meet their clients' daily needs. In Japanese this type of kindness is called omoiyari, which roughly translates into English as "altruistic sensitivity". The omoiyari revealed in each dish shows the owner's feelings for his clients: he makes each dish a powerful vehicle for communication. Omoiyari doesn't only work one way (owner-client), though. It also works the other way (client-owner), with clients showing their gratitude through the way they eat their food or place their chopsticks.

Through the ritual of eating, Japanese people are not only satisfying a basic physical necessity: they are also sharing their feelings with one another. In a country where rigid social rules don't help to establish fluid and sincere relations, food has become one of the most important weapons of communication.

For me this is one of the reasons that food, in modern Tokyo, is getting more and more important for its citizens: it's an easy way to communicate one's feelings to others and receive a gesture of kindness in return. Going back to our izakaya example, it's a way to go back to the homey warmness of the past and to find refuge from the often hostile environment of Tokyo.

Anyone who has travelled to Tokyo knows that its citizens are navigating a delicate and dangerous balance between tradition and modernity. They are trying to maintain their strict traditions while digesting an individualistic and consumerist culture that has come, partly, from abroad. This eternal conflict has a lot to do with the feelings and communication deficit in the city. The fear of losing one's status and the difficulty of cultivating sincere relationships have left just a few "safe zones" where citizens can feel confident and calm just being themselves. Food is one of these "safe zones": it fulfills a basic need, and the satisfaction obtained from it is immediate and powerful. It recalls lost traditions and happy memories in every Japanese subject.

Of course this is not the only reason that food in Japan is so important. Food has traditionally been central to Japanese culture. But people are slowly going back to these little family-run restaurants of the city, which express their omoiyari in each prepared dish. These restaurants are little "safe zones" in a warlike everyday. I'm sure this is the reason I go back to the same izakaya every year and make the same breakfast every morning. Little comfort zones we can buy to get away from the conflict outside.

TOKYO HOMES

For those interested in architecture, Tokyo is a fascinating place. Tokyo is famous for all sorts of eccentric, sometimes bizarre, architecture and this is especially true of its housing architecture. In many European countries, outstanding architecture can often be observed in public buildings, and sometimes in corporate buildings as well. In Japan, innovative architects seem to be more active in the field of housing architecture, or more precisely, detached-housing architecture. Looking at architecture books, one gets the impression that almost every Tokyoite lives in one of those very individualized houses.

This impression is deceiving, however. Most of Tokyo's, and Japan's, population settle for rather standardized homes. The majority lives in detached houses, which are, in many cases, constructed by one of the prefab homebuilders. Others, mainly in the metropolitan areas, live in flats that are even more standardized. Almost all of these flats are designed in the "nLDK" manner, which refers to a living-dining-kitchen-room structure, with "n" being the number of the additional rooms. Most flats have an "n" of 3 ("3LDK"), which is thought to be ideal for the standard Japanese family, composed of a couple and two children: the parents occupy one bedroom and each of the children has his or her own room. These flats are usually constructed as a longish rectangle, with two small dark rooms facing north, and a third room as well as a bath and toilet squeezed between them. A rather narrow hallway connects these rooms to the living room, facing to the south, where a balcony is located. The living room is often the only room with sufficient natural light.

東京の住宅

東京の人口の大部分はハウスメーカーが建てた戸建て住宅か、規格化された集合住宅に住んでいる。第二次世界大戦後、とてつもないスピードで工業化と都市化が進んだ結果、膨大な住宅需要が生じ、住宅は規格化された。「住宅すごろく」の上がりをめざすことが国民的スポーツになった。多くの人にとって、郊外に戸建て住宅を所有することが目標になった。1990年代初頭の人口構成の変化とバブル経済の崩壊により、多くの人にとって住宅を所有することは不可能になった。今日、住宅建設の中心はワンルームマンションだ。単身者の居住が増加傾向にあるようだ。

Maren Godzik は福岡大学准教授。九州に移る前は、東京に居住し仕事をしながら、東京の住宅事情を研究していた。

Looking back in history, one finds common features of housing throughout Japan, but before the Meiji Restoration houses were built following local traditions, which took into account the region's climate and culture. Compare, for instance, the traditional houses in subtropical Okinawa to those in the snow-rich regions of Niigata or Toyama. With modernization these regional differences have largely disappeared. The same is true of many other countries, but it seems that Japan's rapid process of modernization and the short life-cycles of its houses have supported more effectively the spread of standardized types of housing. Given that about 60 percent of households own their homes, and that most of these homes are in detached houses, this is even more astonishing.

For sociologists, this uniform housing style may relate to the emergence of a standardized course of life following World War II, which produced (perceived) similar needs in housing. Economists, however, may refer to the housing market in which standardized houses sell best, despite the fact that the second-hand housing market is small: only 13.5 percent of Japanese houses that were traded in 2008 were not newly built, in contrast to 66.4 percent in France and 88.8 percent in England and Wales.

The incredible tempo of industrialization and urbanization in Japan following World War II created the need to house tens of thousands of people, who moved from the countryside to the urban centers, especially from the 1950s until the early 1970s. The Japanese government was quick to formulate a housing policy and coordinated the construction of hundreds of thousands of houses. Eventually, by the end of the 1960s, there was (statistically) one house or flat for each household.

Japanese housing authorities were fascinated by the enormous and incredibly fast production of housing in Khrushchev's Soviet Union. Even if the proportion of households living in state- or regional-government-supported housing never reached the Soviet Union's or Eastern European levels, the production process and the high level of standardization in Japan show similarities, according to Takeshi Hara.[69] Especially since the middle of the 1960s, variation among multiple-family housing (with regards to the number of stories, exterior design and layouts) was replaced by the nation-wide standard of a five-story block-type.

In contrast with socialist countries, however, these houses were supposed to house not the working class, but the newly-emerging middle class. Compared to the average housing situation, the newly-built public-housing complexes (the so-called "danchi") were of a relatively high standard and provided privacy for each household. They became symbols of the modern urban life that many young couples and families strove for as an alternative to the lives of their parents.

Mrs Maekawa, now 74-years-old, told me about the popularity of the mass-housing schemes provided by the public-housing association from her perspective. She also told me about the way of life she and her neighbors led in the second half of the 1960s. "We finally got chosen for one of the public-housing association's flats. We applied nineteen times. The nineteenth time we finally got a flat. It was a lottery. At that time everybody wanted to move into the housing association's houses. Everybody admired the danchi lifestyle—all the "salaryman", everybody in his or her twenties and thirties. It was during the time of Japanese economic growth. That's why it was so competitive getting a flat there. And everybody had children once they started living there. Those who got the flat and started living there probably felt that it was safe to have children."

Family sociologist Yuko Nishikawa emphasizes the importance of these public-housing complexes to the development of a standard postwar family—that is, a nuclear family composed of parents and two children. In her view the housing complexes were not built to suit the needs of various forms of family; their specific layout and size significantly determined the size of families, and thereby produced the dominant family model of the postwar years.[70]

Mrs Maekawa's son was also born shortly after she and her husband were able to get a flat; before that, they had been living in a relative's house. What people found in the public-housing complexes were high-quality standards, the protection of privacy, and the feeling of being part of a new urban middle-class, which strove for a better, modern way of life.

Mrs Maekawa also talked about what was later dubbed "climbing housing ladders". "Later we bought a bigger 3LDK flat, and then moved once again to a new flat. Prices began to rise during the time of economic growth, so we got more for the flat than we had paid for. Again, after two years, we got one-third more than the price we had paid for it, and could use what we had gained for a down payment on the next flat, which was really huge and of a better standard."

Climbing housing ladders has become a national sport, so to speak; it reflects upward mobility or the aspiration to upward social mobility. At the beginning of the 1970s, construction companies began flooding the market with the above-mentioned "nLDK" flats, which are now the most common form of living in urban areas.

Mrs Maekawa, who has worked her whole life, and has had a rather successful career, preferred living a short distance from her workplace. This was rather unusual by Japanese standards. The goal for many people was to own a detached house in the suburbs. In order to stimulate suburbanization the government made sure low interests for home ownership were granted. Over 19 million houses were built using this scheme until 2003, with people paying back their loans over a period of 35 years. Here, the housing system was interwoven with the employment system of the "salaryman": life-long employment in one company, with salaries growing in accordance with seniority. It gave people the security of being able to both fulfill their housing desires and pay back their loans.

Housing became a highly standardized consumer good. The standard floor-plans were designed in a way that made the most efficient use of plots. They were also easily adapted to specific places. Design and construction served the developer's interests, rather than those of the dwellers.

In her younger years, Mrs Maekawa improved her housing situation step by step, as did many urban inhabitants of her generation. She is an exception insofar as she never had the goal of acquiring a house in the suburbs. Housing prices reached their peak during the 1980s. With the burst of the bubble economy in the early 1990s, owned flats seldom got a price that made them worth selling—let alone an amount that could be used as down payment for a detached house. Today, taking the last step of the ladder, which ends in an owned detached house, has become impossible for many.

Japan's housing system never had much room for those who deviated from the standardized course of life. Demographic change and economic stagnation, however, have started to become a social problem. For many, buying, or even renting, a house is no longer affordable.[71] Job insecurity makes the prospect of having to pay back loans over the forthcoming decades less attractive. Young people postpone or give up the decision of buying a flat or a house and tend to spend longer living in their parents' houses. Though home-ownership rates have not dropped overall in recent years, younger age groups show markedly lower rates than those of earlier generations. Demographic change—a shrinking number of younger people and later marriage (if marriage occurs at all)—has had additional negative repercussions for the demand for housing, and has started to affect suburbs at the edge of the metropolitan area. We can only speculate about what the future of housing in a shrinking and aging society will look like. Housing construction during the last one or two decades has had a strong focus on one-room apartments. Single living takes up more and more years of people's lives and seems to be a still-growing trend.

Recently Mrs Maekawa took a decision that is unusual by Japanese standards: She now lives in a "collective house", where people own flats independently but share parts of their space and time, for example, in a common dinner. Alternative lifestyles, however, find more and more consent among all age groups—a sign of economic constraint as well as of changing preferences. While it is unlikely that this new demand will create more diversified housing in the short-term, the way existing space is used will differ considerably from its use in the past.

SIGNBOARD MACHIYA

Today most commercial spaces are anonymous. Air conditioning makes it possible for them to be everywhere; the huge development of chain stores and konbini underline this fact. These places are staffed with mostly part-time workers, to whom the commercial transaction as a meaningful form of communication is irrelevant.

Usually no significant connection is established between the client and the shop or its staff. In generic spaces of mass-consumption, the value of the connection between the host who is serving and the guest who is receiving is lost. Here no personal relationship arises out of selling goods or making the products.

A typology that stands in contrast to generic consumerism is the traditional shop-house of Tokyo. They incorporate both working and living within one architectural unit. These houses may host a wide variety of small businesses, bars or restaurants.

In Tokyo these shop-houses are mostly represented in so called Signboard Architecture (Kanbankenchiku). These buildings present a flat, front facade attached to a wooden machiya-type building. This architectural style became popular among stores from the middle of the Taisho Era to the early Showa Era (the 1920s and 30s). After the Great Kanto Earthquake in 1923, a lot of houses had to be reinforced for fire protection. The front facades were generally tiled, covered with copper sheets or plastered in a range of Western decorative elements or Japanese patterns.

Due to the strong interrelatedness between the owner, the shop, the home and the neighborhood, one can still find a lot of these shop-houses in traditional parts of Tokyo.

The structure of the shop-houses sets an intimate stage, and allows for inclusive activity. The shop space is almost an extension of the living room, and customers are invited into a personal realm. Perhaps these spaces can be a starting point for the renaissance of a new kind of commerce, where small businesses, personal shopping, one's living environments, and the local neighborhood can intertwine. A shift of focus from anonymous to communal transactions.

看板建築

今日、商業空間のほとんどは匿名的（アノニマス）だ。クライアントとショップやそのスタッフの間に意義あるつながりはほとんど構築されないのが普通である。ジェネリックな商業主義と対峙関係にあるタイポロジーが、「看板建築」に代表される東京の伝統的な店舗住宅だ。仕事のための空間と生活空間を1つの建物に統合した建築である。

オーナー、店舗、住宅と近隣地域の間に強い相関関係がある「看板建築」は、東京の伝統的な地域に今でもたくさん見ることができる。店舗部分はリビングルームの延長のような空間であり、客は個人的な領域に招き入れられることになる。おそらく、こうした空間は、アノニマスな取引よりも共同社会的取引を重視していく、新しい種類の商業活動というルネッサンスの出発点となりうるだろう。

NIKLAS FANELSA

Niklas Fanelsa は建築家であり、かつて東京に暮らし研究をしていた都市の散策家。東京スリバチ学会のメンバーでもあった。現在はベルリンに仕事と生活の場を写し、ベルリナー・ベルク（ベルリンの山）という名の都市景観研究グループを設立した。

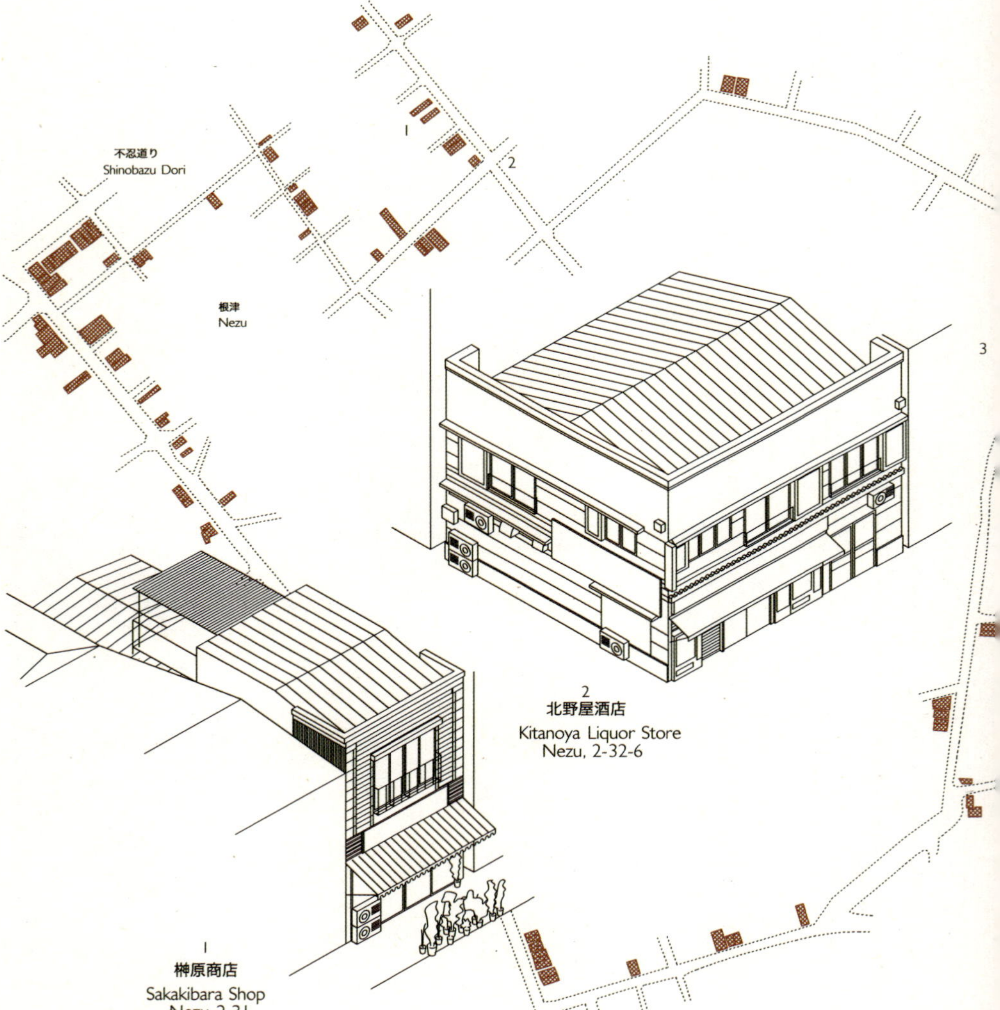

1
榊原商店
Sakakibara Shop
Nezu, 2-31

2
北野屋酒店
Kitanoya Liquor Store
Nezu, 2-32-6

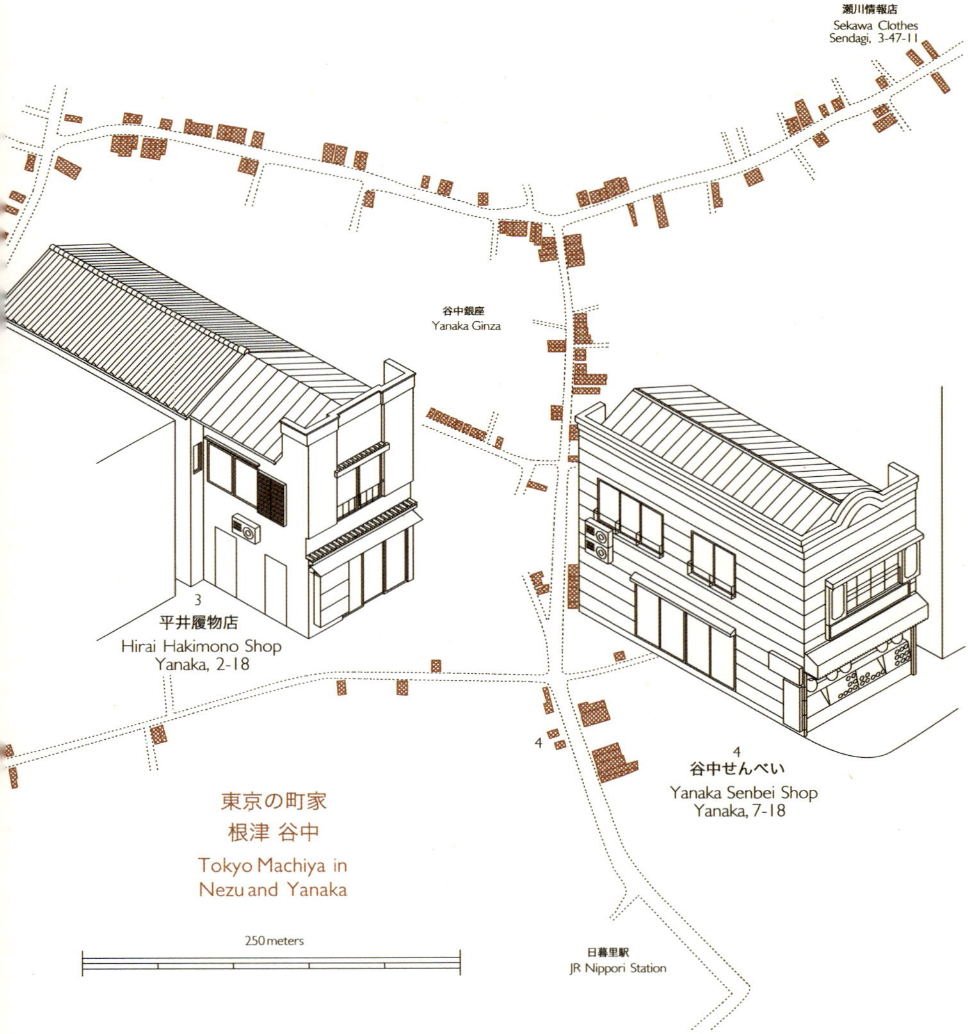
瀬川情報店
Sekawa Clothes
Sendagi, 3-47-11
谷中銀座
Yanaka Ginza
3
平井履物店
Hirai Hakimono Shop
Yanaka, 2-18
4
4
谷中せんべい
Yanaka Senbei Shop
Yanaka, 7-18
東京の町家
根津 谷中
Tokyo Machiya in
Nezu and Yanaka
250 meters
日暮里駅
JR Nippori Station

ENJOY HOUSE

エンジョイ・ハウス

Nanae は Enjoy House を少なくとも週に4回訪問する。仕事は歯科助手をしている、と彼女は言う。私は彼女のいるテーブルの前に跪き、これ以上ないほど丁寧に飲み物を注ぐ。彼女の自分語りを一言も聞き漏らさぬよう耳を澄ませる。彼女が話しかけている相手は私ではない。このクラブのナンバーワンホストの Ryu だ。Ryu は最低の男だが、女の子はみんな彼に夢中になる。Nanaeは売春婦か、多分ソープ嬢だ、と Ryu は言う。私は Ryu の話などどうでもよかった。私はNanaeに恋をしていた。ホストという仕事で、私は消耗し切っていた。疲弊した心を紛らわすために、何時間も歩かずにはいられなかった。歌舞伎町から都庁前まで歩き、また戻ってくる間に、Nanaeのことを考えた。ある日、彼女を見た日から、全てが変わった。

Charlotte van Zanten はフィクション作家、文化的起業家で、3年以上東京に暮らし、研究を行っている。Tokyo Ohayo という小説を書くため、ホステスとして働いた。

Nanae visited Enjoy House at least four times a week. She always came in early and left before midnight. She didn't come on Wednesdays or Thursdays. The reason she would leave early was her job, she once said. She worked as a dental assistant. On weekdays she had to wake up early in the morning.

I wanted to ask why she couldn't come on Wednesdays and Thursdays. By using the most nuanced method, I wanted to find out how a dental assistant could earn enough money to drink in a club like this. Sadly, she wasn't talking to me when I learned about her work. She was talking to Ryu, who sat next to her, and who had put his arm loosely around her shoulder. I had simply overheard the conversation.

Kneeling at their table, I poured the drinks with utmost precision. Shochu, lemon, ice, and soda. I tossed the ice-cubes gently in the long glasses. Soundlessly. Careful not to miss a word of her story.

Her lips were painted a deep red. She articulated her sentences with the same precision with which I prepared their drinks. When she noticed me watching her, I promptly began to focus on the bottle of soda.

Through the glass I followed her small hands. Like a cat, she pulled her red-as-her-lips fingernails in and out the fake leather of the sofa slowly. Though she seemed confident, there was something mechanical to her speech. I realized soon that she had to be lying.

Ryu said and asked nothing. He just gave her that sheepish smile of his.

Later, when I confronted him with my observation, he laughed at me and told me Nanae was a prostitute, or perhaps a Soapland girl.

"Just like all of them," he said.

I didn't listen to him.

"Why?" he continued. "Have you already fallen in love? Already? You are stupid; you are so fucking naïve."

Nanae looked like Mathilda from the film Leon: The Professional: the same haircut, the same necklace, and the same earnestness in her eyes. There must have been some of the same sensuality, but she never showed it, at least not to Ryu. She often sat with Ryu. Sometimes, if he was busy, she sat with other top hosts like Kenchan or Tetsu. However, as with most of the girls who came on a regular base, Ryu was her favourite.

That didn't mean anything. I was convinced that it had nothing to do with romantic love. More with feeling at home. Nanae needed someone who knew her, at least to some extent. Ryu had to be able to ask not only how her week had gone, but also how her father's birthday had been, whether she had finally watched the film he had recommended, and whether her boss was still in a bad mood. That's how it works in here. We sell the intimacy and comfort girls lack in their daily lives. They pay us to do so, Making Ryu's response more of a force-of-habit kind of thing.

Then again, I might have just been trying to comfort myself.

Ryu could be an asshole, because he had appropriated a position in which he could do anything he wanted. It seemed as though he didn't have to make an effort when it came to being empathic or understanding, or at least not anymore. He was simply cool, and for the girls that was enough. He wore his coolness as naturally as the maple trees wear their red leaves in autumn. As though the other seasons didn't matter for him. As though he hadn't grown up in a small village in Gunma Prefecture, and hadn't worn his big brother's discarded clothes or these thick, unfashionable glasses Three-quarters of his life. As though he had always been glamorous, confident and well dressed.

Insidious as he was, he was the number-one host at our club. All the girls adored him.

I lived near the club, and shared a room with my childhood friend Taka and two other colleagues. The room was small, the walls between us and the outside world were paper-thin, and our rickety bunks were uncomfortable. But if you worked in a club six nights a week, as we did, you too could have slept anywhere. I never complained, and neither did Taka.

Born in Chikuma, Nagano, a small village with far more apricots than inhabitants, Taka and I had been best friends since elementary school and had dreamed of something bigger and more exciting since we were kids. Taka especially. He had grown up without a mother and was taken care of by an indifferent and miserable father. He had always waited for the day when he would be free to live the dream. After we graduated we watched the apricot trees come into blossom. As soon as the flowers had evaporated, he left for Tokyo. He found a job as a host within a week.

Of course he tried to convince me to follow, but it took thousands of apricots, hundreds of apples and even an earthquake before I finally did. My uncle owned a few yards in the valleys that surrounded our village and he had employed me right after I graduated. Contrary to Taka's non-existent family, mine was big and warm and well—slightly officious, I would say. To please them, I spent weeks pulling off unwanted, misshapen fruits and later I picked the heavy, symmetrical ones. Halfway through December, when the trees looked bare and miserable, I understood that there was nothing left for me in Chikuma. But the reason I eventually left was the big earthquake in March. Disasters have the unfortunate habit of not only destroying all that is in their way, but also of reminding its bereaved how transient life is.

I occasionally relive my time as a fruit-picker. Then I think about those meditative daily rhythms. But even though my life at this moment is far from meditative, I'm happy I left Chikuma.

And so was Taka.

He was on fire. Tokyo, Shinjuku, working at Enjoy House: they had served him well. I couldn't believe my eyes when I met him almost a year later. He wore fancy clothes, had died his grown-long hair and seemed more confident than ever before. I wondered how it was possible that I had never seen this Taka before. When he picked me up at Tokyo Station, he had just joined the top ten hosts of the club.

He was good at his job. While I had been picking apricots, Taka had discovered the magic of liquor and smooth talk. He found his way easily using words and moves I could never imagine him using in Chikuma. It was good to see him so confident and I never questioned his motives. We had this dream, Taka and I—a greater plan. One day we would open a restaurant in the middle of Tokyo where people would come together to have a good time. If one of us couldn't see the wonders of the world anymore, the other would always remind him. Unlike prominent figures like Kenchan, Tetsu and Ryu, who pretended to be wise but who in reality were gloomy and frustrated, Taka was a bright and optimistic force. He seemed to enjoy working and he liked the girls.

Or, at least, he felt some sympathy.

I wondered whether Kenchan, Tetsu and Ryu had ever been like him.

The first time Nanae spoke to me, it cost me 5,000 yen and another month of slaving.

It was a busy Saturday night and I had been working in the club only a month or two. My job was to make sure hosts like Ryu could work as smoothly as possible and that included, among other things, taking our customers' coats, pouring drinks, lighting cigarettes, and guiding girls to the powder room or the pay desk. As usual, Nanae had been sitting with Ryu, but shortly before midnight he had had to join a birthday bash in one of the private spaces upstairs. He told me to take over, to keep her company. He would be back in twenty minutes. It was the first time since I had begun working in the club that I had been able to actually sit next to a girl.

And she wasn't just a girl.

She was Nanae.

And she looked like Mathilda from Leon.

"Smoke?" she asked when I moved next to her, trembling. Her thin fingers searched for a cigarette in the white pack of Kool Menthol Lights. She had trouble picking it out of the tightly packed new box. Most women smoked Virginia Slims; Nanae didn't.

"I'm not allowed to smoke during working hours," I said carefully. Smoking was only for the real hosts.

"So what?" she laughed. "If I want you to smoke, you should smoke. I don't like to smoke alone. Do you want to make me feel lonely?"

"No," I answered, ashamed. "Of course not."

She handed me one of her cigarettes and asked me how old I was.

"Twenty-one," I lied.

"You are nobody," she concluded, bored.

"I'm very sorry," I said. I couldn't imagine what she would have called me had I told her my real age.

Maybe she wanted me to be her Leon.

I lit the cigarette she gave me and handed it to her. Then I took the cigarette she held for herself, lit it up and inhaled deeply. I could at least take care of her, I thought, and suddenly I felt confident. Though she had told me I was nobody, for the first time since I had set foot in this club I felt like a man.

Nanae was a bored smoker, not an addicted one. Mostly, she smoked half her cigarette before dumping the remains in the ashes of its predecessor. Since it had been my job to light her cigarettes for the past five months, I should have known lighting one after the other simply wasn't her style, but the sudden, misplaced confidence must have poisoned my brain. Instead of paying attention, I welcomed the second Kool, took a sip of the Chu-hi I had prepared for Ryu earlier that night and fell back in the cheap leather of the sofa.

When Ryu came back and found the two of us smoking on the sofa (me sipping his drink), he smiled in a way I had never seen him smile before. All I could interpret in it, was that I was in trouble.

When I helped Nanae into her beige raincoat later that night, I discovered something had changed. Something small. Something so delicate you would hardly have noticed it, but I did. Her eyes had softened and her shoulders and arms were not as stiff as they were usually, but bendable like the willows in Shinjuku Gyoen.

She smiled at me. Had I not already fallen in love with her months before, it would have happened then, at that precise moment. She didn't intend to smile; she was forced by the power of recognition. It was a smile like a wink, and it hit me like thunder.

She knew who I was now.

I had a name.

I was nobody.

And we shared a story.

Made a memory.

She left me there, nailed to the ground—so ecstatic I didn't even realize Ryu had marched straight into the manager's office and would soon Judas me into trouble. Another penalty from my wage, another month of slaving instead of upgrading, a month of cleaning soiled powder rooms…

But who cared? She had smiled at me.

It had only been a few weeks since I had begun working as a real host and I had already realized I would never be as good as Taka though I would never speak or move with his flair, I had some young girls who seemed to like me. One of them was a girl we called Teacup. She was young, very short and always brought along her Teacup Chihuahua. The dog was stuffed into a tiny doggy-bag that had "Louis Vuitton" printed all over the leather. Initially, I felt sorry for the animal, but soon

I learned it was so apathetic it was more like a teddy bear than a flesh-and-blood dog. Besides, she seemed to love it as though it were her own child. In 80 percent of our conversations, the Teacup Chihuahua was either the main subject or set as an example.

To be able to sit with Nanae was the only reason I tried to become better at my job. It wasn't easy being a good host if you weren't Ryu. We had to be creative to keep our customers coming. Every now and then, Taka slept with one of his girls. Most of the time because he felt they were losing interest. Ironically, most of the time they never came back after he fucked them. Perhaps he also did it because he felt bored. Working six nights a week, there wasn't much time to meet girls outside of Enjoy House.

My new position wore me out. I had been physically dog-tired during my slaving period, but now I was emotionally exhausted. Sleep couldn't cure the emptiness the way it had once cured my sore muscles. The only thing that could make me forget everything temporarily was walking. While walking I would, step by step, forget time, place and temperature. I would become insensitive to sound. All the noise of the outside world would entirely proceed into the rhythm of my footsteps. I would forget I was tired or thirsty or hungry. I would forget I had a body filled with a network of nerves and that I was a tiny, meaningless puppet in a billion-person city. Gradually I would forget what emptiness felt like. The meditative pace would take me back to my hometown. I was a child again. I was a picker of apricots in the valley of Chikuma.

But wherever my thoughts went, I always ended up thinking of Nanae. I imagined running into her down in the streets of Tochomae. I imagined how I would discover her from miles away, between hundreds of people all finding their way to work. I would recognise her raincoat. I would recognise her smooth willow-like, resilient tread. In the blue light of the morning, I would discover her silky, black hair and her fresh, clean face—her earnest eyes, narrow from the brightness of the early sun. I wanted to see her going to her day job.

One day my feet brought me from the wide business lanes of Tochomae, where peak hour had just begun, back to the winding streets of Kabukicho. I wasn't there; my mind was somewhere above the clouds. I was only my feet, marching without direction. I don't remember the traffic lights, or the dozens of people I must have passed before I finally noticed her.

She was not in the lanes of Tochomae, not near the station, not on her way to work. She was in the depths and dirt of Kabukicho. 7:08 a.m., and she walked out of a windowless room, guided by an elderly man. It was as though someone had punched me right in the stomach. I was close to vomiting in the middle of the street. And all I could hear was Ryu laughing at me.

"Just like all of them," he yelled. "Have you already fallen in love? You are stupid; you are so fucking naïve. She is just like all of them."

Just another nobody.

PUBLIC TO PRIVATE

Bounded by the yellow line I wait my turn to enter its confines. The roar of its approach wakes me from the morning delusion. As the entrance appears a strong gust reminds us of the reality we face.

Mind the gap.

The steel frame of this structure is perfectly engineered for its purpose. Implicit borders divide it into individual sections. The desire to interact with one's neighbors is dissolved by the heavy silence. Inches away they sit in the same trance as all who have faith in its function. The unspoken agreement maintains order, in exchange for comfort. We sit motionless as instructions are relayed.

The bell sounds.

The positions we decide on remain in place until we retire. This space no wider than oneself has become the studio in which our duties are fulfilled. The devised barriers work in our favor. Outside of our vision, the ones beside us cease to exist.

The public has become private.

We become ignorant of the time spent inside its expanse; it is no longer questioned. Moving from instinct as the repetitious cycle turns us into creatures of habit. Waiting to be woken from the unconscious disengagement by the chimes that speak our code. When the end has become written.

Those who have been given the orders now rise. The pace slows as the end comes into sight. We line up, ready to take our leave. Stop. The door sounds. Carefully we depart.

To welcome the yellow line.

Public transport in Japan transcends the limits of travel. The average commute time is one hour a day, adding up to over 20 days spent each year in public transport. Transport is not only a space of travel but an office, study, studio, and bedroom. Since attending university I have spent a month each year in commute. This has forced me to develop rituals with which to pass the time. To create a productive space within the train's small confines. I draw, read, write… sometimes sleep. These drawings and thoughts are based on my observations in commute.

I wrote this on the train

パブリックからプライベートへ

東京を走る電車は隠された記号(コード)に支配された公共空間(パブリックスペース)だ。しかし、このパブリックな領域にいながらにして、人は自分だけのプライベートなオフィス、書斎、アトリエ、ベッドルームに引きこもる。私も、電車の中で身を小さくしながら、まるで儀式のように決まった行動をとるようになった。ドローイングを描き、本を読み、ものを書き……そしてときには眠ることもある。これらのドローイングと考えは、通勤途中の私が観察したことに基づいている。

Will Robinson はアーティストであり、この6年にわたり東京に暮らし、作品を制作している。これらのドローイングは、電車の中で描いたもの。

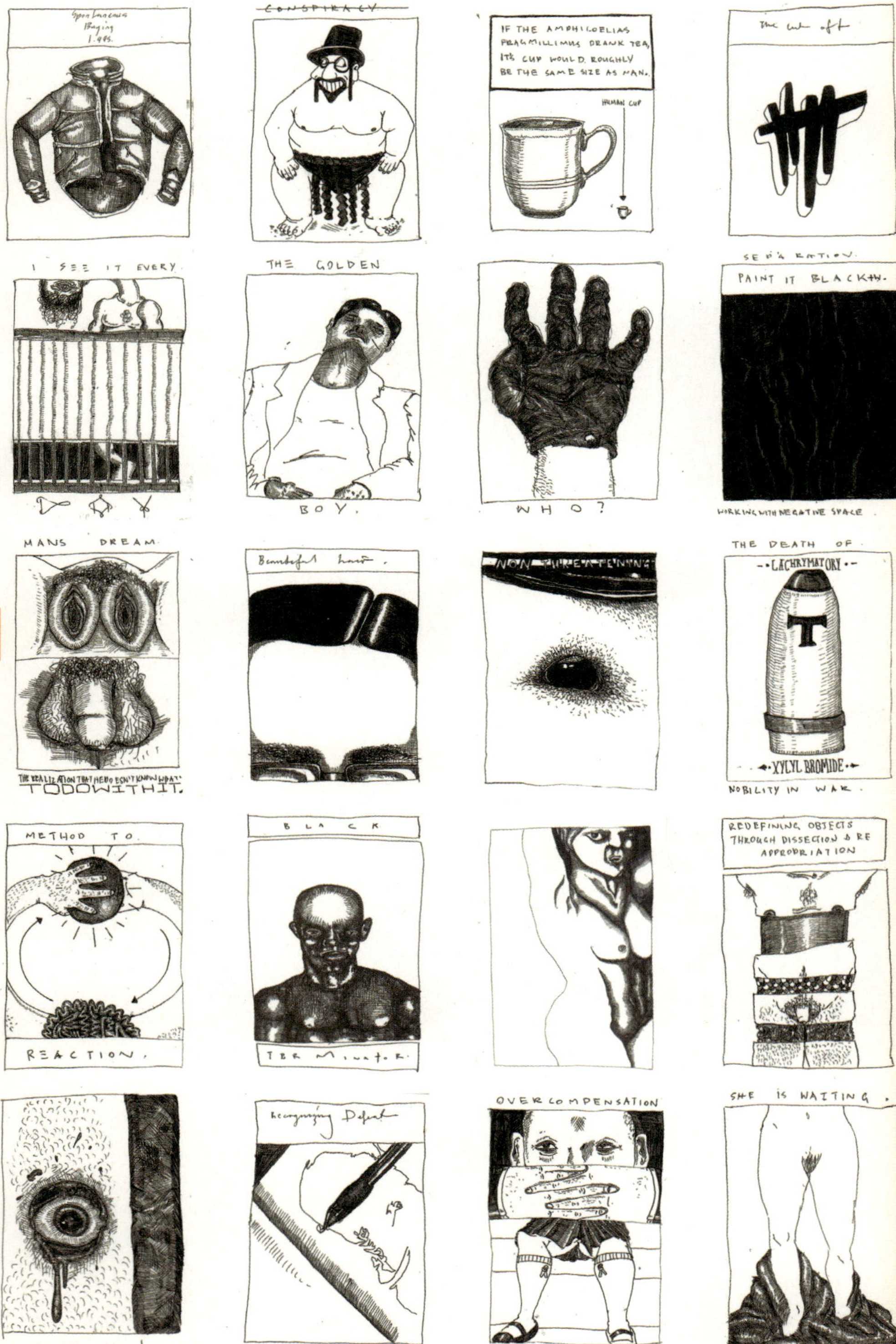
CONSPIRACY
IF THE AMPHICOELIAS FRAGMILLIMUS DRANK TEA, ITS CUP WOULD ROUGHLY BE THE SAME SIZE AS MAN.
HUMAN CUP
I SEE IT EVERY
THE GOLDEN
BOY.
WHO?
SEPARATION.
PAINT IT BLACK
WORKING WITH NEGATIVE SPACE
MANS DREAM.
THE REALIZATION THAT HE DOESN'T KNOW WHAT TO DO WITH IT.
Beautiful hair.
NON THREATENING
THE DEATH OF
LACHRYMATORY
T
XYLYL BROMIDE
NOBILITY IN WAR.
METHOD TO
REACTION.
BLACK
REDEFINING OBJECTS THROUGH DISSECTION & RE APPROPRIATION
SHOT YA!
Recognizing Defeat
OVERCOMPENSATION
SHE IS WAITING.

1.17-31

SINGLE LADIES

Tokyo is always changing. Older buildings are easily scrapped and new buildings quickly take their place. The current transformation, however, is not entirely driven by market forces or real-estate developments. Changing cultural customs, related to domestic and urban lifestyles, are another important driving force of the transition.

Demographic shifts in central Tokyo—from population loss in the 1970s and 1980s, linked to suburbanization, to population recovery after the 1990's—have caused a dramatic transformation in both urban land use and lifestyle. Initially, people moved out of Tokyo to enjoy a suburban lifestyle with large, detached houses. Today, people move into central Tokyo, and into ever-smaller houses, to enjoy a diverse cultural lifestyle.

The last 20 years have witnessed a drastic change in Tokyo's urban housing market. Small-sized households have historically been marginalized in the Japanese housing market, with multiple generations of one family—children, parents and grandparents—often living under one roof. In rural areas this is still common practice. Furthermore, in the 1950s, a romantic image of an ideal-sized nuclear family took hold in the Japanese psyche. People longed for a modern, middle-class lifestyle where the family would slowly climb the so-called "housing ladder". In this ideal lifestyle, dad worked in a corporate environment, with lifelong job security, and mom took care of the house and the kids. In the last two decades, however, this ideal has shifted. The prolonged demographic and economic slowdown of the last 20 years has changed how people consider their choices in life. Changing lifestyles and an increase in condominium construction have contributed to increased homeownership by single persons—especially single ladies—and dual-career couples.[72]

独身女性たち

郊外化の時代は終わった。今日、人々はさまざまな文化的ライフスタイルを享受するため、都心にある、これまで以上に小さな家に移り住んでいる。20年という長きに渡る少子高齢化と経済衰退は、人生における選択肢をめぐる人々の捉え方を変えた。結果として、独身者、とくに独身女性の住宅所有が増加した。集合住宅の70％以上の買い手は30代から40代前半の独身女性だ。こうした女性たちはよく働き、個人の自由を楽しむ。彼女たちは、日本人の結婚や子供に対する関わり方を変えつつある。彼女たちは、伝統的な家族の価値が未だに非常に強い影響力をもつ国における、新しいスタンダードを開拓しつつある 。

久保倫子は都市地理学者、岐阜大学助教。

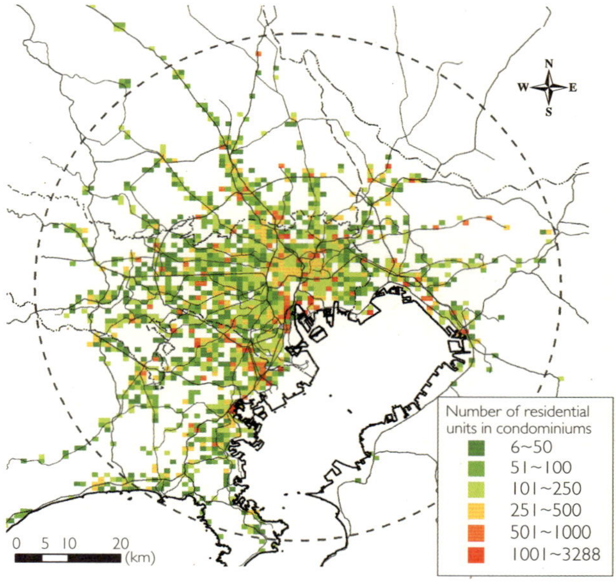

Number of condominiums sold in Tokyo (2005~2009)

Source: Real estate economic institute, 'Condominium Market Trend Search 2005-2009'.

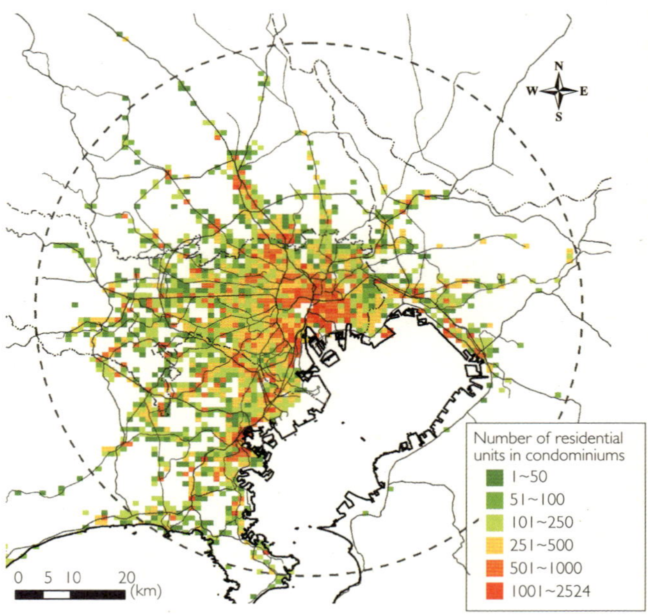

Number of condominiums sold in Tokyo (1999~2004)

Source: Real estate economic institute, 'Condominium Market Trend Search 1999-2004.

In the 1990s and 2000s, something changed. The 2010 Population Census of Japan revealed a surprising fact: In central Tokyo, the percentage of single-person households, especially single-woman households, had reached almost 50 percent of all households, and the percentage of married couples living with children had decreased gradually.[73] Singles and childless couples were increasingly choosing to live in inner-city condominiums. People seemed less interested in detached, suburban houses. These suburban homes used to remind buyers of their childhood family homes in the countryside, but apparently this reminder was no longer necessary.

More astounding was the fact that more then 70 percent of the condominiums were bought by single women in their 30s and early 40s.[74] These women took advantage of the growing supply of increasingly cheap condominiums being built in convenient locations. In particular, the supply of "compact" condominiums—very small-sized living spaces—became larger.[75] The single women who purchased these condominiums were not necessarily rich, however. They seemed to have chosen owner-occupied residences because the monthly rent of their previous residences was so high that occasionally the monthly mortgage payment was less than, or equal to, the rent. These women wanted to improve their living conditions by purchasing their own homes.[76]

Usually, rental apartments have small living spaces and low-quality equipment in their bathrooms and kitchens, and are built with materials that are worse than those used in owner-occupied condominiums. Rental apartments were historically built for students or young people who were expected to climb the "housing ladder" and move toward owning a house after they marry. But those who didn't marry still longed for better living conditions. So it was a natural development for single ladies, who outgrew their student living spaces, to buy a place of their own. In a country were traditional opinions on gender and gender roles still carry tremendous weight, this development was nothing short of a seismic cultural shift.

As condominium purchases by single women became an emerging phenomenon in Tokyo, major condominium suppliers began to build more compact condominiums with this target group in mind. Most major developers even embraced the housing needs of single women. They started cooperating with interior-design shops that were popular among young women, modifying the interiors of the housing units to meet the aesthetic housing needs of young women.

Compact condominiums are mostly built in central Tokyo, with Ochanomizu, Ebisu, and Ginza the most popular areas. These are well-established suburbs with a mature culture and a wide selection of restaurants and bars that cater to single women. Many single women dream of a fashionable lifestyle. They imagine something like the life of Carrie Bradshaw, the main character in *Sex and the City*. They want to be independent career women, wear high-fashion clothes, party with girlfriends, and date good-looking guys.

Ebisu especially is well known as a "livable town for single women". There are many good restaurants that stay open late, and the suburb is filled with fashionable streets with high-fashion boutiques. It is a place where (wealthy) single women can enjoy their lives. But Eastern Tokyo, which includes Ginza and Ochanomizu, is also in high demand, since it is considered the center of high culture. There are many museums, large halls for classical music and ballet, theaters for kabuki and other dramas, and many good restaurants and bars that people can visit before or after a show or exhibition. The condominiums in central Tokyo were built especially for single women who wish to enjoy this kind of mature urban life-style.

Kanako, a condominium resident in the Tokyo Bay area, is a single woman in her 30s and a company employee. She decided to leave her parents' house when her mother passed away. She says, "Mother passed away when I was 30, and that's why I started to search for my own place. I was basically a parasite before leaving my parents' house. The life with my parents was so comfortable that I'd never thought about leaving. If my mother hadn't passed away, there would have been no reason to leave and start living independently."

She searched for rental apartments and then condominiums, and gradually felt like buying one. At first, she entered a provisional contract and paid a deposit for a housing unit in central Tokyo, a compact condominium designed for a single woman. However, she eventually gave up the unit because it was too small, and the developer's financial conditions were not good. "There were no houses with well-arranged rooms. Rooms for families are easy to find, but rooms for singles: no." Kanako devoted one year to search for her new dwelling. At last, Kanako decided to buy a condominium in the Tokyo Bay area.

I asked why she wanted to live alone. She said that she had "longed for an independent urban life in a condominium." She grew up in a detached house, which increased her desire to live in a condominium. "Besides, detached houses are very expensive."

Today Kanako's weekly planner is filled with cultural events. On weekends, she cleans her place and then goes to Ginza or other areas in central Tokyo for shopping, yoga lessons or meetings with friends. It is rare for her to use local facilities such as the library, theaters and gyms, but she does take piano and singing lessons.

Although she is quite ambivalent about it, Kanako also participates in konkatu, or "marriage activities". These include any activity aimed at meeting "marriageable" men, such as attending special parties for people who wish to get married. "I just wonder if I can fit into married life. It will be completely different from my life right now. I've been working for more than 10 years and I've lived my own life. Being a housewife? No way. I'll keep working as hard as I can because it'll be good for me."

Kanako enjoys her single life, and she hopes to have a good marriage one day. But, as she mentioned, independent life is very comfortable, and she has a stable job that helps her sustain her lifestyle. She feels that she has built her own castle and that she is the queen of her kingdom. Many women today don't feel a strong desire to get married. They fear their mother-in-law would hate them and try to limit their freedom. Moreover, many Japanese men still expect their spouse to take charge of the housekeeping, take care of the children, and look after the parents. Many still expect women to quit their jobs when they get married or when they become pregnant.

This divergence of expectations among men and women is becoming ever-more problematic. Now that single women in Tokyo are establishing new urban lifestyles, traditional housing customs and cultural pressures to live a "normal" or traditional life are gradually fading. In the end, Japanese culture must adjust to this new urban reality. But since Japanese society is not known for its social and cultural flexibility, it is uncertain how our culture will evolve.

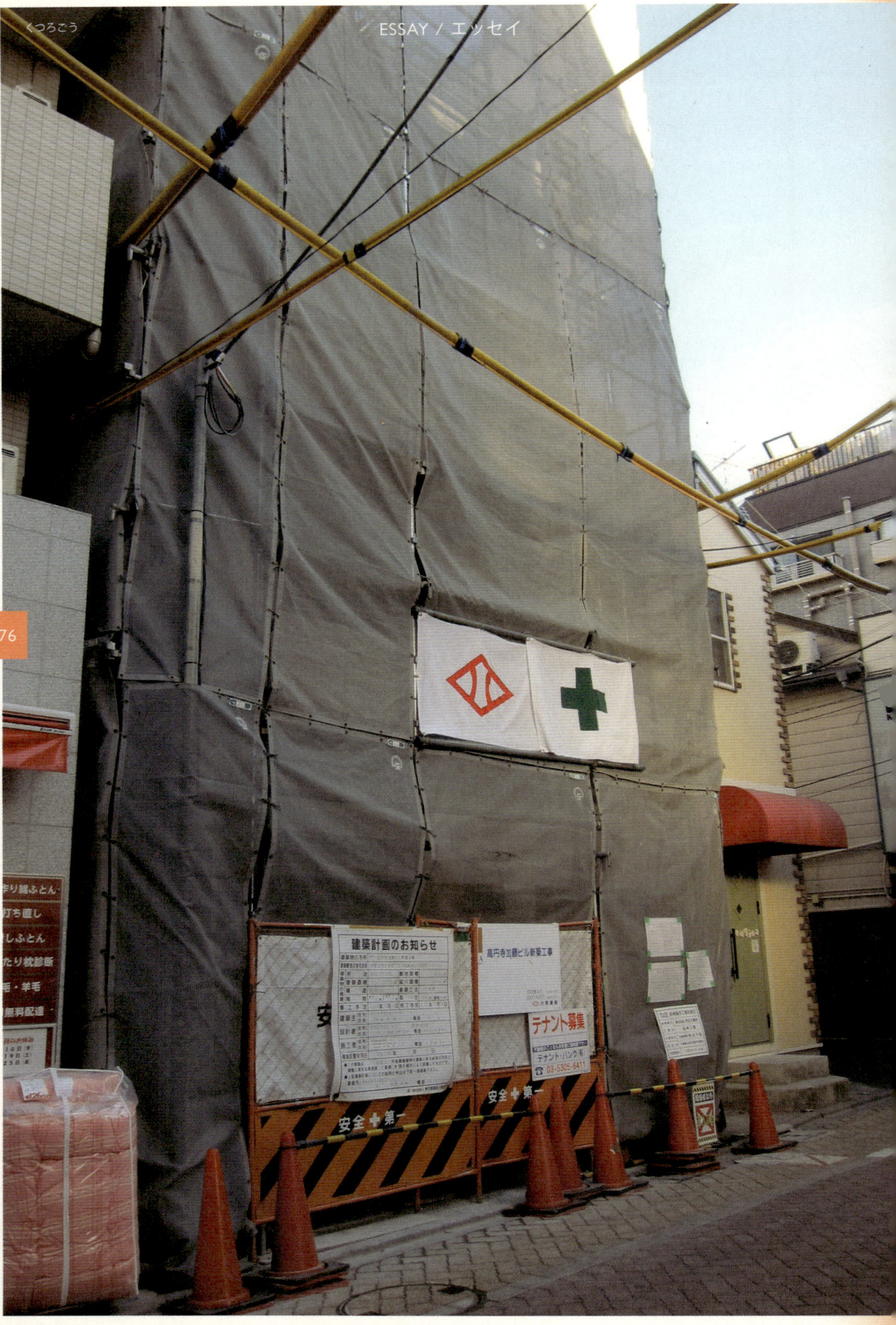
建築計画のお知らせ
高円寺加藤ビル新築工事
テナント募集
テナント・バンク(有)
03-5305-6411
安全第一
安全第一
打ち直し
無料配達

SHAKEN SPACES

We needed a place. Something affordable that would accommodate us both, in an easygoing neighborhood if possible. When an old lady told us Koenji was dodgier than other areas in Tokyo we were certain it was the best neighborhood for us. People played music on the streets, scruffy artists wandered about, and the garbage men were a little more relaxed about how we separated our five types of rubbish. But away from the busy shopping streets with their kooky bars and restaurants lay a labyrinth of suburban housing similar to every other neighborhood we'd seen in this sprawling city.

The suburbs present you with layers of uniformity. The apartment buildings are a clutter of staircases, exterior garbage containers and bicycle parking slots. Doors are lined up one next to the other, with no distinguishable difference other than the number and name on the mailbox. There is no apparent social interaction between tenants. Although the building structure is shared, nothing else is: there is no shared entrance, no hallway, no doorman, no meetings and no noise. Though these buildings are almost naked, with front doors opening directly to the exterior world, there is a great sense of disconnect between individuals' private worlds and the rest of the city's inhabitants.

When we visited an available apartment with a real-estate agent we saw construction work in progress in front of the building. Worried we'd be woken up every dawn with pneumatic drills, we approached one of the laborers. He assured us that the work would be completed in two weeks. Satisfied, we decided to take it: there was a reasonable eyeful of the horizon, no children screaming through the paper-thin walls, and two spaces created by a sliding door. Two weeks of building work opposite wouldn't stop us from entering our lovely matchbox.

An apato is a typical lower-middle-class apartment. It's less sophisticated than a "mansion," which has thicker walls blocking unwanted contact, better insulation, and more seismic safety. Our apato lost out on all these points—but at least it was refurbished. The tatami floor had been changed to "wood" (read: linoleum) floors, and it had a mysterious bathroom design: one room

揺れる空間

高円寺の小さなアパートに暮らした経験を通して、私たちは東京における「家」の概念の明白な特異性に対する感性を育んでいった。家という概念は、厚くて頑丈な壁のなかにあるわけでも、不変的な場所をもつものでもないようだ。快適性は、より流動的な存在になったように思われた。家具やお風呂、電気毛布が仕込まれたこたつ、電気マット、導入すると加湿器を買わざるを得なくなるエアコンなどがつくりだすものなのだ。隣の工事現場では何かを建てているのか、壊しているのかわからなかったけれども、少なくとも私たちは、自宅の流動的な内部空間をだんだん快適に感じるようになっていった。

Mara Duer は社会学者、David Labi は映像作家。二人は東京で共同生活をし、高円寺の小さなアパートでの生活体験と観察をまとめてくれた。

for the toilet, one room for the ofuro—Japanese bathtub—and a little space for the washing machine. Something missing? The bathroom sink. Common in Japan, we were told.

Basic utilities such as central heating and insulation are not the customary means of making your home warm and comfortable. Coziness is instead achieved through extra appliances that allow you to be warm in specific sections of your own home. These include the ofuro, the kotatsu table with a built-in electric blanket, the electric mattress, and the hot/cold air conditioner that forces the additional purchase of an electric humidifier.

After a week in our new dwelling, something wasn't right. Instead of the neighboring house taking shape, the opposite was happening. The walls were disappearing before our eyes. Doors swung in the air; half a kitchen sat poised above the abyss. We witnessed what turned out to be not a construction—but a demolition.

As we watched the neighboring house's entire bathroom torn to rubble, tears fell from our eyes. Surely we could have given a home to that disembodied sink, so we wouldn't have to brush our teeth in the kitchen?

We began to appreciate the distinctness of the concept of "home" in Tokyo. For instance, the bedroom is not a stable place. In a traditional apartment dwelling with a tatami mat, where the occupant sleeps on a roll-out futon, the room functions by day as living room, by night as bedroom. Traditionally, the bed is taken out from the wardrobe every night and rolled up again every morning. For most Japanese people, the bedroom is not their shrine, and their homes are not their palaces. Perhaps this fluid relationship with sleeping places explains the common sight in Tokyo of people sleeping soundly anywhere and at any time.

In two weeks the house opposite our apartment had disintegrated—its composite materials whisked away to destinations unknown—and a ploughed patch of brown earth lay in front of us. A hole in the city was born. A few weeks later our antiquated 24-hour local launderette, furnished with "shower capsules" where you could wash yourself for ¥100, met the same sad fate. It was dismantled with amazing alacrity by a band of workers. People continued to stop for a smoke in front of the vanished building as if they were still waiting for their clothes to be ready.

We started to spot these empty lots all over the city, tufty patches of land gazing at passersby like puppies in a pet-shop window longing for a new owner. This city does not expand outward like an oil stain as most other cities do. It grows within itself, reinventing itself again and again in the same spot. It expands and contracts vertically, up and down. It's as if the little cells of the organism implode, only to be reconstituted in a more practical way, meeting new needs, confronting new dangers, adapting to new demands of the economy.

These sites of "destructive construction" can be seen everywhere in the city. In public areas, like the uniform pedestrian shopping streets shared by every neighborhood, the first step for demolition and reconstruction is the dressing up of the building. A massive tarpaulin veils the structure like a curtain concealing a stage. When the curtain is pulled back, the production within proceeds unnoticed. It's as if the structure in its current form has always been there. A new tile fits seamlessly into the city's mosaic.

Once the house across the street had disappeared, we understood this was just another beginning. A team of construction workers would soon start to assist the rebirth of an old chunk of city. We no longer feared the construction noise. A shiny new building would appear overnight, housing a new family that we would never meet.

NEW FAMILY

I travelled to Tokyo to interview young architecture practitioners about the future of Japanese cities. My standard set of questions, meant to structure the conversation, was often abandoned for a personal story on Japanese society, tradition and behavior. Rather than talking about the future of physical architecture, many designers seemed fascinated with emerging ideas about what they called "a new type of family".

"For decades Japan was trying to follow Western ideas and focus on the self-realization of the individual," says Kumiko Inui. "Before the period of post-World War Two economic growth, we lived in bigger families. Today, we have predominantly single households and a historically low birthrate. Soon a third of the population will be over 60. Japan might become a country with either old or single people. Only recently the debate on the future of our social system started to be held more openly. We realized that individualism is not good and the way we work and organize social activities must be changed. Due to the stagnant economy it is proving difficult to raise the birthrate. Rather than reintroducing the classic family household, we can try to bring individuals together and invent a new type of family. This will be the tendency, I hope. Not only young people will be sharing a house, elderly people as well. These micro-communities will become very important as self-supporting islands within the greater system."

新しい家族

私は日本の若い建築家たちとこの国の都市の未来について語り合うために東京を旅した。多くの建築家たちは、物理的な建築の未来を話すよりもむしろ、彼らが「新しいタイプの家族」と呼ぶ、最近登場した概念に魅せられているように見えた。これこそが、日本の大多数を占める核家族と、少子高齢化問題に対する回答なのだ。私はここ数年、一緒に暮らしながら仕事をしているタケシ、タクマ、トオルの都心にあるアパートメントを訪問し、彼らが「新しい家族」として暮らしているようすを目にしたのだった。このアパートメントは彼らのデザインプロジェクトの1つであり、彼ら自身が1つの社会実験の中心物となっている。

Inara Nevskaya はアムステルダムのDUSアーキテクツに勤務する建築家。2004年から2005年にかけて東京の芝浦工業大学に留学。2012年には、さまざまな若い建築家にインタビューするため、日本を訪問した。

Choreography of a standard family. Collective tatami rooms and dining room, small private hideaways in bathroom, kitchen and ooshire.

標準的家族のふるまい。家族が集まる畳の部屋とダイングルーム、バスルーム、キッチン、押入れは、個人が篭もる小さな空間。

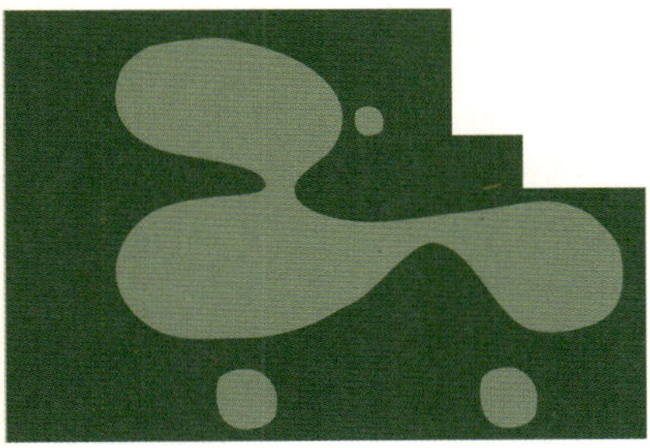

I got curious about what this new type of family could look like. Does it really go beyond people sharing rent and will this have an effect on spatial design?

I was advised to get in touch with the partners of 403 Architecture. I meet Takeshi, Takuma and Toru in their urban apartment, where they have lived and worked together for the past few years. The apartment is one of their design projects and they themselves are the center of a social experiment. Over time they have transformed the standard 50-square-meter apartment, laid out for a modern Japanese family of three, into a space accommodating a young architects' collective day and night, seven days a week.

The apartment is presented as a seven-room dwelling: a meeting/dining room, an office, three bedrooms, a kitchen, a bathroom and a balcony room. Takuma shows me around. We start in the entrance hall, where a table and three chairs serve as the meeting and dining area. The central common room with three identical working tables and shelves, aligned along the wall, is the office studio. The bedrooms, not larger than 3 square meters each, surround the common area and are the only private spaces in the apartment.

Takuma's favorite place in the house is the balcony. Normally the balcony in Japan is used as a utility room: a space for the washing machine, washing line and air-conditioning unit. What Takuma shows me is more like a cozy outside room with a couple of chairs and plants—"a perfect place to be alone, have a cup of coffee or a cigarette".

Unlike many European countries, Japan has no true history of experimentation with collective forms of living. In this apartment more than 80 percent of the dwelling is used in a communal manner. At first, I find it a surprising discovery, knowing the Japanese as mostly very private and reserved people. But when looking at the classic tatami-room house, one realizes that there is a well-established tradition of sharing space. The routine of the family is choreographed in such a way that the tatami rooms can accommodate the diverse and overlapping activities of the different family members over the course of the day. The architects of the 403 collective used this knowledge to construct their own choreography and make their own impermanent, private bubbles within the standard apartment model.

"It started with thinking of an affordable way to live," Takuma explains, "but we do take living together seriously. We share the household and finances, a long-term commitment to our business and most importantly a certain common ground in our ideas and beliefs. We know more about each other than about our traditional family members. I am convinced not only that this lifestyle is emerging because of our overpriced cities, but that indeed another type of family is being born."

Choreography of the new family. Shared working and living with small private sleeping capsules.

ニューファミリーのふるまい。仕事や生活のための共有のスペースと、個別の小さなカプセル的寝室がある。

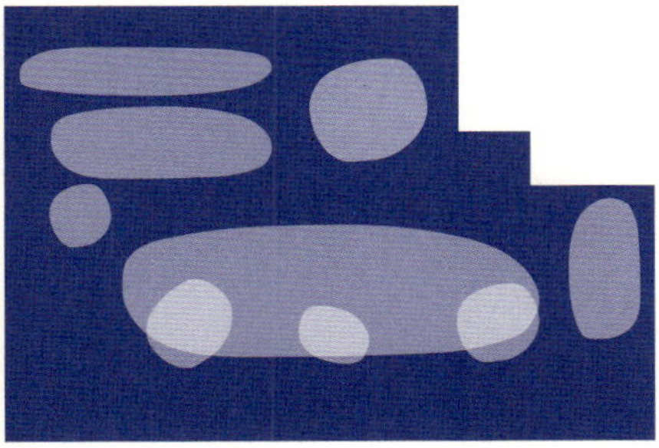

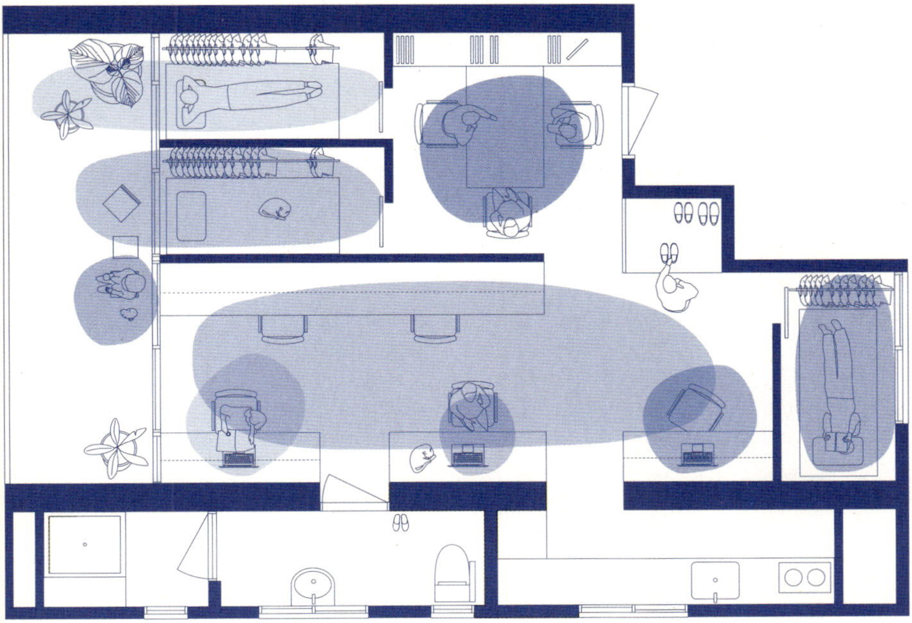

MAPPING KONBINITY

On a quiet evening in a residential Tokyo suburb, the local Lawson is humming with activity. Insects circle the convenience store's roadside sign. Cars and trucks idle in the parking lot. Their drivers slurp noodles, talk on cells phones, and doze after an exhausting day on the job. Half a dozen bicycles hug the store's outer wall. In front of them, a group of young men stand smoking and chatting. A woman, wet, in a loose cotton dress and slippers, scoots past, tossing a small plastic bag into the trash container at the store's entrance before going inside. She joins a clutch of strangers flipping through magazines and manga from the racks along the window.

"Irasshaimase. Konbanwa," two clerks at the counter call out. "Welcome. Good evening." A third clerk chimes in as he emerges through a swinging door with a basket of instant noodles for stocking. Over at the photocopier, a young woman prints photos. Beyond her, in the eat-in corner, a man hunches over his laptop while taking swigs from a bottle of oolong tea. People occupy the aisles. A mother and her son peer into the ice-cream case. An elderly woman fingers packages of breakfast pastries. The basket in the crook of her arm contains a can of cat food and a package of funerary incense. The workman who emerges from the store's bathroom snatches a single serving of sake and a packet of dried squid on his way to the register. He queues behind a woman who is already having a clerk ring up her purchases. With an embarrassed chuckle, she pulls the gas bill she almost forgot from her purse. The clerk scans it with the bar code reader. The woman pays in exact change and wishes him a good night.

KONBINI・コンビニ

Welcome to konbinity—a place of less encumbered attachment and belonging that has reconfigured notions of public space in Japan. Konbini create an "alone together" atmosphere, yet do so without comfortable furniture, low lighting, and customized cappuccinos. For most customers konbini usage is built around short a to pick something up or drop something off. Cafés focuses on coffee and cultivate a customer base through product attention and affect. Konbini, by contrast, seek to be all things to all people. They serve as lunch counters, liquor stores, tobacconists, drug stores, bookstores, newspaper shops, printing and telecommunications kiosks, banks, shipping centers, post offices, bill-collection services, late-night taxi stands, local recycling centers, a branch of city hall, and disaster-relief stations. For most of its users, the konbini is not home, work, or school. Rather, it has been adjusted to maintain a position between such points of commitment and belonging.

「コンビニ」なるものをマッピングする

街角にあるこの場所は何なのか?仕事の後、帰宅する前に、あるいはランチタイムに行く場所。タバコを吸い、漫画を読み、いろいろな料金を支払う場所。あなたが行くあらゆる場所の間のどこかに存在している、このコミュニティは何なのか?

Gavin H. Whitelaw は日本で生活し、仕事をしている社会文化人類学者。日本のコンビニにおける社会的生活や人間文化的エコロジーを研究しており、フィールドワークとして1年間コンビニで働いた。

❶ THE STORE FRONT

The front of the store can appear empty, but return at the right time in the morning, or at lunch, or just after school lets out, or around sundown, and there may be several groups of people milling in front of the store at once. If the konbini has a parking lot, then the number of people may actually be twice what is readily seen. Watch carefully and you will see that the people leaving their cars to go into the store will usually throw something in the trash and recycling bins that flank the door. These receptacles are bane and boon for the store management. They allow the store to remain in the good graces of the local community and city planners, but frequently become the target for people to anonymously dispose of other things: household trash, old car tires, and even murder weapons.

❷ THE MAGAZINE DISPLAY

In a recent poll, 32 percent of people surveyed said they used konbini as a place to read magazines. The magazine rack creates a particular eddy within the social space of the store. Customers are typically permitted to stand and read material for as long as they want. Half a dozen or more people may be seen engaging in such an activity at a given time. Some customers may remain at the rack for close to an hour at a time. The magazine rack is where we find a symbiotic relationship between the konbini and its denizens. Positioned against the store's large plate-glass windows, magazine readers create a living billboard that attracts customers into the store and helps discourage potential criminals from entering the store.

❸ THE BATHROOM

The bathroom adds a more fundamental dimension of convenience to the konbini. New konbini offer separate facilities for women and men. It is not required that people using the washroom buy something from the store, but stores will often request that those availing themselves of the facility check with a clerk at the counter, a additional step that may leave the customer with a slight sense of obligation. Konbini bathrooms are sometimes the places where students will change into suits for a job interview or truck drivers will seek to "wash up" after an overnight in the store's parking lot. Even in the wake of a disaster, konbini will keep their doors open to allow the public access to the toilet.

❹ THE COUNTER

The konbini counter is the main stage for myriads of verbal and non-verbal exchanges between people. Products and services are paid for at the counter. Customer data is collected at the counter's Point of Sales (POS) registers. The counter is where new clerks are broken in and foreign workers get the chance to practice their Japanese. It is also the place where children learn the ritual interactions of commodity exchange. A four-year-old girl on her first errand for a family parts with money at the counter and collects her change. The owner may even put the coins in a plastic bag to ensure they don't get lost on the way home. Counters place clerks on the front line by exposing them to a range of interactions. Most exchanges are rapid and forgettable. Others may be more memorable, accompanied by an interested party's email address or phone number being scribbled on the back of receipt. Then there are the stalkers whose interest triggers staff solidarity and a wall of defense that allows the victim to escape into the backyard until the danger has passed. At worst, clerks can always alert the police using the red button beneath the register.

5 THE BACKYARD

The word, "backyard" is a misnomer. Usually these spaces are cramped and dark, but they offer staff a backstage in which to unwind, eat a meal, check email and even sleep. The backyard is where meetings are held between the store owner and chain-service representatives. It is also the space where interviews with new staff are held.

6 THE WALK-IN COOLER

The walk-in cooler is yet another layer of interiority to the konbini. The walk-in is where workers retreat to when they want to be alone and cool off. The walk-in may serve as the private refrigerator for workers' own food and drink. It can also be the perfect place to observe customers without being seen.

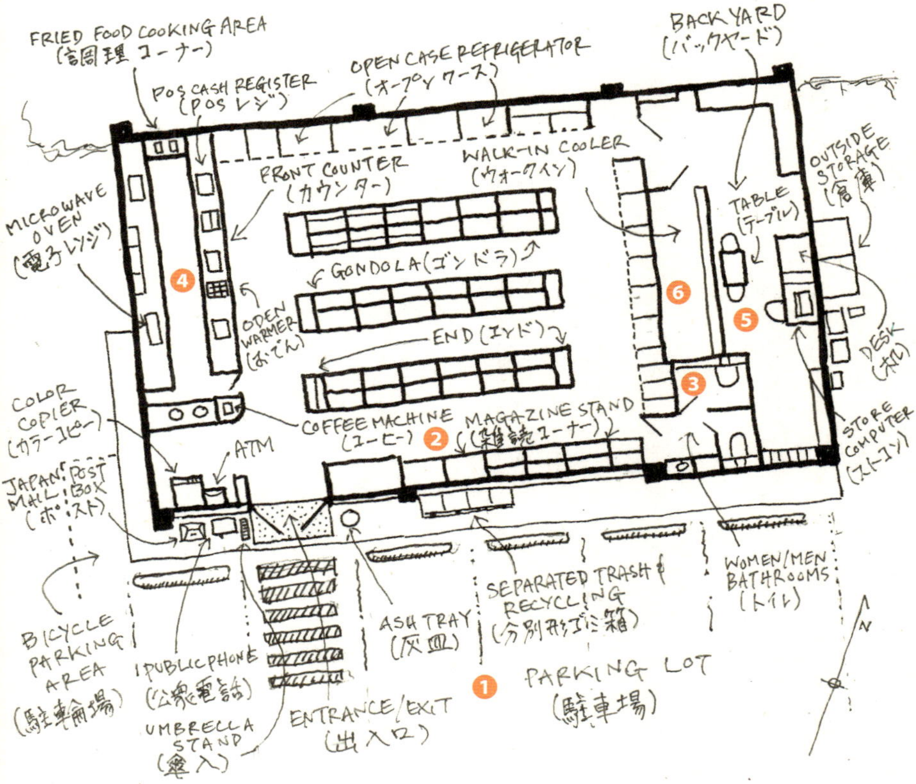

THE SHARED TOWN — TOKYO'S FUTURE

シェア・タウン—東京の未来

日本と東京の人口動向を研究すると、ゆっくりと小家族化が進み、中高年のおひとりさま社会に向かっているのがわかる。この傾向が進むと、家族どうしで助け合って暮らすという、ある意味で日本的なライフスタイルは難しくなる。友人知人、隣人が助け合う形へとライフスタイルも変化せざるをえない。そこで私は近年、他人同士が集まって一つの家に住むシェアハウスに関心を持ち、取材をしてきた。シェアハウスの多様な実践形態を調査するうちに、シェアするという概念を、家を超えて地域や町全体に広げていく必要があることがわかった。このエッセイでは、必ずしも1つ屋根の下には暮らしていないが、リソースをシェアし、ローカルなコミュニティに貢献している例を論じていく。

三浦展は社会デザイン研究者。消費社会、家族、若者、階層、都市などの研究を踏まえ、新しい時代を予測し、社会デザインを提案している。著書に、80万部のベストセラー『下流社会』のほか、『第四の消費』、『郊外・原発・家族』『これからの日本のためにシェアの話をしよう』『東京は郊外から消えていく!』『東京高級住宅地探訪』などがある。

HAGISO

Japan and Tokyo are becoming middle-aged and elderly, single-person societies. Japan's population is getting smaller; it is estimated that its 51.9 million households will decrease by 3.5 million from 2020 to 2035. Over that same period, single-person households will increase from 16.8 million to 18.5 million—nearly 7 million more than the total number of married-couple-with-children households. In the age group of 45 years and over, single-person households will increase from 9.4 million to 13.1 million. In the Tokyo metropolitan area, where the population will also start to decline in the very near future, over-45-single-person households will increase from 1.2 million to 2.0 million. In a certain sense, this will make it harder to maintain the traditional Japanese lifestyle, which is based on family members helping one another out. The lifestyle in Japan will need to change to one in which friends, acquaintances, and neighbors come to one another's aid.

This is why, in the last few years, I have gotten interested in the sheahausu, or "shared house", a house in which several people who would otherwise be strangers live together. From 2005 to 2012 the number of people living in a shared house increased tenfold. In a survey conducted in 2013 by the Building Research Institute, 42 percent of unmarried women living alone aged 20 to 24 and 31 percent of women aged 25 to 29 said they did not mind living in a shared house.

What are the benefits of a shared house? First off, living with other people is enjoyable, and for women especially it provides security in terms of crime prevention. Moreover, since a shared house comes with furniture, appliances, eating utensils and the like, moving is less costly. So a shared house is convenient for the self-employed, people doing temporary work, those who travel for long periods, and even for foreigners. An additional appeal of many of the shared houses is that they are renovated houses with distinctive exteriors and interiors that range from modern to retro to old traditional houses.

The shared house is not only for young people. More and more middle-aged single, divorced, and widowed people, as well as the recently married and people with children, want to live in a shared house. In fact, in the typical Tokyo suburb of Kichijoji there are now shared houses in which elderly couples and young people live together. The elderly members of the shared house are stimulated by the young, while the young acquire wisdom and experience from the elderly. It is a lifestyle that we can expect to increase in popularity in the years ahead.

Home-sharing arrangements—where empty rooms in multi-room homes, occupied by one or two elderly persons, are rented out—are also gradually increasing. Besides rental income, the owner benefits from the home-sharing through the interaction with young people and the creation of a community. Rather than relying on social-welfare programs in the strict sense of the term, where the corporation or the state is the provider, Japan and Tokyo in the years ahead will need to think about creating communities in which citizens can live with people outside their own families at a modest expense, providing help and stimulation to one another.

Still, I am someone who enjoys quietly reading alone. I personally would not want to live in a shared house. At the same time, I think my life is enriched by having some kind of shared component, and I would like to see more lifestyle elements that are shared by the entire community. In other words, I would like to see communities evolve into "shared towns". Sharing a portion of one's time, space, resources, and the like would be easier than living in or managing a share house. Everyone lacks something and everyone has more than enough of something. Someone with a den full of books might open her room as a private library just on Saturdays. A person who has a tearoom he only uses once in a while might loan it out just on Sundays. Someone who loves children might look after someone else's children for a couple of hours while that person goes out to tend to personal business. Loaning out just a little bit of the extra space or resources that we have is how the shared town grows.

Otagai-sama Shokudo, common-meal program.

おたがいさま食堂

おたがいさま食堂は、杉並区で行われている共同食堂プログラムだ。おおよそのメニューは決まっているが、料理を教える人がいるわけではなく、レシピもない。目的はただ「みんなでおいしいご飯をたべること」。作る人・食べる人といった役割をあらかじめ分担しているのではなく、参加者同士がコミュニケーションをとり、それぞれ自分の役割をみつけながらご飯をつくる。

Okatte Nishiogi, a public meal-oriented common space in a family home.

okatteにしおぎ

杉並区にある戸建住宅をリノベーションしてにつくられた、食を中心にしたパブリックコモンスペース。会員制で、平日夜はメンバーが思い思いにご飯を作って食べ、平日の日中や土日はメンバーによるワークショップやイベントが開催される。

Maison-aoki, apartment complex with a common space, shared office and a pop-up grocery store.

メゾン青樹

豊島区にある賃貸マンション。住む人と一緒に選んだ壁紙をオーナー会社負担で貼ってあげることで人気を得た。さらにオーダーメイド賃貸住宅、住民同士が一緒にパーティなどを開けるコモンスペースをマンションの中につくった。
3LDKの部屋は、女性3人が住むシェアハウスにリノベーションした。マンション２階の貸しオフィスはシェアオフィスにリノベーションし、地域のイベント会場としても利用される。

Over the last few years, I have proposed the "comubini" as the nucleus of the shared town. A comubini is not a place of consumption like the convenience stores (kombini) found all over the country. It is a "community convenience place", "comubini" for short, that meets the specific needs of a particular community. Rather than being next to a station or in the entertainment district, a comubini is built in a residential area easily accessed by senior citizens. It has a small shop where people can buy the most basic essentials for daily living as well as a modest restaurant where locals can freely get together, even without a particular occasion for doing so. Solitary people tend to end up eating alone, and for them it serves as a kind of local or simple set-menu restaurant that they can go to whenever they feel like it. And at night it can serve a little alcohol. The restaurant need not be privately operated; it can be managed by local residents or an NPO, for example.

The comubini courtyard has several chairs and tables, where visitors can eat food they buy at the restaurant. Moreover, it is recommended that the comubini have a facility where people can get a massage, receive a basic medical exam via the Internet and a pet-grooming studio. But it should also provide a space for people who can offer a particular service, like a barber, a beautician or a handyman. For a senior citizen changing a light bulb or merely moving something heavy can be arduous. The ability to request handyman services from the comubini at any time would solve general daily living and household problems for residents.

Thus a comubini is not just a place where people can buy things: it is a place that provides the most basic services needed for daily life. It is a place where the old, the young, people living alone and those married with children can gather together to eat, relax, teach, and learn from one another. In the comubini, the "common meal" and "common learning" improve the community's quality of life.

Lately there has been an increase in comubini-like projects. For example, N9.5 Incorporated, a real-estate planning company based in Tokyo's Suginami-ku, has started a common-meal program called Otagai-sama Shokudo. The fact that most of the menu is fixed means that no one supervises its preparation, and there are no recipes either. Its purpose is simple: getting people together to eat good food. The role of each participant in the meal—to cook or to eat—is not decided in advance; instead the participants communicate among one another about who takes which role. For this project they use a kitchen studio in the shopping area, while the neighborhood itself is considered the shared house. The otagaisama shokudo is the common kitchen and community living room of the neighborhood. Participants include everyone—children and adults, people living next to the shopping district and people coming from distant places just to attend the meal. Anyone who applies in advance can take part.

Another example from Suginami-ku started this year is Okatte Nishiogi. It was born out of the idea to create a public meal-oriented common space in a family home. The owner had decided to renovated her single family home into a place where people can get together to eat and prepare meals after her husband had died and her children had set off on their own. People can join through a membership system and are free to prepare and eat whatever they like on weekday evenings, while on weekday afternoons and Saturdays they can hold workshops and other events.

A place like Okatte is not counted as a shared home. Needless to say, people who live in a shared house regularly eat meals with the other people who live there. But in the above examples, the notion of the shared house is expanded to provide the opportunity to share meals with people who live in the surrounding community.

Residents of Maison Aoki picking wallpaper.

メゾン青樹

住む人とオーナー会社（代表・青木純）とデザイナーが一緒になって、壁紙を選ぶ。

Toden Table is a crowd-funded cafetaria where the residents of Maison-Aoki eat together.

都電テーブル

都電テーブルはクラウドファンディングでできた食堂で、一般客はもちろんメゾン青樹の住民たちも、れ仕事帰りなどに子供連れで食事をとれる。

Hagiso is an office, café, a gallery and in the future a check-in point for nearby hotels.

HAGISO

若手建築家の宮崎晃吉がオーナーと出資金を出し合い、台東区・谷中の古いアパートをリノベーションして自分のオフィス、カフェ、貸しギャラリーなどからなるHAGISOをつくった。さらに今彼が考えているのは、近くの、やはり古いアパートをリノベーションしたホテルに客を泊めるというビジネスだ。チェックインはHAGISOで行い、宿泊者の希望に添った谷中の店情報を提供する。ただ宿泊するだけでなく街をたくさん歩いてもらい、入浴は銭湯を使ってもらう。

A larger shared-town project is Maison Aoki. It began with a rental-apartment complex in Tokyo's Toshima-ku. Four years ago, 27 percent of its about 70 units were unoccupied, but today it is a tremendously popular property. The reason for this turnaround is that residents were allowed to choose and install any wallpaper they liked with the consent of the landlord at the expense of landlord, Jun Aoki. Later Aoki built a common space in the complex where residents could gather for parties and other activities. Three-bedroom units were renovated into shared houses designed specifically for a three-person female household. And the unoccupied office space in the complex was renovated into a shared office and is used not only as an office space but also as a location for community events. As a result freelance workers and other working people who reside in the apartment complex use the space as their office. Even Aoki himself has his office in the complex's shared office space, and people can bring their children to the office. Aoki has created a space for children where they play with each other while their parents work. A colleague of Aoki, who runs a grocery store, regularly opens a pop-up store inside the office area where people can buy things to take back home.

Maison Aoki also includes Toden Table, a cafeteria financed through cloud funding. It serves dishes cooked with fresh ingredients supplied directly from farms without using synthetic seasonings. On the way home from work, after they've picked up their kids from daycare, residents have organic and safe food here. This place is popular among working mothers. Housewives living in the apartment can go back to work shortly after they have a baby. Chefs and workers in the kitchen are also women; mothers cook while their kids play in a corner of the cafeteria. It is as if the apartment complex has become a self-contained community. Indeed, Maison Aoki is a community based on a shared-lifestyle model—a "shared town".

Our last example is a true experiment in shared-town design. Its focal point is Hagiso. In the temple district of Yanaka in Tokyo's Taito-ku, Mitsuyoshi Miyazaki—a young architect who started out at the office of Arata Isozaki—renovated an old apartment building. Financed by himself and the building's owner, Miyazaki turned the old apartment building into Hagiso, a place that contains his own office, a café, and a rental gallery. Miyazaki's latest business idea is to make Hagiso a central check-in point for guests staying at various nearby hotels, which are also housed in renovated old apartment buildings. Guests come to Hagiso to check in and receive information of interesting spots and shops in the neighborhood. Many kinds of events that are held in the Yanaka district, including a workshop to create a shakuhachi bamboo flute and play it. Guests are encouraged to walk around in the neighborhood and find something interesting and feel the real charm of Japan. So instead of simply staying at the hotel, guests are encouraged to really walk around the neighborhood and patronize its shops and businesses. For example, hotels do not have a bathroom, so guests are introduced to a nearby public bathhouse (Sento), which is just the kind of thing that a foreign visitor would enjoy. In other words, instead of tearing down and replacing several old apartment buildings, the neighbourhood is being renovated and woven together in the shared framework of a special kind of hotel.

As these examples show, the shared-resource lifestyle is steadily growing in Tokyo as people make use of and renovate all kinds of existing resources. What am I doing to promote the shared lifestyle? I have several thousands of books, so I am loaning some of them to cafés in the neighborhood where I have my office. I have loaned around 300 books on architecture and design to a shared architecture office and café, 200 old magazines to a book café operated by a couple who used to work at a bookshop, and about 100 books on community design and regional planning to a café operated by a bookstore very interested in the topic. Making these books available to others ought to make both the cafes and their customers happier. And since all three shops are within five minutes of my office, it's no trouble to go to one of them to read one of my books if I need to. But the best part of it all is that I can now have a smaller office and save on rent!

Wine
Monte: classic series
Red & White (チリ産)
KAGUA
HAGISO代表、宮崎がデザインした
クラフトビールです。山椒と柚子を使用
した香り豊かなビールです。
ワイングラスでお楽しみ下さい。

HAGISO

日本の人口は既に減少し始めており、2010年時点では5195万世帯だった総世帯数も2020年から2035年にかけて350万世帯ほど減少すると推計されている。しかし一人暮らし世帯は1679万世帯から1846万世帯に増加し、夫婦と子の世帯よりも700万世帯近く多くなる。年齢別では45歳以上の一人暮らし世帯が936万世帯から1308万世帯に増える。東京都でも近いうちに人口が減り始め、45歳以上の一人暮らし世帯は123万世帯から199万世帯に増える。つまり日本も東京も中高年のおひとりさま社会になるのだ。

そうなると、家族どうしで助け合って暮らすという、ある意味で日本的なライフスタイルは難しくなる。友人、知人、近隣住民同士が助け合って暮らすライフスタイルに変えていく必要がある。

そこで私は近年、他人同士が集まって一つの家に住むシェアハウスに関心を持ち、取材をしてきた。2005年から2012年にシェアハウスに住む人の数は10倍に増えた。独立行政法人建築研究所の2013年の調査でも、未婚一人暮らしの20－24才女性の42%、25－29才では31%がシェアハウスに住んでみたいと回答した。

シェアハウスの利点は何か。まず、みんなが一緒に住むから楽しく、特に女性が住む場合、防犯面でも安心感がある。また、家具、家電、食器などが備わっているので引っ越しに伴うコストが少ない。したがって自由業、非正規雇用者、長期出張が多い人、外国人でも住みやすい。さらに、中古住宅をリノベーションしたものが多いため、モダンなものからレトロな古民家まで、外観も内装も個性的である。

若い人だけでなく、中高年の未婚・離別・死別者、あるいは新婚や子どものいる人でもシェアハウスに住みたいという人は増えている。実際、東京の代表的郊外都市吉祥寺には高齢夫婦と若い世代が一緒に住むシェアハウスができた。高齢者は若い人から刺激を得るし、若い人は高齢者から知識と経験を学べる、これからの時代に増えるべき住み方である。

部屋数の多い家に一人か二人で住んでいる高齢者が、空いた部屋を貸しに出すホームシェアという活動も少しずつ増えてきた。オーナーは家賃収入が入るだけでなく、若い人との交流、コミュニティが生まれることがホームシェアのメリットである。

このように、これからの日本および東京は、狭義の福祉政策に依存するのではなく、家族以外の人びとが、あまりお金をかけずに、相互に助け合い、刺激し合いながら暮らすためのコミュニティづくりを考えていくべき時代になっている。

だが、私個人は、シェアハウスに住みたいとは思わない。私は一人静かに本を読む方が好きだからだ。しかし、自分の生活の中に何らかのシェアの要素があることは自分の生活を豊かにすると思っている。だから、街全体にシェアの要素が広がっていくこと、つまり街がシェアタウンになっていくことを私は望んでいる。

また、シェアハウスに住んだり、シェアハウスを経営したりしなくても、時間や空間や資源を部分的にシェアをするほうが、誰でも気軽にできるだろう。

誰もが、何かは足りないが、何かは余っている。書斎に本がたくさんある人は、土曜日だけでいいから書斎を私設図書館として開放したらどうだろう。茶室があるが、たまにしか使わない人は、日曜日だけでいいから茶室を人に貸したらどうだろう。子どもが好きな人は、親が用事を済ましに出かける2、3時間だけ子供を預かったらどうだろう。そういうように、自分が少し余分に持っている空間と資源をちょっとだけ貸し出すことで、シェアタウンが広がっていくはずだ。

シェアタウンの核となるものとして、近年私が提案しているのが「コムビニ」だ。コムビニとは、全国一律の消費空間としてのコンビニエンス・ストアではなく、地域ごとに固有のニーズを満たすコミュニティ・コンビニエンス・プレイス（＝コムビニ）である。

コムビニは、駅前や繁華街にあるのではなく、高齢者が簡単に行けるように、住宅地の中につくられる。日常の最低限の必需品を買える小さな店があり、その他にも特に用事がなくても住民が気軽に集まれる場所にするため簡単な飲食店が併設される。いつも一人で食事をしがちなおひとりさまが、気軽に立ち寄れる地域内の飲食店、簡単な定食屋のたぐいである。夜は少しお酒も出る。飲食店は企業ではなく住民やNPOが経営してもよい。

コムビニの庭にはイスとテーブルがいくつか置いてあり、売っている食品をそこで食べることもできる。さらにマッサージを受ける場所が併設されているとか、インターネットを通じた簡単な診察ができるとか、ペットのトリミングスタジオがあるとか、理髪店、美容室などが出張に来るといったサービスの場所になることも望まれる。

それから便利屋が必要だ。高齢者になると電球を替えるだけでも、ちょっと重い物を動かすのでも一苦労である。だから、家事を含めた日常生活全般の困ったことを解決する便利屋にコムビニからいつでも仕事が頼めるようにしておく。

このようにコムビニは、単に物を買うだけでなく、むしろ生活に必要な最小限のサービスを提供する拠点であり、住民が老いも若きも、一人暮らしも子ども連れも一緒に集まり、一緒に食べ、くつろぎ、教えあい、学びあう場所である。「共食」と「共学」によってコミュニティの質が高まっていくのである。

実際、コムビニ的な活動は増えてきた。まず杉並区の不動産企画会社エヌキューテンゴが始めた「おたがいさま食堂」。おおよそのメニューは決まっているが、料理を教える人がいるわけではない。レシピもない。目的はただ「みんなでおいしいご飯をたべること」。作る人・食べる人といった役割をあらかじめ分担しているのではなく、参加者同士がコミュニケーションをとり、それぞれ自分の役割をみつけながらご飯をつくる。商店街の一角にあるキッチンスタジオを使うが、まちを大きなシェアハウスと見立て、そのハウスの「コモンキッチン」「コミュニティリビング」としておたがいさま食堂はある。参加者は商店街の近隣に暮らす人から、わざわざ遠方から参加する人まで、子どもから大人まで様々。事前申込でだれでも参加できる。

第二に、またもや杉並区だが、「食を中心にしたパブリックコモンスペースをつくる」をコンセプトにした「okatteにしおぎ」が今年できた。ある女性が、ご主人が亡くなり、子どもも独立したあとの戸建て住宅を改修して、みんなが集まって料理をして食べる場所をつくった。会員制で、平日夜はメンバーが思い思いにご飯を作って食べる。平日の日中や土日はメンバーによるワークショップやイベントが開催される。

またokatteでは空いている部屋をシェアハウスとしても貸している。シェアハウスに住んで、同じ住人と食べるのは当たり前だが、地域の住人とも一緒に食べる機会が提供されるわけだ。

次に紹介するのは、東京・豊島区にある賃貸マンション「メゾン青樹」。ここは約70戸のうち27%が4年前まで空き家だったが、今は超人気物件になった。どうしてかというと、住む人と一緒に選んだ壁紙をオーナー会社（代表・青木純）負担で貼ってあげることにしたのだ。

さらに進んで、青木は住民同士が一緒にパーティなどを開けるコモンスペースをマンションの中につくった。3LDKの部屋は女性3人が住むシェアハウスにリノベーションした。マンション2階の貸しオフィスにも空きが出たので、そこをシェアオフィスにリノベーションし、オフィスとしてだけでなく、地域のイベント会場としても利用することにした。すると、マンションの住人でフリーランスの人などがそこで働ける。イベントもできる。青木の事務所もそのシェアオフィスにある。

しかもそのオフィスは、子連れで来てもよい。隣接したスペースには幼児教室も開いた。子どもは子ども同士で遊ばせながら、親が働ける。かつ仲間の食料品店がオフィス内に出店を出すので、そこで買い物をして帰れる。

さらに青木はクラウドファンディングで資金を集めて「都電テーブル」という飲食店もつくった。全国の生産者から新鮮な素材を仕入れ無添加で調理する。仕事帰りに保育園で子どもを引き取って、食堂で安心安全な外食ができる。子育て中のママに人気だ。食堂で働くのも女性たち。マンションに住む主婦は子供を産んだ後、短い時間で社会復帰することも可能だ。食堂の一角で子供を遊ばせながら働くママの姿。まるで賃貸マンションがひとつの街になったかのようである。しかもそれはシェア型ライフスタイルの街、シェアタウンなのだ。

最後に紹介するのはまさにシェアタウンづくりの試み。若い建築家であり磯崎新アトリエ出身の宮崎晃吉が、東京の台東区・谷中という寺町にあった古いアパートをリノベーションした「HAGISO」がその拠点だ。彼は、オーナーと自分とで出資金を出し合い、古いアパートに、自分のオフィス、カフェ、貸しギャラリーなどからなるHAGISOをつくった。さらに今彼が考えているのは、近くの、やはり古いアパートをリノベーションしたホテルに客を泊めるというビジネスだ。チェックインはHAGISOで行い、宿泊者の希望に添った街情報、店情報を提供する。古い日本家屋でのイベントとか、尺八を自分でつくって演奏するワークショップとか、たくさんの活動が谷中界隈では行われているので、それらを紹介するのだ。ただ宿泊するだけでなく街をたくさん歩いてもらい、街の魅力、日本の魅力を体感してもらうのだ。
朝食はHAGISOのカフェでとってもらうので、夕食には希望に合いそうな所を紹介する。ただ宿泊するだけでなく街をたくさん歩いてもらい、店に立ち寄ってもらうのだ。ホテルには風呂がないので、近くの銭湯に入ってもらう。外国人客ならむしろ銭湯を希望するだろう。つまり、古いアパートを壊したり、建て替えたりするのではなく、リノベーションをして、それらをつなぎあわせ、街全体をホテルに見立ててシェアする仕組みを作るのである。

このように、今あるさまざまな資源を活用し、リノベーションし、かつその資源をシェアするライフスタイルが東京でだんだん広がっている。

それで私は何をしているかって？　私は数千冊の蔵書があるから、その一部を自分のオフィスのある街のカフェに貸し出している。建築家のシェアオフィス兼カフェには建築とデザインの本300冊、書店員をやめた男女が経営するブックカフェには古い雑誌のバックナンバー200冊、まちづくりに関心の深い書店が経営するカフェには街づくり関連の本を100冊置いてもらっている。それによってカフェも客も満足度が上がるだろう。その3店がすべて徒歩5分以内にあるから、私は必要があればすぐに読みに行ける。何と言っても私は自分のオフィスの床面積を減らせるから家賃を安くできるのだ！

NEW URBAN COMMONS

Japan is a country undergoing profound social and demographic transformation. During the boom years of the 1980s, a firm belief in unrestrained, perpetual economic growth and material prosperity evolved around mass consumerism. This cozy illusion vanished suddenly with the bursting of Japan's infamous asset price bubble in autumn 1991, leading to economic stagnation and anxiety about the future. The years following the "bubble economy" thus came to be known as the "lost decade(s)".

Such a pervasive sense of crisis and gloom was heightened by other subsequent social developments, such as the growing number of elderly living and—increasingly—dying in solitude, unnoticed by their neighbors (kodokushi), as well as the disintegration of established social institutions and neighborhood communities, and an eroding trust in government and public security.

Successive governments sought to remedy Japan's lingering economic crisis with neoliberal reforms: deregulating the job markets, privatizing public enterprises and encouraging private initiative. Side effects have included has been rising youth unemployment, a widening income gap, growing poverty, and an expansion of precarious, irregular labor. Job uncertainty and stagnating wages have intensified social stress, which has in turn lowered the country's already low birth rate and contributed to other social pathologies.

In 2040, one third of Japan's population will be older than 65 years, and the number of children is in constant decline. At the same time, the country's spiraling debt is likely to cause a further retreat of the welfare state.

新しいアーバン・コモンズ

日本は現在、社会的に、また人口構成の面でも、大きな変容を遂げようとしている。衰退は免れないとする憂鬱な見通しが未だ主流だが、代わりに、はるかにポジティブな読みを行うことも可能だ。未来の住人とともに計画されたコレクティブハウス「かんかん森」、スペースやリソース、さまざまなアクティビティを通して、集団的に自分たちを管理していくという、新しい都市の共有地(アーバン・コモン)の好例である。

Christian Dimmer は東京大学助教(アーバニズム・都市研究)であり、コレクティブハウス「かんかん森」の住人の一人である。

This essay has has appeared partly in: Collective House Kankanmori Residents' Union (Eds.), 'This is a Collective House - 12 Years Collective House Kankanmori, Domesu Publishers, 2014

Children in Kankanmori grow up, sharing many of daily chores that are needed to run a community.
かんかん森の子供たちは、コミュニティの運営に必要な日々の雑事をみんなで分担しながら育っていく。

Growing, preparing and eating together are one important practice at Kankanmori to perpetually renew community ties.

かんかん森では、みんなでいっしょに野菜を育て、食事の準備をし、食べることが、コミュニティの絆を常に新しくしていくうえで重要な活動になっている。ていく。

While this gloomy narrative of Japan's inevitable decline is still prominent, an alternative, far more positive reading is possible: it is the encouraging story of a dawning post-growth society whose seeds we may be seeing in Japan's quickly multiplying new urban commons. It is a story of empowerment, of the careful treatment of natural resources, of a newly awakening do-it-yourself spirit, of creative problem solving, and of sharing precious time, space, and goods.

According to Carl Cassegård, empowerment "occurs when people regain the sense that their actions and opinions matter and that they have the power to influence things in society which they deem to be important."[77] Often unaware of the political implications of providing new social models, the producers of these new urban commons nevertheless engage in prefigurative politics. When people experiment with new forms of social relations, decision-making, culture and human experience that are beyond the state and the logic of the market, they prefigure a more inclusive, just, and sustainable future society. In Japan's new urban commons, the word politics is hardly ever mentioned, and the old ideological thinking of the past has given way to a fresh, healthy, and collaborative pragmatism.

While the old, growth-obsessed Japan of the 1980s had become synonymous with an insatiable hunger for individualized consumerism and the commodification of every aspect of life, the recent social transformations have given rise to a new appreciation of community, sociability, and the cultivation of practical skills. Indeed, young and older people today seem to seek active authorship of their lives—less inclined to sacrifice personal fulfillment to the service of one's company, as previous generations had dutifully done. Life is now seen as a perishable and precious resource that is better spent on socially conscious, meaningful projects.

Superficially, Tokyo's new urban commons can be interpreted as civil society's response to growing social problems and an eroding welfare state that doesn't want to, or no longer can, take care of its citizens. Beyond their obvious significance, these evolving new commons also reflect a profound change of values. Rather than being just a reaction to the threats of poverty, uncertainty and isolation, these projects show that well-educated, motivated individuals with high levels of social capital enrich their personal lives, seek happiness and contribute to the formation of new communities on a local level.

The "producers" of these new community spaces, often ordinary people, pragmatically responded to concrete issues and real problems; very few initially aiming at changing the broader society. New forms of collective living seek to reconnect the young and the old; co-working spaces create new ecosystems in which a variety of creatives from diverse backgrounds stimulate innovation; community cafés provide daycare for children, social contacts for elderlies, or multi-functional spaces for everyone; adventure playgrounds carve out an experience of nature for city children within otherwise over-regulated public parks; artists open their ateliers to take part in community-revitalization projects; farmer markets sell fresh and healthy agricultural produce and reconnect urban consumers and rural producers. Out of this new desire for personal empowerment and creative problem solving, communities of interest are evolving around Japan's new urban commons, almost as a by-product.

Planned together by all future residents, Kankan Mori is a prime example of such a new urban common. It took over one year of careful preparation with dozens of workshops to design the physical configuration, and to develop a differentiated program that would ensure that residents would be able to live a fulfilled community life, without compromising individual privacy or personal space.

For David Harvey, a common is not simply a particular thing or place but "an unstable and malleable *social relation* between a particular self-defined social group" and those aspects

Children grow up in an extended family and regular interact with people of different ages and walks of life.
子供たちは拡大家族の中で育ち、さまざまな年齢、背景を持つ人々と交流しながら育っていく。

The common meal is one of the central features of the intergenerational community Kankanmori.
かんかん森の世代を超えたコミュニティにとって、コモンミールは中心的な存在。

of its social and physical environment that the members themselves consider central to the livelihood of their common pursuit.[78] The process of commoning is then the practice of continuously renewing these social relations, of negotiating the rules for the use of common recourses and for solving conflicts.

Kankan Mori and its diverse residents form such a self-defined community. The residents not only share ample common resources—such as a shared office, a communal kitchen, a living room, two garden terraces, a laundry room, and a wood workshop—but they also engage in diverse commoning activities in order to collectively manage these resources.

A pivotal aspect of Kankan Mori's community life is the practice of common meals. Once a month, every adult resident engages in the preparation of a communal meal and, while eating together, people of all ages and walks of life share space and time together; they reaffirm the diversity of contemporary Japanese society, and practice civility in the common.

This diversity is also important for the upbringing of creative, happy and apt children, something particular crucial in Japan, where parents tend to be very focused on their own children, and where kids are often given over to state-owned or private institutions that submit them to a strictly structured and highly regulated education. Children tend to grow up among peers of the same age, and, as tight-knit neighborhood communities and extended families are a thing of the past, they are rarely exposed to other groups and views in society.

A common is never stable but constantly emerging. Because the number of children has sharply risen in the last years, new rules have to be negotiated that harmonize the divergent demands of a growing number of children with those of elderly residents and other families in need of peace and quiet. At the same time, a new support system has evolved through which residents with time at their disposal offer to care of the children of working parents, outside of the public daycare hours, thus allowing for a more flexible work-life balance.

How Kankan Mori and the other of Japan's exciting social experiments will develop in the future remains to be seen. Commoning is an open-ended, contingent process that always entails the risk of failure. Contrary to many bleak visions of its future, however, Japan is moving forward, if only in small but forceful steps.

The garden terrace of Kankan Mori.
かんかん森のコモンテラス。

Kankan Mori's common meals.
かんかん森のコモンミール。

INVITATION / お誘い

CLOSE TO HOME

SHIBAURA HOUSE
3-15-4 Shibaura, Minato-Ku, Tokyo
108-0023 Japan
Tel +81-3-5419-6446
support@kohkoku.co.jp
www.shibaurahouse.jp

Let us tell you about a special place in Tokyo that has grown dear to us since we first started coming to Tokyo in 2012. It is seven stories tall, light, translucent and white. At night it shines like a giant lampoon, a beacon calling in the night. The architecture is very different from the surrounding buildings, that are bulky, tiled closed volumes. From the other side of the street you can literally see everything that goes on inside. The activities inside are on display, tempting you to come inside and participate. This doesn't only occur when it's dark, also during the day the large open space with trees, picnic tables, a bar and a little library is buzzing with activity. All visible, the only thing separating you from the action is glass sheet.

This place is called SHIBAURA HOUSE and it offers a public space, a kind of village square to the Shibaura neighbourhood, Tokyo and the World. Salary men, mothers with children and the elderly, come here to have their lunch, chat, play and read. And for international designers, artist and other creatives it is a foothold from where to venture into the city to explore, research and develop their projects.

But SHIBAURA HOUSE is more than just a place to meet. They form a bridgehead for international collaboration between Japan and the rest of the world. For the outsider, not speaking the language, and unaccustomed to local conventions Japan (like us), as for the insiders interested in expanding their horizons beyond Japan. SHIBAURA HOUSE was our first totem in Tokyo, a thing we could connect and attach to. A place that made us feel at home, we kept coming back to, and from where we felt confident enough to go on adventures. The fact that this book exists in the form you have in your hands now, is the result of their collaboration and support.

So to good Japanese custom with a straight-forward Dutch twist, we would like to introduce you to SHIBAURA HOUSE, and to their lovely staff and director, Mr. Ito. Send them an email, drop them a line, or give them a call. Tell them about your project. We're sure you'll get by with a little help from our friends, and that this house in Shibaura will soon feel close to home.

わが家のような居場所

2012年に東京を訪ねるようになってから、私たちにとって大切な場所となっていった、東京にある特別な所を紹介しよう。それは7層から成る、とても背が高く軽やかで、透明で白い建物。夜には巨大なランプのように輝き、それは夜に光を放つ灯台のよう。周辺にある厚ぼったくタイルで覆われた閉鎖的な建物とは違い異彩を放つ。向かいの道からは、文字通り中の様子が丸見えだ。建物の中で起きていることが、ディスプレーされていかのように、見る者を招き入れている。これは夜だけでの話ではない。日中でも、植栽、ピクニックテーブル、バーカウンターや小さな図書館がある広く開放的なスペースは、人々の活気で満ち溢れている。全てが見え、中で起きていることと外を隔てているものはガラスだけだ。

ここはSHIBAURA HOUSE。芝浦界隈、東京、そして世界をつなぐ、村の広場のようなパブリックスペースだ。サラリーマン、子連れのお母さん、お年寄りが集い、ランチをしたり、おしゃべりをしたり、遊んだり、読書をしている。そして、国際的なデザイナーやアーティストなどクリエイターたちにとっては、都市を探索し、リサーチを行い、プロジェクトを展開するための足がかりとなる場所だ。

だけど、SHIBAURA HOUSEは出会いの場にとどまらない。日本と海外との国際的なコラボレーションの橋渡しをする。私たちのように言葉が話せず、地元の習慣になれない外国人のために。そして、国を超えて可能性を広げたいと思っている日本人のために。SHIBAURA HOUSEは関わりを持つことのできる、私たちにとって最初の東京のトーテムポールだった。私たちが落ち着くことができ、出かけても戻れる安心感を与えてくれるところ。今あなたがこの本を手に取っているのも、SHIBAURA HOUSEとのコラボレーションとサポートがあったから。

ということで、皆さまに、SHIBAURA HOUSEとその素晴らしいスタッフ、そしてディレクターの伊東さんを紹介する。日本の慣習にならいつつ、オランダ人のストレートさをもって。ぜひメールをしたり、声を掛けたり、電話をしてほしい。あなたが抱えているプロジェクトのことを話してみてほしい。きっと私たちの友達が手を貸してくれるはず。そして間もなく、この芝浦にある家が身近な場所に感じられるようになるだろう。

ENDNOTES / 注釈

CONVERSATIONS IN A TEASHOP
WILLEMIEN DORRESTEIJN

1. Sorensen, A., 'Neighborhood Streets as Meaningful Spaces: Claiming Rights to Shared Spaces in Tokyo', *City & Society* 21-2 (2009) 207-229.
2. Wissink, B. and Hazelzet, A., 'Social Networks in Neighbourhood Tokyo', *Urban Studies* 49-7 (2011) 1527-1548
3. Sorensen, A., 'Liveable Cities in Japan: Population ageing and decline as vectors of change', *International Planning Studies* 11-3/4 (2007) 225-242

THE CITY OF CHILDREN
CHRIS BERTHELSEN

4. Superstudio and The Moriyama Editors Studio, 'Superstudio & Radicals. Tokyo', *Japan Interior Inc.* (1982) 52.
5. Tuan, Y., *Space and Place: The Perspective of Experience* (Minneapolis and London 1977) 10-11.
6. Ward, C., *The Child in the City* (New York 1979) 27.
7. Tuan, *Space and Place*, 31-33.
8. Masten, A, 'Ordinary magic'. *This Emotional Life* (2012). http://www.pbs.org/thisemotionallife/blogs/ordinary-magic
9. Gill, T., 'Celebrating ordinary magic and everyday adventure', *Rethinking Childhood* (2012) http://rethinkingchildhood.com/2012/04/26/everyday-adventures/
10. Gaarder, J., *Sophie's World* (New York 1994) 15-16.
11. Certeau, M., *The Practice of Everyday Life* (Berkely, Los Angeles and London 1984).
12. Ward, *The Child in the City* 27.
13. Ibidem, 94.
14. Ibidem, 88.

THE EMPTY SIGN
ANNEKE ABHELAKH

15. Barthes, R., *Empire of Signs* (New York 1970).
16. White, E., 'From Albert Camus to Roland Barthes', *The New York Times, Sunday Book Review* (12-9-1982) http://www.nytimes.com/books/97/09/14/reviews/1419.html

CITY BEYOND TIME
JORIS BERKHOUT

17. Berque, A., Japan: *Cities and Social Bonds* (Paris 1993).
18. Maki, F., *Nurturing Dreams* (Cambridge 2008) 153-162.
19. Sorensen, A., *The Making of Urban Japan: Cities and planning from Edo to the twenty-first century* (London 2002).

THE NAKED NEIGHBORHOOD: EXPLORING THE METROPOLITAN BATHSCAPE
GREG DVORAK

20. Clark, S., Japan, *A View from the Bath* (Honolulu 1994) 47.
21. Some artists, such as Nagashima Morio, are known primarily for their reputation of painting sento walls. www.morionakajima.com

DOCUMENTARIANS OF CHANGE
DAPHNE MOHAJER VA PESARAN

22. Kon, W., *Ginzagai Fuzoku* (Tokyo 1925).
23. Aoki, S. *FRUiTS* I (Tokyo 1996) 19.
24. *Kon Wajiro Retrospective*. National Museum of Ethnology (Tokyo 2011).p
25. Usui, K., *Marketing and Consumption in Modern Japan* (London 2014).
26. Mansfield, S., *Tokyo a Cultural History* (New York 2009)
27. Benjamin, W. *The Work of Art in the Age of Mechanical Reproduction* (London 2008).
28. Interviews with Aoki, S. by Mohajer Va Pesaran, D. (2012-2014).
29. Godoy, T., *Style Deficit Disorder: Harajuku Street Fashion* (Tokyo and San Francisco 2007).
30. Interviews with Aoki, S. by Mohajer Va Pesaran, D. (2012-2014).
31. Saxonhouse, G. and Stern, R., *Japan's Lost Decade: Origins, Consequences and Prospects for Recovery* (New York 2004).
32. Wood, C., *The Bubble Economy: Japan's Extraordinary Speculative Boom of the '80s and the Dramatic Bust of the '90s* (2005)
33. Matsui, M., *The Age of Micropop: The New Generation of Japanese Artists* (Tokyo 2007).
34. Kinsella, S., 'Cuties in Japan.' in Moeran, B. and Scov, L., ed., *Women, Media and Consumption in Japan* (Honolulu 1995).
35. Aoki, S. *FRUiTS* (London 2001).
36. Johnson, G., and Okazaki, M., *Kawaii: Japan's Culture of Cute* (New York 2013).
37. Nichols, B., *Introduction to Documentary* (Bloomington 2001)
38. Interviews with Aoki, S. by Mohajer Va Pesaran, D. (2012-2014).
39. Halbwachs, M., *On Collective Memory* (Chicago 1992).
40. Ibidem.
41. Kinsella, S., 'Cuties in Japan.' in Moeran, B. and Scov, L., ed., *Women, Media and Consumption in Japan* (Honolulu 1995).

TIME IN THE CITY OF TEMPORAL MONUMENTS
JULIAN WORRALL

42. Statistics Division, Bureau of General Affairs, Tokyo Metropolitan Government (2011).
43. Benjamin, W., edited by Peter Demetz, *Reflections: Essays, Aphorisms, Autobiographical Writings* (New York 1986) 162.

IN THE ARENA OF ALTERNATIVE MODERNITIES
JULIAN WORRALL

44. Baudelaire, C., *The Painter of Modern Life* (1863).
45. Marx, K., *The Communist Manifesto* (1848).
46. Okakura, K., *The ideals of the east, with special reference to the art of Japan* (New York 1904) 8.
47. Taut, B., *Fundamentals of Japanese Architecture* (Tokyo 1937) 20.
48. Gibson, W., 'Modern Boys and Mobile Girls.', *The Observer* (2001).
49. Isozaki's interpretation of *"ma" was presented in the exhibition Ma: Space-Time in Japan* in various cities around the world between 1978 and 1980.
50. Barthes, R., *Empire of Signs* (New York 1970) 3-4.
51. Benjamin, W., *Theses on the Philosophy of History* (1938).

HERA SHIBORI
FRITZI PONSE

52. Whittaker, D.H., *Small Firms in the Japanese Economy* (1997).
53. Sennet, R., *The Craftman* (New Haven and London 2008).

LOVE OF NATURE
ANNA BERKHOF

54. Puck Brecher, W., 'An investigation of Japan's relation to nature and environment', *Japanese Studies* 12-12 (New York 2000) 72.
55. Rots, A., *Forests of the Gods: Shinto, Nature, and Sacred Space in Contemporary Japan* (Oslo 2013) 109-110.
56. Kalland, A. and Asquith, P., 'Japanese Perceptions of Nature. Ideals and Illusions', in ibidem *Japanese Images of Nature. Cultural Perspectives* (London and New York 1997) 15.
57. Rots, *Forests of the Gods* 123.

THE SEA WE WOULD LIKE TO SEE
MANAR MOURSI

58. Zhongjie, Lin., *Kenzo Tange and the Metabolist Movement: Urban Utopias of Modern Japan* (New York 2010) 110.
59. Zhongjie, Lin., *Kenzo Tange and the Metabolist Movement* 111.

FEELING AT HOME IN TOKYO
ANNA BERKHOF

60. Daniels, I., *The Japanese House: Material Culture in the Modern Home* (New York 2010) 75.
61. Jonas, M.C., 'Private use of public open space in Tokyo A study of the hybrid landscape of Tokyo's informal gardens', *Journal of Landscape Architecture* 2-2 (2007).
62. Graafland, A., *The socius of architecture: Amsterdam, Tokyo, New York* (Rotterdam 2000) 122.
63. Krusche, J. and Roost, F., *Tokyo. Die Strasse als gelebter raum* (Zurich 2010) 33.
64. Ronald, R., Alexy, A., *Home and Family in Japan: Continuity and Transformation* (New York 2011) 175-176.
65. Daniels, *The Japanese House* 27-29.
66. Ronald, R., Alexy, A., *Home and Family in Japan* 180.
67. Ibidem, 190.
68. Daniels, *The Japanese House* 55.

TOKYO HOMES
MAREN GODZIK

69. Takeshi, H., *Danchi no kukan seijigaku* (Tokyo 2012).
70. Nishikawa, Y., *Sumai to kazoku o meguru monogatari: Otoko no ie onna no ie seibetsu no nai heya* (Tokyo 2004).
71. Hirayama, Y., *Jutaku seisaku no doko ga mondai ka: Mochiie shakai no tsugi o tenbosuru* (Tokyo 2009).

SINGLE LADIES
TOMOKO KUBO

72. Yabe, N., 'Population recovery in inner Tokyo in the late 1990s: a questionnaire survey in Minato Ward.', *Geographical Review of Japan* 55 (2003) 277-292.
73. *Population Census of Japan 2010*. Statistics Bureau of Japan.
74. Kubo, T. and Yui, Y., 'Diversification of the condominium supply in central Tokyo: Supply strategies of 'compact' condominiums.', *Geographical Review of Japan* 84 (2011) 460-472.
75. Yui, Y., 'Housing purchase by single women in Tokyo Metropolitan region.', *Bulletin of the Graduate School of Education, Hiroshima Univ. Part. II, Arts and Science Education* 48 (2000) 37-46.
76. Yui, Y., 'Housing purchase by single women in Tokyo.', *Quarterly Journal of Geography* 55 (2003) 143-161.

NEW URBAN COMMONS
CHRISTIAN DIMMER

77. Cassegård, C., 'Play and Empowerment: The Role of Alternative Space in Social Movements.', *Japanese Studies* (2012). http://www.japanesestudies.org.uk/ejcjs/vol12/iss1/cassegard.html
78. Harvey, D., *Rebel Cities: From the Right to the City to the Urban Revolution* (New York and London 2013).

Unless mentioned otherwise all images in this volume are owned or made by the authors, or used by the authors with permission from the owners.

INTRODUCTION

2-5	Jasper van den Berg
4-7	Cecilia Hendrikx
8-9	Jeptha Dullaart
10-15	Edwin Gardner
18	Jacqueline Hadel
22	Edwin Gardner

CHAPTER 0,5 / FIND YOURSELF

28-29	Jasper van den Berg, Edwin Gardner
30-31	Edwin Gardner
32,34-35	Aukje Dekker
42-43	Edwin Gardner
52, 54-57	Sabine Lubbe Bakker

CHAPTER 1 / WALK THE LAND

60-61	Edwin Gardner
62 top left	Elmimmo (Flickr-user: elmimmo)
62-63	Edwin Gardner
78-83	All topographic maps are the contemporary maps illustrated by Kashmir 3D using the digital maps of 250m-grid (Elevation), 10m-grid (Elevation of Active Volcanos) and 5m-grid (Elevation) from Geographical Survey Institute Japan, and the fundamental geospatial data 5m-grid fromWater Geographical Survey Institute Japan and Water and Disaster Management Bureau, Ministry of Land, Infrastructure, Transport and Tourism. The coastline and routes of each period are added by the author.
107	Forward Stroke Inc.

CHAPTER 2 / FOLLOW THE RHYTHM

120-122	Edwin Gardner
123	Jeptha Dullaart
124	Courtesy of Asahi Shimbun
136	Screenshot Thermae Romae App
142-143	Japón Entres Amigos (Flickr-user: alfonso1987)
145	Courtesy of National Museum of Ethnology, Japan 2011
147, 149	Courtesy of Aoki Shoichi, 1996

CHAPTER 3 / CHOOSE YOUR CITY

166-169	Edwin Gardner
170, 172	Old Tokyo, Vintage Postcard Museum, www.oldtokyo.com
173	Urban Simulation Team www.ust.ucla.edu/ustweb/Projects/Columbian_Expo/38_JapanesePav_crop.htm
174	Wikimedia Commons user: Kirakirameister
175	Courtesy of Warner Brothers
187	Jasper van den Berg
189	Tim Adams (Flickr-user:36217981@N02)
211	Gabrielle, illostrophy.com
221	Anna Berkhof
222	Anna Berkhof
223	Cameron Allen McKean
227	Courtesy Kiyonori Kikutake

CHAPTER 4 / MAKE YOURSELF AT HOME

234-237	Edwin Gardner
242	Kimon Berlin (Flick-user: kimon)
249 bottom	Ogino Taro
290 middle	Daisuke Kurihara
299-303	Michiko Matsumoto
304	Forward Stroke Inc.

CONTRIBUTORS / 寄稿者

Tokyo Totem is a co-creation by the following people:

Anna Berkhof is an architecture and landscape historian and photographer.

Anneke Abhelakh is a Balsthal(CH) based architecture and design curator, wanderer and writer.

Arne Hendriks is a wanderer between the world's of art, science, speculative design and radical ecology.

Arthur van Beek is a visual artist, graphic designer and co-founder of the Eddie the Eagle Museum in Amsterdam.

Atsushi Miura is a researcher of social design.

Aukje Dekker is a visual artist and co-founder and director of the Eddie the Eagle Museum in Amsterdam.

Bastian Boss is a service designer, social entrepreneur and loves to ride his bicycle.

Cameron Allan McKean is a journalist, photographer and romantic geographer.

Charlotte van Zanten is a fiction writer and cultural entrepreneur.

Chris Berthelsen researches creative climates for cities, organizations and humans.

Christiaan Fruneaux is a writer, traveler and a co-founder of Monnik.

Christian Dimmer is an assistant professor for urbanism and urban studies at the University of Tokyo and a resident of Kankan Mori.

Daniel Ruigrok is an urban designer, co-founder of Elberfeld and a fan of the French comic artist Moebius.

Daphne Mohajer va Pesaran is a fashion designer, trend forecaster and lecturer in Tokyo.

David Bauer is someone who would rather walk than work.

David Labi is a filmmaker.

David Orkand is an architect who studied, lived and worked in Tokyo for four years.

Edwin Gardner is an architect, researcher and a co-founder of Monnik.

Fritzi Ponse writes and teaches about design cultures and is interested in things that look mechanically produced but are made by hand.

Gabriel Verret is an architect that studied in Paris and Tokyo.

Gavin H. Whitelaw is a sociocultural anthropologist living and working in Japan.

Greg Dvorak is a writer, photographer, and associate professor of Pacific and Asian cultural histories, based at Hitotsubashi University.

Inara Nevskaya works as an architect with DUS architects in Amsterdam.

Jan Rothuizen is a visual artist.

Jasper van den Berg is an artist, designer, husband and a father of three, who is building his own house.

Jephta Dullaart is an expert on urban heritage and founder of Het Erfgoedkabinet.

Jonathan M. Hall is a California-based writer and scholar of experimental media.

Joris Berkhout is an architect working on global business development at a Japanese real estate developer.

Julian Worrall is an architect and writer who divides his time between Tokyo and Adelaide, where he teaches architecture at the University of Adelaide.

Kohei Fukazawa is an editor.

Maiko Arrieta Aoki grew up in Spain and Japan, and is studying in Tokyo to become a cook.

Manar Moursi is an architect/artist and she is the founder and principal of Studio Meem in Cairo.

Mara Duer is an Argentine sociologist, with a master from the International Christian University in Tokyo, Japan and currently doing a PhD at Warwick University, UK.

Maren Godzik is an associate professor at Fukuoka University.

Niklas Fanelsa is an architect and urban flaneur that lived and studied in Tokyo.

Norihisa Minagawa is the president of the Tokyo Urban Basin Society.

Thijs Middeldorp is one of the partners in Partizan Publik and clerk of The Parliament of Things.

The Pink Pony Express is a design collective, based in Amsterdam.

Thekla Boven is an architect conducting research on rural cultural revitalization strategies.

Tomoko Kubo is an urban geographer and an assistant professor in Gifu University.

Will Robinson is an artist living and working in Tokyo for the past six years.

Willemien Dorresteijn is a teacher and a researcher at the University of Applied Sciences of Amsterdam.

Yasutaka Yoshimura an architect and urban designer based in Tokyo, Japan.

Yi Zhang is a Chinese artist and interactive designer who lives in Los Angeles.

COLOPHON

Editors in chief
Edwin Gardner
Christiaan Fruneaux

Editors Japanese
Shinya Takagi
Ryoko Kozono

Copy editor English
Daniela Franca Joffe

Translation from English to Japanese
Junko Kawakami; Summaries, Captions, Dear reader (Introduction)

Translation from Japanese to English
Kei Benger translated *The Formation of Tokyo –Topography and History, Tokyo Jisou Maps, Deciphering Tokyo through its SURIBACHI Topography + A Recommended Tour of Roppongi's Uneven Topography, Super Legal Buildings* Glenn Rich and Junko Kawakami translated *The Shared Town – Tokyo's Future*.

Graphic design
Jasper van den Berg
(Studio Rooiejas)

Special thanks
Vincent Schippers
Klara van Duijkeren
Bas Valckx
Masaru Ito
Miho Shimizu
Kanako Iwanaka
Haruka Yokokawa
Yama Yuki
Anneke Beerkens
Bunka Gakuen University
Partizan Publik
Marc Wesseling
Trainspot
Darko Radovic
Kumi Aizawa
Cameron Allen McKean
Daphne Mohajer Va Pesaran
Christian Dimmer
Shokokusha Publishing
Jiro Motonaga
Ayumi Higuchi
Adam Rakestraw

Publisher
Flick Studio
Akasaka 6-6-28-6B, Minato-ku,Tokyo 107-0052, Japan
Phone: +81-3-6229-1501 / Fax: +81-3-6229-1502
www.flickstudio.jp

Co-publisher
Monnik
Tolhuisweg 1, 1031CL Amsterdam
info@monnik.org / www.monnik.org

Printed in Japan by
Fujiwara Printing

Distributor international
IDEA Books
www.ideabooks.nl

Distributor Japan
TSUBAME BOOK DISTRIBUTOR

Supported by

creative industries fund NL

JAPANFOUNDATION

Kingdom of the Netherlands

SHIBAURA HOUSE

City of Amsterdam

Fifth print, June 2019
Fourth print, November 2017
Third print, November 2016
Second print, December, 2015
First published on October 30, 2015

www.tokyototem.jp

ISBN:978-4-904894-28-6

THE GUIDE PROJECT

This book did not appear out of thin air. The move from its conceptualization to its fruition took about four years. In 2011 we, together with Vincent Schipper, who had lived in Tokyo for a couple of years, decided that it would be really nice if we could make a guide that allowed us to experience Tokyo, the biggest metropolis in the world, in a more in-depth and subjective manner. We envisioned a guidebook that could somehow help the reader transform this enormous urban space into a meaningful place, and that could direct us past the exotic and beyond the spectacle.

In different collaborative constellations, working with Christian Ernsten, Joost Janmaat, Rani al Rajji and many, many others, we have produced alternative guidebooks before—one on Beirut, one on Amsterdam and recently one on Warsaw. These guidebooks were partly based on workshops where we invited architects, artists, writers, designers and other urban explorers to co-create a guide with us. Not all contributors to the guides were involved in the workshops though, some became involved afterwards. The workshops were just the beginning of the guide-making process. The results of all our collective efforts became *Beyroutes* (Archis 2010), *Mokum* (Archis 2011) and *The Make Yourself at Home Guide to Warsaw* (Centrum Sztuki Współczesnej Zamek Ujazdowski 2015).

In November 2012 we organized the Still City workshop in Tokyo's SHIBAURA HOUSE. During the workshop we invited a diverse local and international group of makers, designers and thinkers to co-create this guide with us. We asked them to look through the lenses of 'growth' and 'stillness' at this city and translate their findings into a contribution for the guide. These lenses, although abstract, initially made sense to us. Tokyo was both the biggest city in the world and the capital of a graying nation that had experienced economic zero-growth for almost two decades. Aware that the human population and its produce couldn't grow indefinitely, we hoped that Tokyo could somehow provide hints about what a post-growth society could look like. How-ever, after we read and looked at all the contributions and examined our own questions and experiences, we discovered that the book we wanted to make actually emerged from another central question: How to feel at home in a massive city like Tokyo?

Exactly three years, to the day, after the Still City workshop kicked off on the 30th October 2012, Tokyo Totem will hit the bookstands on the 30th October 2015.

Between the workshop and this book launch, the coalition changed again. Vincent Schipper, who guided us through his Tokyo, left us to successfully found an art residency in Kama City in Kyushu, Japan. This book is also his brainchild and we are very much indebted to his efforts. On the other hand our team was strengthened by graphic designer Jasper van den Berg, also part of the Still City workshop, and who joined us in making this book a reality.

ガイドプロジェクト

この本は構想から4年を費やして完成したものだ。始まりは2011年。我々は東京に2、3年住んでいた男、Vincent Schipperとともに、メトロポリス東京をもっと自由に、主観的に体験できるような、ある種のガイドブックをつくりたいと心に想い描いていた。それは、読者がこの茣とした都会に意味を見出せるような、そしてよくある異国情緒やスペクタクル表現を超えたような本だ。

しかし我々は、その前にベイルートとアムステルダム、最近ではワルシャワの本を、Christian Ernsten、Joost Janmaat、Rani al Rajji、その他大勢のコラボレーターとともに出版した。いずれの本も建築家、アーティスト、ライター、デザイナー、リサーチャーらに集まってもらったワークショップを元にしている。ワークショップは、ガイドブックづくりの始まりに過ぎない。そうしてできたのが『Beyroutes』(2010)と『Mokum』(2011)、『The Make Yourself at Home Guide to Warsaw』(2015) だ。

そして2012年11月、我々は再びこの仕掛けを実現させることができた。東京「SHIBAURA HOUSE」での「静止都市(Still City)」ワークショップである。国内外からアーティスト、デザイナー、作家に集まってもらったこのワークショップでは、参加者に次の依頼をした。東京を「成長」(growth)と「静止」(stillness)という観点から見ること、そしてそこで発見したことを出版のために寄稿すること。ふたつの観点は抽象的だが非常に意味のあるものだ。東京は世界最大の都市であると同時に、この二十年間経済のゼロ成長を続けている熟年国家でもある。世界は人口や生産力がいつまでも成長することはないとわかってきた今、東京にこそポスト成長社会の姿を示すヒントがあるのではないかと考えている。しかしすべての寄稿を読み、これまでの見聞を整理した結果、我々がつくりたかったこの本には、別の中心的なテーマも生まれつつあることを発見した。それは「東京のような巨大都市で、どうしたらアット・ホームな状況を生み出せるのか?」というものだった。

「静止都市」ワークショップのキックオフがあった2012年10月30日からちょうど3年後の、2015年10月30日、その書籍『トーキョー・トーテム』が刊行される運びとなった。

この3年で制作体制も変わった。我々に東京を案内してくれたVincent Schipperはアートレジデンスのプログラムを見つけて九州の嘉麻市へ移った。この本は彼のアイディアから生まれたものでもあり、彼の努力に負うところが大きい。彼は去ったが、我々制作チームは、グラフィックデザイナーのJasper van den Bergや「静止都市」ワークショップの参加者、そしてこの本づくりのために新たに参加してくれた人たちによって、強化されてきたのだった。

Tokyo is a dense city, there seem to be no space for expansion, no more space for life. But this is actually not true, there is lots of space, just look at the city in a different way: the typographical way.

By looking at a letter's negative space a typographer defines the contour and shape of the character. To be able to see what's right and wrong about the letter, typographer's use an old trick. Turning the character upside down.

THIS SIDE UP

こちら側を上に

東京は密度の高い都市であり、拡大の余地もなければ、生命が育まれる場所ももはやないように見える。しかし、実際はそうではない。違った視点、タイポグラフィーという視点で東京という都市を眺めてみれば、たくさんの空間が存在している。

タイポグラファーは、余白を見ながら文字の曲線や形を決定していく。文字が間違いなく正しく表現されているかどうかを見るために、タイポグラファーが昔から使っている方法がある。逆さまにして見てみる、という方法だ。

Jasper van den Berg はアーティスト、デザイナー。2012年と2015年に東京に滞在した。本書のデザインも担当。

The still city knows. An illuminated scene. All in memory.
A large vessel. Floats on an anchor attached. To swamps and cinders.
Tokyo moves on. No fear for changing tides. Still with confidence.

The dragon threats him. It's the fire of shaking earth. New architecture.
The soldiers tried too. Bombs only called for revenge. War of industries.
The trader moves in. Quietly, like a sniper. Deadly without guilt.

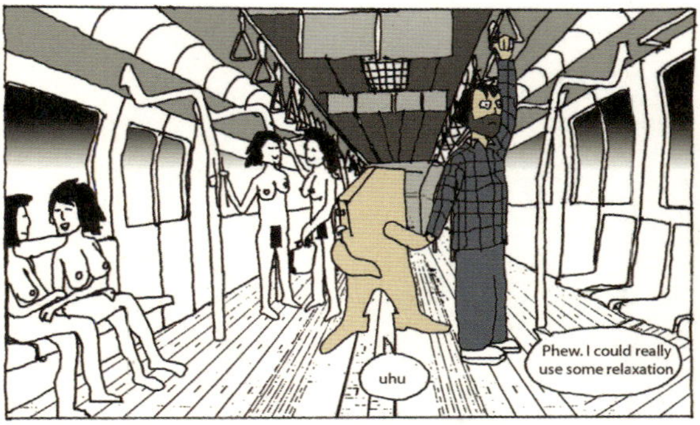

Like fish in the sea. Moving in the waves all day. The train helps to rest.
Mountains are nearby. They release voices and sounds. Echoes of downtown.
Big man hears the sun. Large trees bellow in the wind. Like the weeping sea.

Streets of clear asphalt. With electric masts for trees. Trees for receivers.
Silence clears the streets. A pack of snow muffles sound. The power of still.
A turtle roars loud. Or a dragon's cheerful cry. You hear what you know.

DANIEL RUIGROK

LUST IN TRANSLATION

The stilted rivers. Boats with wheels on all levels. Streams of the city.
Dykes of tall buildings. To prevent calm polder fires. Stations as Windmills.
Small streets in silence. Hard board walls and sliding doors. White and blue collars.

monnik

flick studio